W9-BNS-438

A
BREED
APART

Mike Helm

A BREED APART

The Horses
and the Players

HENRY HOLT AND COMPANY

NEW YORK

Copyright © 1991 by Michael Helm
All rights reserved, including the right to reproduce
this book or portions thereof in any form.
Published by Henry Holt and Company, Inc.,
115 West 18th Street, New York, New York 10011.
Published in Canada by Fitzhenry & Whiteside Limited,
195 Allstate Parkway, Markham, Ontario L3R 4T8.

Library of Congress Cataloging-in-Publication Data
Helm, Michael
A breed apart : the horses and the players / Michael Helm.
—1st ed.
p.   cm.
Includes index.
ISBN 0-8050-1326-1
1. Horse-race betting—United States.   2. Horseplayers—United
States.   3. Horse racing—United States.   4. Race horses—United
States.   I. Title.
SF332.H45   1991
798.401'0973—dc20   90-20921
                                                               CIP

Henry Holt books are available at special discounts
for bulk purchases for sales promotions, premiums,
fund-raising, or educational use. Special editions
or book excerpts can also be created to specification.
For details contact:
Special Sales Director, Henry Holt and Company, Inc.,
115 West 18th Street, New York, New York 10011.

First Edition

DESIGNED BY LUCY ALBANESE

Printed in the United States of America
Recognizing the importance of preserving the written word,
Henry Holt and Company, Inc., by policy, prints all of its
first editions on acid-free paper.∞
10 9 8 7 6 5 4 3 2 1

Parts of chapters 2 and 3 appeared, in different form,
in the East Bay Express.

The author would also like to thank Felicia Eth, Jack Macrae,
and Amy Robbins for their help.

For Panama and the horses

CONTENTS

1

IN THE
GRANDSTAND

*I*t was a glorious spring morning, and Panama and I were soaking up the sun at Golden Gate Fields an hour or so before post time. Behind us San Francisco Bay glistened like a million-carat jewel and the Golden Gate Bridge seemed close enough to touch. Our spirits were bolstered because the track had been playing fast and there were a couple of horses we liked. With us was Panama's sidekick Ed, a blues critic and first-time horseplayer from west Texas.

Though it was early, we weren't alone. Scattered about the grandstand were several dozen other early birds. Some were loners, while others like us made up small clusters of friends. We were all diligently studying our *Daily Racing Forms* and trying—like rabbinical students reading their Bibles—to divine the future. Only in our case, prophecy involved the modest hope that we pick a few winners and break even; more ambitiously, that we catch a long-shot exacta or daily double and put a dent in our credit cards; or—the ultimate horseplayer-goes-to-heaven fantasy—that we hit the Pick Six and pay off the mortgage.

Besides the seductive challenge of winning some money, the racetrack has other allures for the confirmed horseplayer. Near the top is the fact that it's a great escape. However fleeting and illusory, you are momentarily free. Though horseplayers compete against each other for a cut of the pari-mutuel pool, that doesn't prevent them from enjoying each other's company. There is an irreverent camaraderie at the track that is largely missing in outside life. In fact, it's not unusual for one handicapper who's just met another to say, "You like the one horse? I like the two horse. Hey, why don't we split a one-two exacta box?" And they do.

There is also a scholarly side to handicapping that attracts a diversity of talents. Fans with a mathematical bent play horses by the numbers and spend hours composing elaborate speed figures and track variants. Genetically inclined students of the game trace and assert the importance of pedigrees and breeding nicks. Video freaks watch the reruns in hope of spotting a troubled horse whose ability is better than would otherwise appear in the *Racing Form*. Amateur kinesiologists study the body language of each horse, while would-be criminologists study the workout and past performances to ferret out a trainer's cagey intent. The simple truth about the appeal of horse racing is that it is the most complex and interesting form of gambling.

For our part, Panama and I have been pondering the *Racing Form* and playing horses for a number of years. We've read the handicapping books, dabbled in speed figures, watched the reruns for troubled trips, and studied trainer patterns as clues to picking winners. Still, we stopped short of becoming professional handicappers because we realized that path runs the considerable risk of turning a pleasure into a full-time, low-paying job.

These days we're generally content to bring around fifty bucks to the track and have a good time. This, of course, doesn't mean we've abandoned our interest in coming home winners and improving our handicapping skills. It just means that even when we lose we consider playing the horses a lot more fun than blowing a comparable amount in some other more socially acceptable pursuit. More than once I've heard Panama disarm a critic of horse racing by saying, "You think the horses are a waste of money and time? Compared to what? Listen, by the time you buy a ticket to a 49er or Warriors game, pay for parking and food, you're going to spend at least fifty bucks. And after the game, what do you have left? Horse racing's got some tradition, it goes back hundreds of years, probably to the dawn of civilization. At its best, you get to see one of nature's fastest and most majestic animals run and compete. You get the thrill of watching an Affirmed and Alydar, Alysheba and Ferdinand, Sunday Silence and Easy Goer duel down the stretch with a ten-spot on their nose. And the jockeys who ride them are unmatched as athletes. It takes intelligence to play the horses. It's not just a passive spectator sport. Every race tests your powers of observation and analysis, as well as your intuition. And the bottom line is, if you exercise a little restraint, you have a decent chance of coming home with more money than you left with."

Panama's friend Ed had heard a version of this spiel, too, and it was one of the reasons he had decided to tag along. While he listened in, Panama and I focused our attention on the upcoming daily double. We had already gone over our *Racing Forms* the night before and made our tentative picks for the first and second races, but we enjoyed the leisurely pace of arriving early and comparing notes.

It's always a pleasure to glance at Panama's *Racing Form* and see the artistic way he has marked it up with his set of color-coded pens. Like many handicappers he has invented his own arcane geometry. Circles mean one thing, boxes another, squiggly lines, stars, and so forth yet another. Out of sloth or perhaps a sparer spirit, I stick to a single pen in recording my own hieroglyphics.

Panama and I take turns sharing insights into each race, because there is so much information buried in the *Racing Form* that often one of us gleans a significant nugget that the other has missed.

When there are several contending horses in the double we sometimes pool our bets to cut down on the initial overhead. If our opinions are too far apart, we just go our own ways.

One thing is for sure though: hard experience has taught us to go easy on the double. Too much enthusiasm early on and you can wind up tapped out later in the card when there is a race you particularly like and want to play. Also, it is prudent to check for any changes in the running surface before wagering much of your bank, because track conditions vary notoriously from day to day. Different horses, as the saying goes, truly like different courses.

After considering our options for the double, Panama and I decided to pool our bets and play a modest eight-dollar combination. We chose two horses, No Illusions and Pleasantly Naughty, in the first race and hooked each of them up to two other horses, Winged Idol and The Irish Look, in the second. There was a lot of early speed in the first race, and we figured it would set up for a couple of horses who could close from behind. In the second race, we picked two front-runners, figuring that one of them might forget to quit. Our payback, according to the pari-mutuel prices listed on the tote board, would range anywhere from twenty-five to seventy-five dollars. The final payoff would depend upon how many dollars the public had bet on the winning combination in the pari-mutuel pool.

It is a delightful peculiarity of horse racing and the pari-mutuel betting system that the odds on a horse in any specific race are determined not by the house but by the wagering of the fans, and that big money works against itself by lowering the odds. Each handicapper in the grandstand is literally betting his or her judgment against that of everyone else. The fewer dollars bet out of the total pool on a particular horse or combination, like the daily double, the longer the odds and the higher the payoff. A horse becomes a favorite and gets the lowest odds on the board simply because more money has been wagered on it than any other horse in the race. Since favorites win only a third of the time, the perceptive or lucky gambler can go against the collective sentiments of the crowd and often be rewarded handsomely for doing so. Of course, there are all kinds of long shots. There are nonfavorites that "figure," and horses that haven't won a race since they last outran the cows.

Ed, who had been listening dubiously to our speculation about early speed, quitters, and closers in the daily double, finally summoned up a judgment. "No Illusions, indeed," he drawled in reference to the first of our selections. "I think I'll just skip the first two races, watch them blackbirds peck through the manure out there on the track, and see what happens to *your* money."

Panama nudged me in the ribs and said, "Pay no attention to Ed here. He's like all those Cajun blues singers, full of suspicion and complaint."

But before Ed could reply, the bugler signaled the beginning of the first race, and the horses began to file out of the paddock. Our attention immediately swung out to the track. Post parade time! That most seductive moment for a horseplayer, when the horses snort and prance in front of the grandstand and the jockeys bob in their saddles. The moment when the anticipation and adrenaline sweetly build, the cheeks flush, the breath shortens, the fingers itch, the heart skips a beat, and a horseplayer's in love again. Regardless of how badly he may have fared on his last visit, the first race offers the possibility of redemption and renewal. It signifies a new day and confirms the horseplayer's ultimate mantra, "There's always fresh."

In the post parade our two choices, Pleasantly Naughty and No Illusions—a couple of six-year-old mares—seemed alert and ready to run. No Illusions did, however, have bandages wrapped around her front legs, and that concerned us. We wondered whether she had some tendon problems, or if the trainer had wrapped her up to pump up the odds and scare away any other trainer from "claiming" her out of the race. But, since her recent races had been pretty good, we decided to stay with her.

When I returned from placing our bets, Frisco had joined us just in time to play the double. He was breathing hard because he had sprinted in from the parking lot. "Man, I just got down," he croaked. "This sure beats the daily grind! I just had to get out. I couldn't deal with one more five-year growth plan. I needed the company of some fellow degenerates!"

A transplanted street artist/grant hustler from the Bronx, Frisco delights in puncturing the pretensions of San Franciscans by referring to their fair city as Frisco—hence the moniker we have given him. Like a lot of artist types, Frisco has a love-hate relationship with the philistines he has to raise cash from and exorcises the money demon by throwing a few dollars at the horses. And, like many people, Frisco also loves to be right, which means he tends to play "the chalk," or favorites.

There was a delay at the starting gate for the first leg of the double, so I took the opportunity to explain the conditions of the first race to Ed. It was a bottom-of-the-barrel $6,250 "claiming" race for female horses, and only fillies and mares four years old and up were eligible to run in it. The fact it was a claiming race meant that any horse entered into the race could be purchased for the stated value of the race.

"What?" Ed asked incredulously. "You mean, if she's my horse and she's in a claiming race, I have to sell her to anyone who wants her?"

"That's right," I explained. "Owners who enter their horses in claiming races enter them for a 'tag' with the full knowledge they may lose them. All that is required to claim a horse is a valid owner's license, the conviction the horse is worth the claiming price, and a strongbox full of cash deposited twenty minutes before the race—no checks are accepted. If an owner doesn't want to risk losing his horse, he shouldn't enter it in a claiming race."

We had been waiting impatiently for the horses to break from the gate when the track loudspeakers blared out, "Ladies and gentlemen, by recommendation of the track veterinarian and order of the stewards, the number three horse, No Illusions, has been declared a nonstarter. There will be a slight delay, and cash refunds are now available at the windows."

"Damn," Frisco muttered, "I had that horse singled to three horses in the second race in the double. Still, I guess I was lucky. If they'd let the three horse run, I would have had all my money on a cripple."

Since Panama and I also had the horse, we too were relieved it had been scratched from the race. We considered switching our bets to another horse. But the lines were long, and it seemed likely we'd get shut out before placing our bets. Besides, last-minute picks, in races comprised of cheap stock, hardly ever pay off. We decided the gambling gods were sending us a message and sat on our refunds.

And a good thing, too. Two long-shot horses dropping in class from more expensive races, Chief Belle and Roxie's Ahs Lahn, won the double. The combination paid a hefty $226. But shrewder or luckier handicappers than us were the only ones who got it. Pleasantly Naughty, our lone entry in the first race, made a brief move then hung in the stretch.

Panama and I failed miserably in the third race, but Frisco caught King Skipper, the two-to-one favorite. "You guys will never learn," he crowed. "Always playing those long shots." Clamping on to our wallets, we turned our *Racing Forms* to the fourth race. It was a $20,000 maiden-claiming affair for three-year-old colts and geldings bred in California going six furlongs, or three-quarters of a mile. The "maiden" designation meant that *none* of the horses in the race had ever won a race before, at least on any recognized track. When either a male or female horse wins its first race, it "breaks its maiden," according to racetrack parlance. After that, the horse faces its sternest class jump, because it has to enter a race populated by horses *all* of which have won at least one race before. It takes a horse with unusual ability to go from breaking its maiden to winning its next race.

Nevertheless, Panama and I are partial to maiden races for three-year-olds in the spring, because you never know when a mystery horse will pop out of one of those races at a big price and climb the class ladder to stardom. One of the joys of being a racing fan is to catch a young horse on the way up and follow its career. Despite the best efforts of high-priced breeders, nobody knows when some ill-bred, lightly raced maiden will become a real runner. Every now and then a trainer with modest connections and an overlooked horse catches lightning in a bottle and wins the Kentucky Derby.

Panama and I felt that there were several first-time starters in the race that maybe could run. They had to beat a horse called Gray Whale, who had run a close second three times in his first six races. As we deliberated, the tractor harrows went over the track surface, smoothing it out, trying to maintain a graded consistency that wouldn't favor an inside or outside post position.

Frisco consulted his *Racing Form* and came up with the eight-to-five favorite, Gray Whale. "I'm playing the chalk," he asserted. "You've got to take what you can get. The horse bobbled his start last time out and still got beat only a neck. He's dropping in class to $20,000 today and should be a lock in this field."

Frisco had a good argument for Gray Whale, but by experience I am suspicious of heavy favorites that finish a close second three times in a row. Often that's a signal the horse lacks the extra heart to win. I was partial to a first-time starter called Just Deeds and pointed him out. "Hey, he's sired by Beau's Eagle, who's been getting a lot of winners lately, and his mare is Shaky Footing, whose daddy was Shecky Greene, a real speedster. Lloyd Mason sometimes hits with first-time starters, and Tommy Chapman is riding him."

Meanwhile, Panama, who works as a chef in Marin County, had riveted his attention on another first-timer, King of the Bayou, a Cajun Prince horse out of the dam (mare) Speed Queen, who was sired by Tyrant. No doubt because of some culinary and ethnic affinity to Bayou culture, Panama is partial to Cajun Prince horses when it comes to breeding. Panama's interest in King of the Bayou was also heightened by the fact he had a "bullet" workout (the fastest of the day) three days prior to the race and was being ridden by Aaron Gryder, a hot young jockey from Santa Anita. But logical or not, Panama usually stretches the odds for Cajun Prince horses. For him, unless they got beat last time by twenty lengths, they are almost an automatic bet.

Now, betting a horse because you like its name is crazy. But, as anyone who has ever been to the track knows, names are magical and often seduce you. This is especially true in maiden races, where you don't have much else to go on. Or in stakes races, where several horses seem more or less equal. I couldn't give you a purely rational explanation, but whenever I see a turf horse that is out of a Stage

Door Johnny, Green Dancer, Grey Dawn II, or Habitat brood mare, I take an extra look. If it's a six-furlong sprint, everything else being equal, I'm partial to horses sired by Sucha Pleasure, Run of Luck, and Beau's Eagle. In past years I've been captivated by Nodouble, Somethingfabulous, Zanthe, and The Irish Lord horses. Over time, I've learned that some of these genetic lines produce horses with early speed, others get horses that can go a route of ground, and still others "throw" offspring that run particularly well on the grass.

This doesn't mean, of course, that just because of its name and breeding a horse is going to win. But is it really an accident that such great foundation stallions as Bold Ruler, Northern Dancer, and Raise a Native were given such captivating names? On some intuitive level, I can't help but feel their owners knew they had a special horse that required a name to match. Even cheap claiming horses have great names: Sleazy Looker, Win for Love, Stretch It Out, and Spin Sum Gold. More than one desperate musician has stolen a lyric or title from a quick reading of the *Racing Form.*

Even Ed, our resident skeptic who had yet to place a bet, wasn't immune to the magic of names. When Panama enthused about King of the Bayou and his daddy, Cajun Prince, Ed's ears and regional loyalties perked up. "Say what, King of the Bayou and Cajun Prince?" he more exclaimed than asked. "Now, that sounds like my kind of horse. If he looks good, I just might put a couple of dollars on his nose."

I started to hand Ed my *Racing Form* but he waved it away. "Keep that cheap rag away from me. I'm not gonna go blind reading it, you-all can do that. I'll just look at the horse and make up my own mind."

Panama and I had to laugh. The eight-point type and blocky appearance of the *Racing Form* inevitably put most first-time racetrackers off. And Ed's insistence on preferring the judgment of his own eyes was not without merit. When it comes to picking a winner, a lot of experienced handicappers become so mesmerized by a horse's past performance charts that they forget to look at the horse. They wind up betting on losers because they underplay the importance of a horse's *current* physical and emotional condition, as can be gleaned from its behavior in the paddock, post parade, and warmups. If a horse looks bad, nine times out of ten he's going to run badly.

Ed's reaction to the *Racing Form* reminded me of my first afternoon at the track, some ten years earlier, when I had been inveigled out by a friend to see the horses run. I had resisted the track's allure for most of my life, but genetics (bad breeding, no doubt) and destiny had finally prevailed. My grandfather on my dad's side had been a handicapper for the *Houston Post*, and my father, according to family legend, had paid for my birth with a trifecta he won while my mother was in labor in a Brooklyn hospital. The three winning horses were named, appropriately enough, Blue Booties, Tell Me Now, and It's a Boy.

When I bought a copy of the *Daily Racing Form* on that first day and opened to the past performance charts, I was—like most first-timers—immediately intimidated by the blizzard of statistics and arcane language with which I was confronted. I didn't have a clue about how to interpret the numbers or the meaning of such phrases as "dwelt last time," "lugged out," "bolted," "blinks on," "steadied," "eased," "suspicious class drop," or "first-time Lasix." In confusion and despair I resorted to Plan B, which was to pick out the horse with the most interesting name or personal association to bet, temper that by how the horse looked in the post parade, and finally keep a tight hold on my wallet.

It didn't take me long to understand that picking winners is tricky. A thoroughbred can run like a champ in one race and be a shadow of himself in his next one. Horses—like humans—are prey to the infirmities of the spirit and flesh. They get tired and hurt, and often run sore, with the result that they don't run their race, and the people who bet on them finish out of the money.

Racing luck plays an important part too. The best horse doesn't always win. He can have what horseplayers call a bad trip. He can get a poor post position or a lousy ride. He can stumble and be left at the gate, be bumped by another horse, get dirt in his eyes, or be forced wide, to mention but a few. When a couple of these things happen to a horse in a race, he can easily lose five to ten lengths off his best performance and look much worse in the *Racing Form* than he really is.

Dick Stoneman, who had just gotten off his early-bird shift at the post office and was still in his uniform, joined us and threw out another possibility. "Just Deeds and King of the Bayou are okay, but what about the ten horse, Forceful David? That Jim Benedict is a sneaky trainer. He's got a small stable, but he brings in some nice-priced horses."

Of all of us, "The Stone" is the dean. He has been playing horses for thirty-five years and has carried the mail for almost as long. He claims that, in all his years at the track, he has yet to meet anyone who is a lifetime winner. "Maybe someone is," he concedes dubiously, "but I haven't met him. Sure people go on a streak or hit a really big payoff—I've done it myself. But, lifetime? I'm way behind. To stick around as long as I have you've either got to be a philosopher, a real sicko, or love the game." After we all have lost a bet, The Stone sometimes enjoys teasing us by crooning the lyrics to an old Broadway tune, "Horses don't bet on people. They've got too much sense."

Ronnie Beauchamp also joined us. He had moseyed over from his favorite spot near the sixteenth pole to say hello. We call him Ronnie Beau because he's a classy dresser and a wine salesman. He pointed to his copy of the *Racing Form* and expressed another opinion. "Look at the six horse, Sharp Envoy. He got bumped at the start last time out and still closed like a mother. He only got beat a half-length. He's being bumped up in class from a $12,500 race to a $20,000 race, and "Cowboy" Jack Kaenel is riding him. Those are good signs. I know he's going off at fifteen to one, but horses don't read the tote board. They don't say, 'Whoa, I'm going off at fifteen to one, I better run at the back of the pack today.' They don't know how good they are until they actually run."

The Stone cocked his head sideways, peeled a jaded eye back to Ronnie Beau, and countered, "I don't know about that. I've seen some horses that *never* seem to run unless they are fifteen-to-one or longer shots on the board. Either they could read the odds or their trainers were playing some games."

Amy, a retired black woman who sometimes sits in our section, listened to our patter and felt compelled to chip in her two cents. "Good thing you fools have jobs. If you had to earn your living around here, you'd starve to death. Better get smart and play the action on the board. Somebody just dropped a bundle on the eight horse, Confiscated Gem. The morning line on it is fifteen to one, and it's gonna go off at five to one. That's my horse!"

By now the horses were leaving the post parade, and it was time to make our bets. There were six of us, and we had six different opinions about who would win the race. It was obviously not a race to put a lot of money into. Most professional gamblers would avoid it like the plague. But as weekend recreational gamblers, we were into it. We liked the action and were destined to back our intuitions. Just Deeds was going off at twenty-eight to one. The long odds worried me, so I decided to put a place bet on him as well. Maybe he couldn't beat Gray Whale, but at least he could come in second.

Panama and Ed were still strong on King of the Bayou, who was going off at eighteen to one. They were playing him to win and place. On an impulse I suggested that the three of us "box" our two picks along with the favorite Gray Whale in a three-way exacta that would cost us four dollars apiece. If any two of the three horses finished first and second in the race, the minimum payoff would be over a hundred dollars.

Ed consulted his pocketbook and nixed that idea. "And besides," he warned, "if I put money on a horse with a name like Gray Whale I might jinx King of the Bayou." Panama and I laughed and, in deference to Ed's foreboding, threw Gray Whale out. Instead, the three of us boxed King of the Bayou and Just Deeds into a four-dollar exacta. For a dollar thirty-five apiece, we were going for it and enjoying the sentimental purity of our bet!

Listening to our selections and betting strategy, Frisco snorted, "If you guys really want to play a long shot, you should try the lottery. Boxing a twenty-five-to-one and eighteen-to-one horse: you must be crazy."

Frisco had a point. Most of the handicapping books advised against betting exactas, let alone long-shot ones. Their counsel, based on sobering experience, was to play only a few races a day and then, when you finally settled on your horse, to bet it only to win and place. For more conservative high rollers, the legendary Pittsburgh Phil had even invented a system of show betting on legitimate favorites that would return twenty cents on the dollar. His critics contended that risking a lot of money to make a little was a form of financial suicide or "bridge jumping." But Pittsburgh, puffing on his cigar, retorted, "Hey, it's better interest than you can get at the bank."

Well, we weren't bridge jumpers or bankers. We didn't have a lot of money. We preferred to risk a little in the hope of making a lot. And besides, it wasn't as if we were betting on proven losers. Though our horses had never run, they also had never been beaten! They had good trainers, good jockeys, and good workouts.

When the horses broke out of the gate, we couldn't believe our eyes. Just Deeds and King of the Bayou broke to the lead and ran head and head around the far turn. They were flying five lengths in front of any other horse. As they came around the quarter pole and raced down the stretch toward the wire, I was up on my feet screaming. Panama was giggling, while Ed tried to maintain his reserve. We were going to hit the goddamn exacta!

Then, out of the corner of my eye, I saw a blur closing fast on the rail. It was Gray Whale, who had broken slowly, making one desperate last rush to catch our tiring horses. Oh, no—that sick, apprehensive feeling of doom, familiar to all horseplayers, shot up from my stomach. It was accompanied by the equally familiar voice inside every horseplayer's head that loves to second-guess. The voice said, "You should have boxed Gray Whale into the exacta, dummy. Now you're gonna lose a couple of hundred dollars just because you tried to save a few dollars. Why didn't you go with your gut intuition? Idiot, you should never listen to your friends. What do they know? You should have known at least one of the first-time starters would tire and get caught at the wire."

I fought the voice off and urged our horses on. And, glory be, the horse gods were with us! As Gray Whale moved up to challenge Just Deeds and King of the Bayou, he began to hang. He couldn't get past them! His furious rush had taken too much out of him. He was going to quit again!

13

The three horses hit the wire necks apart. Though the photo-finish sign went on, and the track announcer warned, "Ladies and gentlemen, please hold all tickets. The stewards will be examining a photograph to determine the exact order of finish," I knew we had hit the exacta. Track officials routinely put up the photo-finish sign in any close race for dramatic effect.

When the photo sign went off and the winning numbers were flashed on the tote board, they read vertically 3-4-11. Just Deeds paid $59.00 to win and $26.60 to place. King of the Bayou came in second, and the $2.00 exacta paid a whopping $438.00. Gray Whale finished third. Panama rushed up to cash the ticket. When he returned, he peeled off $146.00 to each of us. As Ed stuffed his winnings into his wallet, he was still incredulous that he had gotten over a hundredfold return on his one-third share of our $4.00 bet. Pulling himself up from his grandstand seat, he drawled, "Think I'll go get myself a Jack Daniel's with a beer back and just enjoy the glow of this bet."

A wise man, Ed. He wasn't going to be one of those guys who won early and then left the track broke. Panama and I wondered whether or not he could resist another bet. Most racetrack fans get hooked because they hit big the first time out and think to themselves, "Hey, this is easy." The people who lose all their money the first time out rarely come back.

None of us had much luck the rest of the afternoon. Even Frisco was down thirty dollars playing the chalk horses. To get even he decided to stab for a long shot. "I really must be getting desperate," he joked about his selection in the seventh race, which was a mile route. "I'm gonna play Happy Idiot at seventeen to one. He's the early speed stretching out on the rail, and Chuck Jenda is good with routers. Maybe he can wire this field."

Too bad it wasn't a six-furlong sprint. Happy Idiot led into the stretch, then faded to fourth. Nobody cashed a ticket in the feature race. We decided to skip the ninth, beat the traffic, and get a post-race nightcap at our favorite watering hole.

Since Panama and I had managed to keep a hundred bucks of our exacta winnings, we told Patrick, the bartender, to set 'em up.

When he returned with our drinks, out of whimsy I asked him if he had ever been tipped a winning pari-mutuel ticket. "Yeah," he intoned sarcastically, "Martin, over there, once gave me a beauty that paid $5.80."

"And what happened," I asked, "when you went out to cash the ticket?"

"I wound up losing over a hundred bucks."

While Patrick's story cracked us up, Frisco wasn't amused. He was nursing his beer and bruised ego and said, "We can't beat this game by just reading the *Racing Form* or playing the action on the board. You guys were lucky to hit that big exacta. What we need is a mole to get us some real inside information."

The Stone had his doubts. "I can't tell you how much money I've lost betting on hot tips from 'someone who knew someone' on the backside. In my experience, it's the worst bet going. I'd rather take my chances with the *Racing Form*. In fact, if they didn't have one, I wouldn't be a horseplayer. It's what ties everything together. As far as picking winners, I don't think there are any foolproof rules. Horse racing is just plain unpredictable. In fact, that's part of its charm."

Ronnie Beau thought things over and said, "You know, all of us are pretty decent handicappers. We pick our share of winners. Our problem is with money management and the fact we don't stay out of enough races. We need to pick our spots. We can't play every race and hope to come out ahead. Of course, I should talk— I'm the worst offender." We nodded our heads in acknowledgment of one of racing's few basic truths, fully cognizant of the fact that we violated it nearly every day.

Panama, who had been suspiciously quiet, smiled wickedly and offered a twist to Frisco's suggestion of planting a mole on the backside. "What about the scribe here?" he observed coyly. "What we ought to do is send Helm to the backside. He can pose as a reporter and interrogate the horsemen. That's how the espionage agencies do it. Helm can be our spy."

I had to laugh. Though we were kidding around, I had in fact been giving serious consideration to writing a book about the backside. While I obviously wanted to improve my handicapping ability, the fan in me was also interested in exploring the craft and lore of the sport. I wanted to know what really goes on in the mornings, what the professionals think about their jobs, and how they view the racing game. The brief articles in the *Racing Form* just didn't satisfy my interest and curiosity. Maybe, if I spent a season hanging out with the horsemen, I'd find an articulate cast of characters to help me separate the horseshit from the truth. With luck, they'd even answer some hard questions about the shady sides of the sport and where it was headed.

But in order to do that, I'd have to find an angel. It was Panama who came up with the right suggestion: "What you need to do is rustle up a couple of chapters and get some New York publisher to gamble on you. I'll bet some of those guys back there like to play the ponies. Hell, from what I've heard, publishing a book is riskier than betting on a horse. Give it a shot. Send them your stuff and see what happens."

2

WELCOME TO
THE BACKSIDE

*T*he first thing you learn about life on the backside is that it starts early. Real early. Since the races are run in the afternoon, all the exercise and most of the care of the thoroughbreds has to be done between six and ten in the morning. This means the eight-hundred-odd horse people who work at Golden Gate Fields are usually up an hour before dawn.

I arrived a little past six on a crisp April morning and checked in with the gate security. I was still recovering from a party that Frisco had thrown the night before, but could see I wasn't alone. Some of the workers on the backstretch looked as though they had sampled a little Jim Beam, too. A couple dozen horses were already on the main track—some jogging and cantering and others galloping full blast along the inner rail. The latter were being timed with stopwatches by the track's clockers, because it's a rule of racing that no horse is supposed to be worked without having its time recorded and then published in the *Daily Racing Form*. Though the rule is sometimes circumvented by a wily trainer who works his horse in the dark or fog, it is intended to protect the gambling public by preventing a horse whose condition is better than it would otherwise appear in the *Racing Form* from being slipped into a race.

I had a ten-thirty appointment with trainer Bill Morey but had come early to pick up on the morning ambience. A number of horsemen were leaning against the south rail next to the gap where the horses enter and leave the track. They were sipping coffee out of paper cups, and exchanging greetings and friendly insults.

I took a cue from them and ambled over to the track cantina for my own caffeine fix. I filled up on a fifty-cent cup of coffee, a donut, and a quarter refill and walked back to the gap just in time to hear one trainer lament about an upcoming race, "My horse hates the rail," while another, with problems of his own, countered, "Yeah, but it's a short field—she can get to the outside."

It was an ancient lament. Many a trainer has cursed his fate when the luck of the draw is unfavorable to his horse. Depending upon a horse's temperament and experience, the grading of the track—how hard or soft it is—whether the day is rainy or dry, and the distance of the race, there are real advantages and disadvantages to drawing an inside or outside post position.

An exercise rider who looked as if he had lived a hard forty years moved past on his mount and called out to a trainer nearby, "Hey, I heard you lost your filly." Undaunted, the trainer shot back, "Yeah, but she went for twenty grand." They were engaging in claiming talk.

Most of the races run on the daily card at Golden Gate Fields, in fact at every track around the country, are claiming races. Though the claiming idea seems complicated, it's basically horse racing's version of a high-priced poker game. Whenever a trainer enters a horse into a claiming race or runs him for a "tag," another trainer can buy (claim) the horse for the stated value of the race. Claiming races are arranged into a financial hierarchy that roughly corresponds to a horse's ability. The faster the horse, the higher a price it runs for. Trainers sometimes claim horses for themselves, but more often they act as agents for the owners who patronize their stables. Although it sounds odd at first, the claiming structure is integral to the health of the horse racing business. It's a self-protective mechanism that horsemen have evolved over time to equalize everybody's chances at the track and limit the greed of the owners with the best horses.

The way it works is this: If you own Bold Lightning, a $50,000 racehorse, you can run him in a $20,000 claiming race against the likes of, say, Molasses, and easily win the $10,000 purse. But because it's a claiming race, you take the considerable risk of losing Bold Lightning for only a $30,000 return, which is $20,000 less than he's worth. The purpose of the claiming structure is to encourage owners and trainers to run horses in races that reflect their true value. If you run a horse too cheap, it will be claimed from you. If you run a horse over its head, it won't win any races.

As soon as a race begins, whoever has put in a claim for a horse owns it—though any winnings from the race go to the previous owner. When more than one person claims the same horse, dice are thrown to see who gets it.

Whenever an expensive horse is dropped heavily down the claiming ladder into a cheaper race, the *Racing Form* will say something like "suspicious class drop" in its analysis of the race. Usually there is something physically wrong with the horse, and the current trainer is trying to unload it. Other trainers, understandably leery of claiming it, ask themselves the obvious question, "Why is this horse running so cheap?" Yet occasionally a cagey trainer will drop a sound horse and try to steal a race, gambling that other trainers will be too afraid of getting damaged goods to claim it. If that trainer is lucky, he not only wins an easy purse but also gets to keep his horse.

More often than not, horses are claimed on their way up the claiming ladder, which is a gamble in itself. Usually a young filly or colt—one that has shown promise by winning or contending in a race or two—is jumped up from, say, a $10,000 to a $20,000 bracket, and another trainer will put in a claim for it, based on his or her assessment that the horse hasn't yet reached its highest earning potential. If the trainer is right, the claimed horse will win in the higher bracket and move up even further. If he's wrong, he will soon discover that he's paid $20,000 for a $10,000 horse.

When a young horse is of good enough quality that an owner or trainer doesn't want to risk losing it to a claim, it can be entered in a straight "maiden" or "maiden special weight" category. This is a category specifically designed for promising rookie horses that have yet to win a race. Once they win a race (break their maiden), promising horses are eligible for a variety of nonclaiming races, such as allowance races, overnight handicaps, smaller stakes races, and graded stakes races like the California and Santa Anita derbies. At the top of the pyramid are the Triple Crown races: the Kentucky Derby, the Preakness, and the Belmont Stakes. Admission to the very best races is usually limited by a minimal earnings requirement or by an invitation-only policy—though owners who think they have a contending horse can sometimes enter one of these races by paying a substantial supplementary fee. This is what happened when Clover Racing Stables and trainer Julio Canani supplemented fifty-to-one-shot Martial Law for fifty grand and won the million-dollar Santa Anita Handicap in 1989.

Back by the rail a gorgeous chestnut mare trotted by. I exclaimed to an old-timer next to me, "That sure is a good-looking horse!" Unimpressed, he gave me a hard glance and retorted, "Sonny, that horse couldn't outrun a fat man in rubber boots."

So much for beauty. I soon learned that the old-timer was a blacksmith who had been shoeing horses at Golden Gate Fields since the track opened in 1941. Warming to my interest, he filled me in about the craft of first shodding and then shoeing a horse's hooves. "When you're shodding a hoof," he explained, "you don't want to trim too much. Otherwise, the shoe can catch and be thrown during a race. You've also got to be careful to keep the nails away from the tender frog of the hoof. If you puncture the frog, it can abscess and affect how fast a horse will run. There's nearly forty kinds of shoes a trainer can choose from, and you have to custom-tailor each fit. Shoes used to be made of heavy metal, but nowadays—with the emphasis on speed—almost everyone uses the lighter aluminum ones."

Two colts smoked by us along the inside rail. One was a black beauty and the other a bay. Reflecting back upon my initial enthusiasm, the blacksmith mused, "You know, thoroughbreds *are* magnificent creatures. Guess that's why I've stuck around all these years. Every one of them, except for a few bastards slipped in during the Civil War, traces back to the breeding of one Turkish and two Arab stallions to British brood mares in the eighteenth century. Even the cheapest, most run-down claimer has some royalty in him. You can never tell when one of them will wake up and run the race of its life."

Another set of exercise riders ambled past on their horses. One of them turned toward the rail and inquired of a trainer how things were going. The trainer deadpanned with one of horse racing's standard one-liners, "Fast women and slow horses." The rider laughed, then drawled back, "Give me the fast horses—the rest will come."

In the old-boy network of horse racing, sex, women, and horses are never very far apart. Still, even the track has, like the rest of American society, been changing. As I watched the horses work out, I noticed that nearly half of the exercise riders were women. Unlike their male counterparts, they seemed more engrossed in talking to their horses than to the mostly male crew of trainers watching things from the rail.

I moseyed down the rail toward a young man with a baby nestled against his chest. He had a stopwatch in his hand and had just timed one of his horses. He introduced himself as Allen Kemp; he and his wife, Paula, train a small string of Washington-bred horses at Golden Gate Fields and Bay Meadows. Both of them, he said, are at the track each morning and take turns looking after their stock and two infants.

We talked horses and riders, and I learned that a thoroughbred can weigh anywhere from eight hundred to twelve hundred pounds, depending upon whether it's a light-framed filly or a big-muscled stallion. Most thoroughbreds fall between nine hundred and a thousand pounds. While jockeys have to keep their weight at 114 or less in order to get mounts, exercise riders often tip the scales at 140 pounds. A lot of them are ex-jockeys who have tired of starving themselves and now work on contract for the bigger stables. Their heavier weight is one of the reasons workout patterns in some barns always seem to be slower than in others. Kemp said the best free-lance exercise riders make a good living. On a good morning they can ride as many as twenty mounts between six and ten o'clock. At $7 a pop that means they can earn up to $140 for a half-day's work.

Another trainer next to us made a comment about having to geld one of his unruly colts. Kemp explained why gelding is a common practice. "We have too many cheap studs as it is. Proving a stallion as a sire is expensive and takes a long time. And besides, if a horse doesn't have his mind on business, he's unlikely to win any races and will be worthless as a stud anyway. Some horses have become great runners after being gelded. Look how John Henry developed after being cut. He raced until he was nearly ten and gave racing fans plenty of thrills. Up until Alysheba he was the leading money winner of all time."

Our conversation was interrupted when the racing office's loudspeaker clicked on and screamed all over the backside, "Attention all horsemen. We have a maiden $12,500 race for four-year-olds and up, fillies and mares, for next Wednesday that still hasn't filled. We need three more horses. Gentlemen, can you help us out?" Kemp happened to have a filly that qualified and excused himself to enter his horse. The loudspeaker, I learned later, though it seemed crude and raucous and something that might even scare the horses, is a necessary device for contacting trainers who are hardly ever in their offices—and, in any event, hate to answer their phones.

Right after Kemp left, the whole pace of the backside picked up. Horses were suddenly everywhere. It was a little past nine, and trainers who hadn't yet worked their horses were now desperately trying to get them out before the track was closed at ten. Of the thousand horses that are exercised each day, nearly two hundred of them were now out on the track or clopping to and from their shed rows. It looked like an experiment in controlled chaos—an appearance that was reinforced when a spooked horse slipped on the cement near the gap and flipped over onto his rider. A number of horsemen pitched in to offer help, and the track ambulance was called. Fortunately, the rider was only momentarily stunned. He dusted himself off and, true to racing's code, insisted on remounting his horse.

Competitive as it is, the backside is also a real community. Something about it is like a small medieval city. It has its own recreation center, chapel, tack shop, restaurant, and police force and is presided over by its own set of *patrones,* the stewards. Most of the grooms and a number of the stablehands work and sleep on the backside full-time and hardly ever leave the grounds. As one refugee told me, "These fences aren't here to keep us in, but to keep those other people out." Besides the trainer, jockeys, exercise riders, and grooms, most every morning the backside includes a mix of owners, jockey agents, veterinarians, pharmaceutical salesmen, horse vanners, gardeners, tractor drivers, gatemen, culinary workers, and other track personnel hurrying to and from the barns. It takes a lot more people to put on the afternoon racing show than the casual fan realizes.

Approaching ten o'clock, everything began to wind down. Most of the horsemen had already gone back to their barns or headed over to the cantina for one last cup before getting ready for the afternoon races. I lingered at the rail as the last of the horses cantered by and listened as the air exploded from their nostrils. The sound reminded me of the snorts of boxers in training. In the distance I was struck by the casual, almost elegant recklessness of one of the exercise riders, who stood tall in his stirrups to slow his horse down.

3

PEAKS AND VALLEYS
The Trainer

When I arrived at Bill Morey's barn, two horses were being lathered and washed while their grooms joked in animated Spanish. Three more horses, fresh from their workouts, were cooling off on mechanical "hot walkers," and another twenty or so stood in their stalls with mud poultices packed on their legs, stoically awaiting their morning feed. The barn had the sweet smells of liniment and hay.

Morey was on the phone. "Yeah, we're putting him in for twenty grand next Friday," he told some owner. He motioned for me to sit down. Once off the phone he warned that things were hectic and we'd have to work our talk into the gaps of his busy schedule. He called out to one of his assistants, Julie Baker, and asked if the horses listed on the chalkboard outside his office had been shoed yet and whether she had entered a certain horse at the racing office. Baker nodded affirmatively and said she was getting a filly named Ladytron ready for the first race, which was set to go off at 12:30 P.M. The horse would have to be at the receiving barn an hour before post time so the state veterinarian could certify she was sound enough to race.

His immediate business taken care of, Morey settled back and responded to my query about how he had gotten into the horse business. "Horses appeal to me," he mused, "probably because it's in my blood. I'm half Irish, you know. The Irish and horses, it's in their blood. My mother's father drove horses in his day. On my father's side, even though he's not Irish, his family had blacksmiths there. So, probably, my interest is in the genes. I like to be around horses. My father had a horse when I was young. I was sitting on a horse when I was two or three years old."

It also helped that Morey grew up in San Mateo, California, near Bay Meadows racetrack. As a kid he inveigled his way into the hearts of local trainers by doing odd jobs around the stable area. In 1960, by the time he was eighteen, he and a buddy were sufficiently hooked on horses that they leased a four-year-old filly named Ho Annie Lo and took her to Agua Caliente racetrack in Tijuana to try their spurs. Remembering that incident, Morey laughed and said, "We thought we knew something about horses. But we found out we knew nothing. We ended up broke and returned the horse to the guy we leased it from. After that experience, my partner decided to go somewhere where he could get three square meals a day. He joined the army."

I was familiar with the idea of buying and claiming a horse, but leasing one was a new twist. Morey explained that leasing arrangements often involve a shaky marriage between a financially overextended owner, an undercapitalized aspiring trainer, and an unproven horse. At the lower end, leases are often framed in terms of what horsemen call a win out. Morey described a win out this way: "If you're a trainer, an owner or breeder might come to you and say, 'Listen, I can't afford to train this horse, but I know he's a pretty good horse. You can have him to train and if he ever wins $1,500, you can give that to me and the horse is yours.' So the trainer takes the risk of all the training expenses, and if the horse happens to win a race, then the horse becomes his after he has paid off whatever the win out amount in the notarized lease agreement stipulates."

With better stock, there are other types of leasing arrangements. A common one, Morey elaborated, "is where the horse is just leased out for a specified time, for racing purposes only, because the owner might want to breed him down the line. In that case, the owner doesn't want to race him but wants the horse to show some wins so that people will pay more for breeding rights." When it's a "racing only" lease, the trainer and the owner typically agree to split the earnings. The exact percentage each party gets will range from fifty-fifty to ninety-ten, depending upon the quality of the horse.

Morey advises aspiring horsemen to shy away from leasing arrangements. "I recognize that when your bankroll isn't looking too good, sometimes you have to shop around. But it's not a healthy way to go into this business. You're much more likely to get stuck with somebody else's feed bill."

After going broke with Ho Annie Lo at Agua Caliente, Morey returned to northern California and settled in San Carlos, about five minutes away from Bay Meadows. Consulting his wallet, he decided to get into some kind of trade that would pay the rent. "I was determined to stick with horses, but I could see that I would need to have income from some other source than just training horses, because that was pretty lean. I got into a plumbing apprenticeship that took five years. But while I was doing that, I always had a horse or two that I was training on the side. During that time the only thing that kept me afloat was my plumbing job. I was also working as a groom and barn hand with other established trainers too. People like Tex Johnson, Cliff De Lima, and Ted West. I knew I needed to build up my knowledge of the business, things I was missing due to inexperience."

From 1960 to 1981, with the exception of a stint with the marines in Vietnam, Morey worked at both his trades, determined ultimately to become a full-time horseman. "Up until then," he recalled, "I was still training only a few horses. Then one St. Patrick's Day there was a big crowd, and the call came out for a few extra clerks at the pari-mutuel windows. I volunteered. I had a pregnant wife, two horses, and a very light income. From that day I worked myself into a job as a regular clerk and kept training horses on the side, waiting for a break."

Thanks to the union wages Morey made as a pari-mutuel clerk, he could afford to be at the track full-time. He took care of his horses in the morning and late afternoon and worked as a clerk in between. I asked Morey what his impressions of the gamblers in the grandstand were when he was a pari-mutuel clerk. "I didn't see anything real foolish," he replied, "except every now and then people bet more than they should have. For them it was kind of like a disease. I was an information clerk and we used to cash checks for certain parties that would sometimes bounce. That was a sign they were getting in over their heads. You didn't see a lot of that, but you did see some."

Unlike professional wags in the grandstand, Morey seemed reluctant to second-guess the fans. "What happens sometimes in this business, gambling-wise, is that you start to think you know more than you really do. For instance, here on the backside, sometimes I will see a horse and think to myself, 'Gee, that horse doesn't look too good this morning galloping by.' Well, I lock that in and the horse runs a week later and I see people betting on him, and all I've got locked in my mind is what I saw a week before. So I think to myself, 'Why are those people betting on him?' And sure enough here comes the horse and he runs good. There goes my theory shot to hell. My point is that sometimes the more you know, gambling-wise, it hurts you."

Morey reminisced about Mark Roberts, who handicapped for the *San Francisco Chronicle* for a number of years. "Roberts was one of the best handicappers I've seen. Many times the pari-mutuel clerks would take Roberts's top selections for the day and pin them on the wall. The patron would come up to bet and confidentially ask, 'Do you know anything smart to bet here?' The clerk would roll his eyes up and take Mark Roberts's top pick off the sheet, not saying that's where he was getting his tip. The impression given was that the clerk had a hot horse based on some inside information from a trainer or owner about a horse's condition. He would give him Mark Roberts's horses, and many a time the horse won and the patron would come back and thank him with a tip."

Regarding fans that like to play long shots, Morey said, "How can you say what's foolish and what isn't? When a guy bets on a fifty-to-one shot, you don't think he has any chance. But every now and then a fifty-to-one shot wins. The only way you can catch a fifty-to-one shot is by playing him, you know what I mean? Personally, I don't think it's a good roll of the dice. You might say it's like playing double sixes out of the box every time, though occasionally, when you hit, you look smart. Favorites win thirty percent of the races. If I was gonna make a gamble I'd stay closer to that bracket. I tend to favor situations where a horse is going off anywhere from five to one to ten to one. You get a little more return on your money than the favorites. When they get up to fifty to one, I just kind of watch them. If they win, they win and they're on their own."

Morey's rise to prominence as a trainer itself reads like a long shot, though he was sustained by a few bright spots. The first horse he and his wife claimed was for $2,500. Crimson Flag was his name, and he won his next time out. "That was really something. He went off at eighteen to one and paid $38. Then a few weeks later he went off again at about the same odds and paid another $38, on my wife's birthday. So you might say we were driven into this thing with a winner and stayed with it during leaner times."

Reflecting on his long path to success, Morey said, "Our win percentages were always high, but we weren't starting enough horses for people to notice, and you really need exposure in this business to attract some owners who will give you some horses to train. There's a lot of good men in any game, but without exposure you can sit in those trenches a long time."

By the fall of 1984 Morey was running a string of about fifteen horses and had a phenomenal meet at Bay Meadows. Out of ninety starts, his horses won thirty times. "Everything went right at that meet," he recalled. "I didn't lose a photo finish. All my horses stayed sound. Let me tell you, the phone began to ring. And it rang some more. I took on anything and everything I could. I went with the flow. It's peaks and valleys in this business. You've got to go when it's time, and I was ready. I wanted to go. I took on as many horses as people wanted to send me. It's developed now to the point where our stable is built up to a pretty good business. This morning, between our barns at Golden Gate Fields and Bay Meadows, we have fifty-seven horses."

As with any business, growth has its problems. "The more you pick up in this business, the more help you need—which kills you because of taxes and things like Workmen's Comp. Your overhead goes way up, but you have to have the help. If you go secondhand in this thing, you don't do any good. We have, between the two barns, twenty people on payroll right now."

While Morey owns some horses, like most public trainers, the great majority of the horses he trains are owned by other people. In northern California, trainers survive by charging owners $40 to $46 a day to keep their horses ready to run, which means an owner can expect to spend over $18,000 a year to keep a horse in training, excluding vet fees. In addition, trainers, like jockeys, get ten percent of any earnings the horses win. Given the expensive nature of horse racing, a trainer who doesn't win or isn't in the money very often will soon find he's losing his horses to other trainers. So it's a high-pressure job.

"Most owners, you have to remember, have made or are making their money in something else," Morey said. "Now don't get me wrong—there is money to be made in this business. But I compare it to the stock market. There is money to be made in the stock market, but I don't think there are a lot of people just making their living off of it. They're taking money they made in their own business and investing it in the stock market. All of my owners are making their money elsewhere. This is a side business for them. They want to make money in it too, but they also like the thrill of having a racehorse, of bringing their family out and going into the paddock area and having their picture taken in the winner's circle. That really puts them on a natural high."

On the downside, Morey confided, dealing with some owners can be exasperating. "One of the hardest things I've found about claiming is dealing with the guy who comes up to you and says, 'I just want to claim a horse for a hobby' or 'I'm not worried about money. I just want it for a write-off.' When you hear this, look out. This'll be the guy who is on the phone every day wanting to know when his horse is going to run. Or as soon as his horse runs sixth or seventh a couple of times, he wants to know when the heck his horse is gonna start running good, because the bills are starting to mount up. The truth is, everybody who has a horse out here wants to see it pay for itself and if possible put a little in the bank."

Another sticky situation involves people who come into the business on a lark, get a good claim, and suddenly think they are experts. "This is tough." Morey shook his head. "They're actually very green owners and think every claim is going to be a good one. They really don't understand that the facts of this business are, you usually have a bad horse. When you get a good one you should enjoy it and let the trainer do most of the direction, most of the driving. Sometimes new owners think that managing a horse is simple and try to step into the driver's seat. It makes for a bad situation, where you're liable to burn a good horse out by running him too much or destroy his confidence by running him over his head."

Morey considers himself fortunate that he's been in the business long enough to have real horse people as owners. "The people who really didn't understand the business, or who we didn't get along with, we've weeded them out. I lost some good horses by doing it, but I just couldn't see eye to eye with where the owners wanted to place the horse or who they wanted to ride it. We've got good owners now. I don't have any pressure on me other than the pressure I put on myself to have my horses run better."

Though Morey has begun to breed horses in the last few years, like most trainers he makes his living playing the claiming game. "The claiming side is the backbone of this business," he emphasized, "because very few horses are potential Kentucky Derby winners. You have to have the claiming categories for the less able horses. But claiming is also the toughest part of the business. When you claim a horse, sometimes you have to take it from a friend of yours, which you don't like to do. It leads to problems. You end up out here with not too many friends. It's like playing poker—

you try to protect your good hands and dump your bad ones. Sometimes your friends take your good horses and that upsets you. Other times you unload a bad one on them. In that sense, it's every man for himself out here. It's a tough game, a crapshoot. You have to have owners who realize that. The claiming business or even the horse business is not something you want to put your last buck into. The difference between buying a horse and buying a piece of property is that you can go out and look at your property every day, whether it increases or decreases in value. In this business sometimes you'll come out and find an empty stall. Your horse has been claimed or, even worse, has been drastically injured or is sick and dies."

Racehorses are fragile creatures, and Morey emphasized the care they require. "People don't take as good care of themselves as we do of our horses. If we come in in the morning and find that a horse hasn't eaten his evening ration, we stick a thermometer up his butt to see if he has a fever. If a horse sneezes, we call the vet and give him a shot of penicillin. If we get sick with the flu, we still go to work."

Given the $15,000 to $20,000 annual cost of keeping a horse in training; I asked Morey how trainers and owners can afford to run horses in the $6,250 claiming races that tend to dominate the daily racing card. After all, most of these horses, being at the bottom of the racing pyramid, are lucky to win one or two races a year, and the winner's share of the purse is only $3,500.

"Well, every horse that you breed you hope is gonna become a Secretariat," Morey answered. "But they don't all turn out that way. Just like every parent hopes their kid will turn out to be president of the United States, or a doctor or lawyer. But some of us turn out to be horse trainers or reporters. That's life. Some of these horses instead of being a stakes horse or an allowance horse become claimers. And the lower the bracket, the less money there is. At the $6,250 level—you're right—there's no money in it. You don't try and breed these kinds of horses, you wind up with them."

Morey's advice to potential owners runs along these lines: "The first thing in claiming a horse is that a fella has to be comfortable with what his bankroll is. If his bankroll is $20,000, he'd better claim a horse for about $10,000, so he can keep about ten grand in reserve for expenses and a bad day. Number two, the better a horse you can claim, once you get off the $6,250 bottom, the more room you have to adjust a little and make your money back. What I'm saying is, if you take a horse for twenty grand and he steps on a rock and gets a stone bruise, he might be a little off and you can drop him down to $12,500. You've still got a place to go. If you take a horse for $6,250 and he steps on a rock, you've got nowhere to go. You've got to keep him in the barn at $40 a day until things change."

In northern California the fast lane for owners and trainers who like to play the claiming game is between $8,000 and $16,000. "When you run a stable like that," Morey explained, "you run a very busy store, because not only do you have claiming owners in your barn, but so do other fellas. So, what you're doing is exchanging horses quite a lot. Some of these guys may lose two or three horses in one day and when the week is over have swapped eight or ten horses."

Given that kind of turnover, I wondered how it was even possible to train a horse. Morey paused and said, "I think this kind of training is a little bit different. Basically, you try and find a loophole in a horse that you can fix quickly. If the horse is a bleeder, and you take care of it, sometimes you can make that next jump up the ladder and turn a few dollars. That's what a trainer on this level is trying to do, turn dollars fast.

"Horses worth claiming at this level," Morey explained, "are usually proven racehorses. They want to win but have developed some physical problems that have slowed them down a bit. They were probably meant to be better horses than they are, but they've landed in this bracket due to injuries or whatnot. But if you can patch them up, you can run them back. You can take that little jump and make a little profit. You can claim them for ten and bump them up to twelve-five. If the horse is hot, a lot of guys will be going back in for it for twelve-five so they can bump it up to sixteen."

Morey had some thoughts about why there aren't many high-priced claimers running in northern California. "We don't have a good program here to keep our better claiming horses. If you look at the purse structure here, compared to Santa Anita, you'll see the purses are nearly double down south for horses running in the same categories. We ran a horse for $32,000 at Santa Anita and it came in second and earned almost as much as it would've gotten with a win up here. So what you have is a situation where owners are pulling their better claiming horses from local trainers and sending them down south. That's why you are seeing more cheap races in the daily card here. The racing secretary just can't fill the card with better races. A lot of tracks around the country are in the same bind."

Another part of the problem, as Morey sees it: "Too much of the daily handle is going to the state in the form of taxes, and track management is also greedy with its end of the cut." According to the racing office at Golden Gate Fields, 15.3 percent of all straight betting is taken out of the betting handle and divided up as follows: 5.1 percent to state and local taxes, 5.4 percent to track ownership, and 4.8 percent to the horsemen for purse money. On exotic bets like exactas, the Pick Six, and daily doubles, over 20 percent of the handle is divided up among the three parties.

"I think we've lost the horsemanship in management, which we really need," Morey lamented. "It's just a business to them, and they are not adequately supporting the owners and trainers that make the sport possible. We should strive to keep our better horses here by making the purses more competitive at the midrange level."

The problem from management's point of view is that increasing the size of the purses lowers their profit level, at least in the short run. "They should get rid of these $400,000 stakes races, which are won by southern California horses," Morey argued. "That money is taken away from local horsemen. It's ridiculous to have a $400,000 race here. At the most the El Camino Real and Golden Gate derbies should be for $150,000. That would be fine, and the rest of the money should be invested in good allowance and claiming races here to support a better program throughout, rather than putting all this money into a one-shot affair where you get to see one of the top three-year-olds in the country for *one* race.

"I know that management says that racing without the big horse is nothing. That's true—if the big horse stays here. But if the big horse comes from New York or southern California, takes the money, and leaves, he's not going to pick up local fans here. It's not a shot in the arm for business here. You get a couple of big crowds for the one big horse, and lousier cards and less attendance the rest of the time."

Our conversation shifted to the physical problems horses can have and how that affects a trainer's judgment or whether or not to claim them. A major worry for trainers is whether or not a horse is a bleeder, suffering from what veterinarians call exercise-induced pulmonary hemorrhaging. Why horses bleed is unknown, but it's a widespread problem. More than seventy percent of all racehorses in California are bleeders. To combat the problem they are given the controversial drug Lasix, but it doesn't always help.

"Just because you see that a horse is on Lasix in the program, that doesn't mean the horse isn't gonna bleed through it in a race," Morey explained. "Sometimes a trainer has to use other things to deal with bleeding. I have a feed called Respond that I use with my bleeders and horses that have allergies. Trainers have different techniques and approaches they use that may work better on a particular horse. If a horse bleeds or stops suddenly in a race, we scope them when they come back to the barn and often find out that by golly the horse did bleed through its Lasix. So we try something else—change their diet, add some vitamin C or K to their feed, change their bedding from straw to wood shavings to cut out a possible allergic reaction that is affecting their breathing. Every barn is trying something a little different, to get an edge on the guy who isn't trying as hard, to stop a horse from bleeding through its Lasix."

Trainers also worry a lot about conformation—how a horse is built physically. "Conformation is very important to the soundness of a horse, from his feet on up. Now, there's hardly any perfectly made horses around here. Every fault the horse does have in his conformation, he will usually pay a penalty somewhere down the road. For instance, going back to those twelve-five claimers, those horses were probably meant to be $25,000 horses, but because they were maybe toed-out real bad, their knees are offset, or they're crooked-legged, they pay the penalty and they injure themselves along the way. Maybe they have a floating [bone] chip in there or a strained ligament, so they run slower and they're not worth twenty-five grand anymore but are now in the twelve-five bracket. You can claim some of them at that level and bump them up. But it depends upon how much of a conformation fault the horse has. Of course, there's always a horse out there that's gonna make a liar out of you. There's always a horse that's crooked and people will say, 'Well, look at this horse, he made a million bucks.' But you can also go to lay-up farms and see a whole herd of them turned out because a conformation problem has caught up with them."

Morey's comments reminded me of Minutes Away, a stakes horse that Panama and I had bet on and followed over several years. He developed a "bowed tendon" problem, but his trainer kept patching him up and bringing him back to the races. They finally had to drop him into the claiming ranks, where he easily won a bunch of $50,000 races. All the trainers knew the horse was bowed, so no one would claim him. They were afraid the horse would break down right after they shelled out fifty grand for him. Still the horse kept winning. He was finally scratched one day by the track veterinarian at the starting gate and subsequently retired. Morey remembered him well. "He was a horse with a lot of ability. They did a good job with him. Holding tendons together is one of the toughest injuries for a trainer. They'll look beautiful for so long and then all of a sudden they go. Bad tendons out here are looked upon as being 'a little bit pregnant.' It's gonna become a bigger and bigger problem. It's just a matter of time."

The phone rang and Morey said he had to get back to work. But he agreed to let me talk with Julie Baker, one of his assistants, to get a feel for the daily operation of the barn. A couple of days later, during a midafternoon lull, I caught up with her.

The first thing I asked Julie was how she got interested in horses. She shrugged her shoulders and said, "I just think I liked the way they looked. While other girls were playing with Barbie Dolls, I was playing with toy horses." Baker grew up in California in Pleas-anton, and then moved to Manteca and the Modesto area. Her first horse was a Welsh pony she got when she was ten. From there she went on to show hunters and jumpers until she was fifteen. After that she took a couple of years off, got married, had three kids, and filed for divorce. Realizing she couldn't make any money showing horses, Baker went to work breaking colts and fillies at a quarter-horse ranch. That experience led her to galloping horses for a variety of trainers. That's how she met Bill Morey and landed her job.

Galloping Morey's horses in the morning is still an important part of Baker's responsibility. "Given their druthers," she ex-plained, "most trainers would rather have an inside person, con-nected to their barn, work their horses than hire free-lance help. But it takes a barn of about twenty horses to be able to afford to put one on the payroll. A regular rider can detect subtle things about a horse's soundness or running habits that can be corrected by a trainer if he knows about them early on. The typical free-lance rider often doesn't pay attention to that kind of detail.

"You have to understand that riding a racehorse is a difficult and complex job," she continued. "A racehorse is a really fit animal. They're extremely well fed and are given vitamin supplements, minerals, and salts. Racehorses are high spirited, high strung, and really like to run."

Another part of Baker's job is to supervise the six grooms that work with her. Most of them at Golden Gate Fields are green-carders from Mexico who live and work on the backside in generally marginal accommodations and under the paternal eyes of the stew-ards. Because of fear of fire in the highly combustible stable area, grooms are not allowed to cook in their rooms. Each groom gen-erally takes care of five horses and is paid the going rate of $210 a month per horse. Baker speaks enough Spanish to communicate with them.

Of all the people around the barn, a good groom is probably the most sensitive to a horse's condition. Since he spends the most time with him, rubbing him down, feeding him, and consoling him late at night, the groom is most aware of subtle changes. If thoroughbreds could talk, they would probably talk about their grooms—at least that's the way Frisco sees it. On more than one occasion he has torn up a losing ticket on a favorite and remarked, "The groom probably kept my horse up half the night playing mariachi music."

Baker agreed that a good groom knows his animals and can either deter or help a horse to run better. "We have two or three really good grooms who have been around for a long time. Others are just learning—they're young. The ones that don't last maybe get homesick. They just don't care that much and sometimes become drunks."

We talked about the temperaments of different horses. Baker has some pretty clear-cut ideas. "Good horses," she said, "don't do anything wrong. You just love them to death. Bad horses hurt themselves or somebody else." Baker has the scars to prove it. In her experience, the better the horse is bred, the better it usually acts. "They don't try to hurt you. Probably because they're more expensive, they're better trained. That has a lot to do with it. People take more time with an expensive horse and are kinder to him. Horses will do to you what you do to them. They know right away what kind of person you are. They pick it up right away—especially racehorses, because they're more fit, more energetic, feel better, and are real attentive."

Baker is particularly fond of some of the older horses. "We have a seven-year-old and two eight-year-olds here that haven't had any time off at the ranch, so to speak. They've been here the whole time I've been here. These horses amaze me, because racing is the hardest thing you can do to a horse, and these horses have been here for years. And they still keep trying. They're like Duracell batteries—they never stop."

Then, of course, there are the horses with chronic problems. For obvious reasons Baker was reluctant to talk about them. Bill Morey, like every other trainer playing the claiming game, might want to unload them in their next race and wouldn't want the word to get out. It is every trainer's unwritten rule for employees on the backside that the less said about their problem horses, the better.

· · ·

Baker walked me through her typical day. The first thing she does when she arrives at the barn each morning is walk down the shed row, checking each stall to make sure all the horses "are still standing." Though she laughed when she said that, she was actually serious. "If a horse is lying down, it's a bad sign. The first thing you have to do is get him up. Because if a horse can't stand up, something is seriously wrong. Recently we had a horse that was down. You could tell that she had thrashed in her stall during the night because she had dirt and straw all over her. I got her up, put a blanket on her, and walked her around. I also called the vet right away. I could tell she probably had colic, because she kept turning around and looking at her side and biting at it. Horses with colic often do that. It's not that they're trying to tell you something so much as that they don't know what else to do. The vet arrived a little after five-thirty, put some oil in her stomach, and she was fine."

Besides checking for horses that are down, Baker also looks to see if they have eaten their evening rations. A horse that is off its feed may be getting sick. When Baker encounters a tub full of feed, she routinely takes the horse's temperature to see if it's within the normal range of 99 to 101 degrees.

Assuming all the horses are accounted for and healthy, Baker next scans the schedule Bill Morey has posted on the barn wall to see which horses need to be galloped and worked that day. She's also responsible for taking care of all the riding equipment: the exercise saddles, reins, bits, and blinkers. "You don't want any of the straps to break during a race," she explained. "That can be really dangerous."

When a new horse is claimed and comes into the barn, it comes with a card listing the equipment it has been running with. Baker and Morey use their judgment about what else might be needed. Because they can dramatically affect a horse's performance, major equipment changes must be approved by the stewards. The public in turn is informed about such things as the addition or subtraction of blinkers and whether a horse will be running with mud caulks.

It is also important to remember that horses, like people, are creatures of habit. When they are claimed and have to move to a new barn and different handlers, they sometimes act up. Recently a newly claimed filly bolted in the middle of a race, Baker told me. "That's extremely dangerous. The rider had to bail out. You can't have that. So we changed her equipment—went to a more severe bit and added one-eyed blinkers so she couldn't see the outside fence and try to jump over it."

After the horses are worked in the morning, they are cooled out for twenty minutes on the hot walker, a circular turnstile to which they are tethered and which rotates counterclockwise as the horses move. Then they are washed and groomed before getting their morning feed.

Once back in their stalls, most horses have their legs rubbed down with liniment, and then mud poultices are applied to help draw out any soreness and heat that the workouts may have generated. Of all the parts of a horse's anatomy, the legs are the most vulnerable to injury, and trainers pay the most attention to them.

The easiest horses to work with are the geldings. "Stallions are more aggressive and will sometimes bite, while fillies are the most temperamental. I don't know what it is, but they all just seem to want their own way."

In the afternoon, horses generally race against their own sex. Fillies and mares race against each other, as do colts, geldings, and stallions. As a rule the males are bigger and stronger and the females can't outrun them, though Genuine Risk and Winning Colors are two exceptional fillies that gave "the boys" all they could handle and won the Kentucky Derby.

It's also Baker's job to talk to jockey agents and try to get the riders that Morey wants for his horses. And besides everything else she does, Baker takes care of the myriad details involved in getting a horse to the starting gate.

On the morning of a race the track veterinarians look at each horse scheduled to run that day. They take off any bandages and examine the legs, then check for other signs of illness or unfitness. When Baker or Morey bring the horse into the track's receiving barn just before the race, the track and state veterinarians check everything again and verify the horse's identity by looking at the tattooed numbers stamped under the horse's upper lip. The tattoos are necessary because so many horses look alike, and the track has to guard against the possibility of some unscrupulous horseman trying to substitute a ringer into a race.

In contrast to the cynical view of many racing fans, Baker sees the vets as the unsung heroes of the backside. "The vets are here about as much as I am. They work really hard and take good care of these horses. If you want to be a vet at a racetrack, you've got to be better trained than if you are in private practice. Whenever we need them, they're right here. They're real pros."

Baker had to get back to her chores, and I had a couple of horses I wanted to bet. I ambled past the maze of tranquil barns on my way out of the backside to the grandstand. The hot walkers lay idle, the horses stood quietly in their stalls, and hundreds of wet bandages fluttered as they hung and dried from the sides of the barns. By midafternoon the whole backside often looks like one big infirmary.

A couple of days later on a lazy afternoon, when he didn't have any horses running, Morey nursed a beer and elaborated about the claiming game. "I used to claim horses from the rail. Now I don't have the time. When I was up at the rail I watched for horses that looked sound, horses that had won easy last time out or had maybe been boxed in and figured to improve—naturally, a good-looking horse. At this size, my business runs differently. An owner will call me and say, 'My name's Don, and I've always wanted a horse named Don. There's a horse called Don's Park running today. I'll be out at the track. If the horse looks sound to you, let's claim him.' This isn't the best way to claim a horse. But horse racing is a crapshoot. If you're gonna be lucky, you're gonna be lucky. Sometimes you can make your own luck a little by putting more research into it, but I find that people are willing to be a little bit looser about things now."

Once Morey has claimed a horse, I wondered how he decided at what level to run him next. "One good way," he said, "is to work your new horse with one of your horses that you already know the value of. If your new horse can keep up with a $20,000 horse in the morning, you can guess that it will be competitive at that level in the afternoon races."

It's an axiom of racing that good trainers run their horses where they belong, in races they have a chance of winning. It's a testament to Morey's acumen as a trainer that better than half of his horses consistently finish in the money. I asked him if he knew which horses he would be running against before he enters a race. "Sure. We've got our own *Wall Street Journal,* the *Daily Racing Form.* I read that and can guess who we'll be running against. Generally, if you're running in a $20,000 race, you'll get horses that ran at that level last time plus some dropping down from $25,000 or being bumped up from $12,500. You don't know about big class jumpers or droppers, or invaders shipping in from down south. Still, the *Racing Form* gives you a pretty good idea."

What about jockeys? "You try to get the jock that fits your horse. If you're a trainer, you try to figure out if your horse needs a kind hand or a heavy one. Whether you need a speed jockey that runs well on the front end or one that comes from behind. There are different things you try and weigh. I think Russell Baze, before he went down south, covered them all—he was our best jock. Ron Hansen is very good. Roberto Gonzales is an example of a jock who gets a horse out of the gate fast."

I recalled The Stone's skeptical view about how hard some jockeys are trying. "Hey, don't tell me these jockeys don't play games," he'd insist. "I've seen them strangle horses at the gate, deliberately tuck in behind a wall of horses, even burn their horse out on the front end."

Morey disagrees. He believes most of the time jockeys shouldn't be blamed for losing a race. "Sometimes a jockey gets in trouble out there and can't overcome it. Maybe the track is heavy on the outside, so the jock comes in, gets stuck behind a wall of slow horses, and can't get home in time. Or maybe a horse is speed crazy and unratable. When you hear a gambler grumbling about a jockey's ride, more often than not it's just because he lost some money. Rather than admit that he bet on the wrong horse, he'll blame the jockey. Sometimes, right after a race, a trainer will blame a jockey, but when they look at the films, they'll usually see it really wasn't the jockey's fault."

Ultimately, of course, if a horse consistently runs badly, it's a reflection on the trainer's judgment. I asked Morey what his worst claim was. "I remember it distinctly," he replied. "My sister and brother-in-law had just come back from a stint overseas working for General Electric with a pretty good bankroll. They were looking for a tax write-off and a little fun. So we claimed a horse, The Proud Greek. He was a big gray horse, and he turned out to be the worst claim I ever made—and I've made some bad ones.

"This horse wasn't only bad for my business, it was also bad for my home life. I mean this was my sister and brother-in-law we're talking about. The Proud Greek was a beautiful horse, but he had every fault there was—starting from his feet on up. When he walked he acted like he was walking on eggshells. He had a navicular real bad. He had a bad ankle and a bad knee, too. Then he broke a splint bone. He was just self-destructive—a little that way before we got him, but after that he just totally fell apart. This all took place in a period of about a year. What we did for his feet was we 'nerved' him. When I say 'we,' I mean we had the vet at the hospital block the nerves going into his feet. Then we had to take the splint bone out. It was really one thing after another. The vet bills just kept piling up.

"Meanwhile, things were getting really hot in the family because my sister and brother-in-law had also involved some of their friends in the horse. We all started out friends and pretty soon we were looking at each other with daggers because they were very upset with their horse. We claimed The Proud Greek for something in the neighborhood of $12,500 and raced him only a couple of times over a year and a half. He ended up as an absolute giveaway. We donated him to the vet school at U.C. Davis as an animal they could do further research on because he had so many problems. My relatives were rewarded with a small tax write-off for donating the animal. That was a real bad claim."

On the other hand, Morey has had a number of bright spots, too. "Out of claiming races we've had maybe a half dozen or so horses go up the ladder and win stakes races. I mean, you get lucky once in a while in this thing. One of our better claims was To Air Is Equine, a horse that I claimed for the Mitchell Brothers— not the porno guys, but some others. I called them up one day and told them I had seen a horse in a training race that looked pretty good to me. I was very surprised to see the horse entered in a $25,000 maiden claiming race for two-year-olds a week later. I said, 'If you're interested, it takes a big set of balls to go for a first-time starter for twenty-five grand, but this horse can run.' So they said they'd call me in the morning. Sure enough, I got a call the next morning and they said, 'We're putting our balls on the line.' "

The first time Morey ran To Air Is Equine he won a stakes race at the Alameda County Fair. That was followed up with a blazing stakes win on Thanksgiving Day at Bay Meadows. Morey began looking forward to a trip to the Kentucky Derby with him. "He was really rolling in the right direction. He was sired by Shady Fellow. But he did have a conformation fault. His left leg really turned out more than it should. You like to see your horses with their feet correct, pointed straight ahead. Some horses are pigeon-toed and others toe out.

"Anyhow, one day To Air Is Equine's defect caught up with him. But not before we ran him against Snow Chief at Bay Meadows. I thought our horse had a chance. Snow Chief went on to win the Preakness and some other big races. Anyhow, when we ran against Snow Chief it was on a very sloppy track. Our horse didn't like dirt kicked back in his face. We called him 'Airhead' because he didn't like dirt in his face, let alone mud."

Morey had given the jockey strict instructions not to "get down in the 'rooster tail,' where the horse in front on a real sloppy track will be shooting that mud up in a spume and it hits the horse in back in the face. We definitely wanted to have our horse in the clear. Well, as racing luck would have it, we ended up trapped inside and were forced to stay there. To Air Is Equine made a bold move going down the backside but was blinded and covered with mud as he came up. He ended up a distance back. But that was just because he couldn't see. He absolutely lost eyesight and control of himself at the end. Still, he was one of our better claims. He won over $100,000 before he got hurt—he pulled a suspensory. We tried to bring him back a couple of times, but it just wasn't going to heal. He's now a riding horse at Woodside."

I've often wondered where thoroughbreds go when they have to leave the track. Frisco, in his inimitable style, often describes a weak field in a bottom-level claiming race as "one step removed from dog food." "Michael," he'll say, "these horses are so bad that when the race is over—if it's ever over—they're going right into the can."

I asked Morey about what happens to cheap racehorses in northern California when they can't compete anymore. "Oh, you mean the killers?" he whispered in mock horror. "Actually, that's just a myth. When horses can't win anymore and aren't good for breeding, they make excellent pleasure horses. If they have size to them they make excellent jumpers. You'll see them in Grand Nationals in San Francisco. Retired thoroughbreds aren't the best horses for a green hand, though. You've got to have a pretty good rider to take a horse from the track and turn him into a pleasure horse. But once conditioned to that, they're fine. You have to remember that horses are in the fast lane here. We program their diet. We fill them up with ethyl by putting that grain in front of them. That grain just ignites them. So it takes a while to slow them down. Once you take that grain away from them and feed them hay, you're turning them into a different animal."

Morey elaborated on a racehorse's diet. "They have their oats, their sweet feed, their bran, salt, and molasses. I believe in cooking their night grain into a hot bran. Other trainers just like to feed dry. Some horses we give more bran to, others less. We rely on our help to monitor our horses' diets. You have to have good help. You're a dead duck without it. Somebody has to pick up on horses that are being overfed or underfed, whether their bowels are too tight or too loose. Then you adjust their feed to it. I feed my horses two times a day. Occasionally, I'll feed a horse an early can of grain. But he has to prove to me that two meals a day isn't enough. My theory is that you can overfeed a horse a lot easier than you can underfeed him."

This same intense individual attention extends to a horse's exercise. "Let's take a horse that just raced today," Morey said. "After the race it'll spend thirty to forty-five minutes on the hot walker for the next couple of days. The third day you put the saddle back on it and let it jog a bit. Somewhere between the seventh and fourteenth day, you'll work the horse with a stopwatch." Racing takes a lot out of a horse, and generally a sound horse can run consistently only once every three weeks. "There are horses we don't work between races," Morey continued, "but usually you'll see a workout. Your lighter horses, your fillies and mares, need less work. The degree of soundness of your horse also affects how much you work it before a race."

Our conversation turned toward the breeding end of the horse business. With his success on the claiming side, Morey and his owners have begun to take some of their top-earning fillies and turn them into brood mares. "We now have some mares that we raced as young horses that we've retired. We also happened to find a stud that we liked that was for sale for a pretty reasonable price, about $50,000, a horse called Young Commander. He's a proven stallion, but he'd only been bred to a handful of mares, all owned by this one lady. They were all weak mares. I think Young Commander is going to be an up-and-coming stud. At least I hope he's gonna be one, because he's being bred to good mares now. It's going to be real interesting to see what happens to his foals. But you have to remember that in the breeding side of this business it takes a long time to prove a brood mare or a stallion."

If claiming a horse and paying for its training and upkeep seems like an expensive gamble, breeding and raising a horse is even more of one. "When you mate a mare," Morey continued, "that little baby takes a long time. Takes about ten months in the mare, and then it doesn't start racing until it's two and a half years old. You're tying up more than three years with a horse that may come out with some kind of deformity that makes him unsuitable for racing."

The typical boarding farm charges $10 a day for keeping babies. That's $300 a month, plus another $100 per horse for vet fees and trimming and shoeing their hooves. That adds up to a minimum of $400 a month (plus the initial cost of keeping your brood mare and the stud fee) to raise a young horse for its first two years. Another expense comes when it's time to break a horse so that it will accept a rider. "You go through a breaking period of three to four months," Morey explained, "before a young horse comes into a stable like this. That costs $30 a day. Then they come here at $45 a day for a couple more months before they're ready to race. You usually average a minimum of six months' training before a horse is ready to run. That's from the time you first put the bit in its mouth until its first race."

Even six months of training may not be enough for a young horse, at least in Morey's opinion. "We went to Ireland and visited with one of their premier trainers, Vincent O'Brien. He's comparable to someone like Charles Whittingham in this country. O'Brien takes a minimum of twelve months with his young stock before he lets them race. This is where you need good owners. If you don't have patience in this business, you might as well get out. If an owner starts pushing you to run a horse faster than you should, you're gonna end up in trouble down the line. There's an axiom in racing that's really true: 'If you don't wait on the horse now, the horse is going to make you wait on him later.' "

Morey sipped from his beer and added, "You know, what we're all here to do is to develop young horses into winners. Sometimes it happens through claiming, but what you really feel good about is when you have a young horse and you put all your time into him, you program him, you bring him out, and he runs well and he wins. This is your highlight. You love to win. Your real downfalls in this business come when your horses get hurt. This is the part that's hard to get used to. The more horses you have, the more injuries you take. You're going to see it. It upsets you during the day, but you have to go home at night, take a hot shower, maybe a shot of whiskey, go to bed, and the next day wake up and wash your face. It's a new day. That horse might be gone or is maybe on the ranch, and it may have been a super horse. When I lost To

Air Is Equine, it really hurt. But every day you come out here you have to be ready for it."

I asked Morey to compare—from his perspective of nearly thirty years in the horse business—his life now with when he first started out at Agua Caliente. "Caliente is a good place to go for background," he reflected. "They have many good trainers who take these bad-legged horses and win races with them down there. It's a tough place to make a buck. But it's also kind of enjoyable racing there because they only race on the weekends. You can run your whole string on just a couple of days and actually have a couple of days to go fishing, play golf, or whatever.

"Up here, to get a day away is tough. You have to find a day and just take it. I've only just started doing that because we're in a better position. Sometimes you can go three or four years here without a day off. That includes Christmas, because the horses have to be taken care of. They can't take care of themselves."

Morey finished his beer, slapped his thigh, and said it was time to get back to work. It seemed appropriate to end our talk by asking him about gambling. "Luckily," he reflected, "we have people who like to gamble on our horses. Without them we wouldn't have a business. People on the outside think that all of us on the backside are compulsive gamblers. But I betcha not even twenty-five percent of the trainers bet heavy. There just isn't enough profit in this thing to get carried away. The feed man could probably tell you who's gambling and who's not. The guys who are paid up on their feed bills are the guys who are not gamblers. But don't get me wrong: I like to bet a little on my horses. But those are the only horses I'll bet. Still, I probably bet on as many losers as anyone out there—and I'm only playing my own horses. At the end of the year, if I shook out my Levi's on all the bets I made, on all the tickets I cashed on my own horses, I'd be even, or maybe a dinner or two ahead.

"Hey, it's a tough game."

4

HAPPINESS IS A LIVE MOUNT
The Jockey

*F*risco, Panama, and I were watching the feature race that Saturday afternoon when Big Conviction, a speed horse from Santa Anita, opened up a three-length lead going into the far turn. At that point "Cowboy" Jack Kaenel, who was in the irons, moved Big Conviction in toward the rail for the run to the wire while Rob An Plunder—the odds-on favorite—began to close on the outside. The two horses fought it out the last sixteenth of a mile with Big Conviction prevailing by a neck. However, a steward's inquiry soon followed and the results were reversed. Big Conviction's number was brought down for interference and bumping in the stretch. In disgust Frisco tore up his ticket and lit into Kaenel for his ride. "Did you see what he did?" he bitterly moaned. "The rail's been dead all week, and Kaenel takes a horse with a three-length lead and not only moves it to the inside, but also keeps Rob An Plunder from having to go wide. Then, as if that's not bad enough, he whips his horse on the left side, he drifts into Rob An Plunder, and gets his number taken down. That's the worst ride I've seen this meet."

Panama challenged Frisco's analysis. "Hey, Big Conviction has a tendency to quit." He pointed to the past performances in the *Racing Form.* "The Cowboy was probably just trying to cut the corner and save some ground. Unless I was in the saddle I wouldn't want to second-guess his ride. Kaenel didn't win the Preakness on Aloma's Ruler and set the world record for six furlongs with Zany Tactics by not knowing what he's doing."

Frisco, Panama, and I, like a lot of racing fans, enjoy the pleasure of having an opinion. When I suggested Panama might be right, Frisco snorted. "Even Stumes of the *Chronicle* says the rail's been dead for the past ten days. You guys have been mesmerized by the Cowboy's reputation. Just because Kaenel has won some big races doesn't mean he can't screw up."

Frisco had a point. Panama and I *had* been following Kaenel's career since he had moved his tack to northern California in the spring of 1988. In fact, we were in the grandstand the afternoon that Trevor Denman, who was filling in at Golden Gate Fields after the Santa Anita meet, first introduced the Cowboy to local fans. When Kaenel won his first two races and went on a tear for the next week, I sensed an interesting story and called him up.

It was nearly ten o'clock that Sunday evening, and "Cowboy" Jack and I were stretched out on lawn chairs back behind the Golden Bear Motel on San Pablo Avenue in Berkeley, sipping a little Jim Beam. For the Cowboy it had been a good first week at Golden Gate Fields. He had won eight races, and now, with a couple of days off, he confided, he was enjoying the afterglow of a rare meal—steak and potatoes with all the trimmings. The rest of the week Kaenel, like most jockeys, would have to eat like a bird or "flip" (throw up) like a fashion model to keep his weight down.

Kaenel and his family were hunkered down at the Golden Bear because it was close to the racetrack in Albany, and they hadn't had time yet to scare up a small ranch to settle into. Besides Jack, there was his wife, Debbie, their three kids—Mike, Jacklyn, and Kyle (who had been "foaled" in January)—two quarter horses, and nine mules to consider. Then, too, there was his dad, Dale, and his wife, Debby, and their two kids, as well as fellow jockey Gary Boulanger and his girlfriend who had come out from New York with them to try the California lifestyle. There was a gypsy-caravan feeling about the Kaenel clan that had a nice draw to it, though one could see that it would require an unusually understanding landlord, probably another horse person, to accommodate this bunch.

When I mentioned this gypsy feeling to Jack, he chafed a bit at the comparison. "I guess you could say that, but all I've ever tried to do by movin' around is improve myself, increase the amount of money I make."

Kaenel was articulating a basic truth about the world of horse racing: racetrack life is inherently transient. In northern California the racing season opens at Bay Meadows in San Mateo in the fall and continues into winter. It next moves to Golden Gate Fields in Albany from late January to the end of June, and then concludes with the summer county fair circuit of two weeks each at Pleasanton, Vallejo, and Santa Rosa. After that, for the real diehards, there's even a meet in Humboldt County at Ferndale, just before Bay Meadows begins the year anew in late August.

But it's not unusual for jockeys, and even trainers, to move from one regional circuit to another when they get a better offer or run into a cold streak and can't win any races where they are. There's an expression among horsemen, "Horse racing is like gunfighting: second best isn't good enough. If you don't win you're dead and had best move on."

For most jockeys life isn't easy. According to John Giovanni, the national manager of the Jockeys' Guild, Inc., there are some three thousand licensed jockeys riding across the United States. Of these, fewer than half make a living at it. In fact, only around a hundred jockeys make more than $15,000 a year. While the media focuses attention on millionaire riders like Pat Day, Jose Santos, Angel Cordero, Jr., Chris McCarron, and Gary Stevens, the great majority of jockeys supplement their income by exercising horses in the morning and hope that one of the trainers will give them a "live" (contending) afternoon mount.

Kaenel, who is usually in the top three percent of his profession and earns close to $200,000 a year, comes from a horse racing family. When I asked Jack how old he was when he first got on a horse, he laughed. "I don't remember. Probably before I could walk. I had my boy, Mike, on a horse when he was a week old—of course, I was holding him on."

Jack was riding horses on his own at six and entered his first competitive race when he was ten. "I raced ponies," he reminisced, "between pari-mutuel trotting horse races in Pennsylvania and Ohio where my dad was training horses. The pony races were for half a mile. There was no starting gate, you just had what they called a handler, and they'd fire a pistol into the air to start the races. It was a pretty hairy situation. I rode with just a bridle and no saddle. That's where I learned to ride with my hands rather than my feet, how to keep my balance, too, by keeping my knees tucked in hip-high."

When Kaenel turned eleven, he and his dad hitched up their six-horse trailer and hit the bush circuit. Before long, Jack graduated to riding bigger horses at the county fairs in places like Rocky Ford, Colorado; Woodward, Oklahoma; Ak-Sar-Ben and Atokad, Nebraska; and Yuma, Arizona. Though the legal age for riding is fourteen, nobody bothered to check Jack's age. "My father took me to those bush tracks just to teach me and let me get experience. He took time off from his career as a trainer to help me learn mine. We had a small string of about half a dozen horses. We didn't go having to make money and win races. Of course we did win some, and pretty soon I was riding other people's horses, too—riding almost every race on the card."

Later, when Dale Kaenel and I were watching a video rerun of Aloma Ruler's victory in the Preakness, his fatherly pride came through about those early bush experiences. "Look at the way Jack is rating that horse on the front end, so he doesn't use him all up! He learned how to rate [ration a horse's energy] at those bush fairs. Sometimes we'd run the same horse in five races over nine days. Jack had to learn how to get the most out of a horse without using him up so much he couldn't win his next race."

To this day, Jack told me, "You'll hardly ever see me win a race by more than a length or so. I'm not just riding this race but thinking about saving something for the next one."

By the time Jack was fifteen he had served his apprenticeship and was ready to do some fast riding at recognized tracks. In the fall of 1980 he and his dad headed up to Winnipeg, Manitoba, with four horses. "I got my gallop license at fifteen, even though I was supposed to be sixteen. Gallop licenses for exercising horses in the morning aren't nearly as well checked as anything else. I soon developed quite a good business because I was a light rider. Pretty soon the trainers asked me to start ridin' for them, so I did. I took out my license one day, and when the entries came out that afternoon I was named on thirteen horses on the overnight sheet."

Jack finished up the Manitoba meet, stopped over in St. Louis and won two races, then headed to New York. Because he had already been riding at established tracks, nobody at Aqueduct asked him to prove his age. At fifteen Jack rode Aqueduct in the daytime and the New Jersey Meadowlands at night, and nobody asked any questions because he was winning a lot of races. By the first of the year he was tied for leading rider at Aqueduct.

Kaenel rode at Aqueduct from October 1980 until mid-April of 1981, with a month off in between for a broken wrist. He and his dad then decided to move south to Pimlico, in Maryland. About that decision Jack reflected, "I had the 'bug'—the five-pound weight allowance given apprentice jockeys—at Aqueduct, but in the spring all the 'heavyheads,' the established New York riders, were coming back from their winter meets in Florida. It was much tougher getting any decent mounts. I was still ridin' good, but hell, there were fifteen of the best riders in the country coming back to New York, and a lot of business was drying up. We had an opportunity to ride for some good people, with large purses, in Maryland, so we chose to go down to Pimlico. I rode at Pimlico for less than a month when I got caught for being underage."

Kaenel was leading rider at Pimlico when he got caught, but he didn't get his license back until the last day of the meet. From there he went back up to New York for the summer Saratoga meet, then on to the fall meet at Aqueduct. He returned to Pimlico in the spring of 1982 just in time for lady luck to smile on him.

Originally, Angel Cordero, Jr., was slated to ride Aloma's Ruler in the Preakness for trainer Butch Lenzini. However, Cordero, being a heavyhead, could afford to pick and choose. He had ridden Aloma's Ruler in a prep allowance race that the horse had lost. Unimpressed with its performance, Cordero opted to ride another horse in the Preakness.

Here's how Kaenel tells the story: "Cordero didn't think Aloma's Ruler was a good horse, seeing as how he got beat in a much cheaper race. So I went over the next morning and talked to Aloma's owner, who I knew because I was ridin' some of their other horses. I told them, 'I'd like to ride your horse in the Preakness if Angel don't ride it.' They said, 'Angel's riding it.' I said, 'Well, if he don't, I'd sure like to ride it.' Well, sure enough, Angel didn't ride it, and they told me they'd give me a shot on it. They said if Aloma's Ruler ran well in the Withers Stakes, they'd give me a shot on him in the Preakness. We won the Withers, and the horse ran the slow time of 1:35.2. But even so, we beat some nice horses in the Withers, so they decided to take a shot with me and the horse in the Preakness."

What followed was drama made for television. Jack "the Kid" Kaenel rated the swift Aloma's Ruler perfectly on the front end and outfoxed the legendary Willie Shoemaker, who was on the three-to-five favorite Linkage. It was at the Preakness that Kaenel earned his nickname, "the Cowboy." The owner of the Pimlico track, jubilant that a Maryland horse had won the race, gave Kaenel a cowboy hat as he approached the winner's circle. Instead of wearing his jockey cap, Jack donned the cowboy hat when all the pictures were taken, and he has capitalized on the moniker ever since.

Despite his sensational ride, Kaenel discovered that one race does not a career make. Between the spring of 1982 and the fall of 1985 he continued to ride counterpoint to the schedules of the New York heavyheads. He alternated riding between Aqueduct and Pimlico—with side trips for stakes races at Keeneland, Ak-Sar-Ben, Sportman's Park, and Canterbury Downs in the Midwest. Then, in the summer of 1985, Kaenel decided to work his way west. "I had been planning to come to California when I left the East Coast. I was working my way through the Midwest planning to hit southern California at the right time. I hit the last half of the Pomona meet as a way to break into the Oak Tree meet at Santa Anita."

The Cowboy did well at Santa Anita but developed a reputation as the "long shot" rider. "When all you ride are long shots," Kaenel observed, "it's hard to have your name high up in the jockey standings. It wasn't that I wasn't ridin' good, I just wasn't getting enough good, live mounts. When you're not at the top of the standings and don't get enough live mounts—regardless of how good a rider you are—you can't do no good. I was getting sixth call on all my horses. If Laffit Pincay, Gary Stevens, Eddie Delahoussaye, Chris McCarron, or Fernando Toro all passed on a horse, then I got to ride him." Kaenel discovered that southern California had its own heavyheads and a hierarchy to match. He rode at Santa Anita and Del Mar for two seasons, then accepted an offer to ride the winter meet in 1987 at Aqueduct for his old trainer Butch Lenzini, who had a large stable back in New York and promised to put Jack on some live horses. Kaenel rode at Aqueduct, winning races and freezing his ass off until the spring of 1988, when he decided to give northern California a shot.

Kaenel got down to the main truth about racetrack life. "A good horse is what you have to start with," he emphasized. "That's what makes an owner, trainer, and a jockey look good. You can't take anything away from a good horse. What you have to do is get all you can out of him. You can't make a slow horse run fast. I've won over a thousand races, and I've yet to pick a horse up and carry him across the finish line. I've always been on the horse. That's why any winning picture ever taken of me, I'm patting the horse. I'm giving him appreciation. I didn't win the race, he was doing the running. My job is to get the horse from the gate to the wire in the fastest possible time."

Of course, getting a good horse to ride—a "live mount" in racetrack vernacular—is not so easy in the highly competitive racing world. Talent, hard work, a good agent, and luck all play a role in securing one. The process of getting live mounts begins anew every day for a jockey with the morning workouts. Kaenel routinely gets to the track on racing days by six A.M. "For some horses," he emphasized, "I need to get out real early. I get up, go to the track, have myself a cup of coffee, read the *Racing Form* and see what horses I'm on that afternoon. I also talk to my agent and line up the mornin' workout schedule. He usually sets things up for me, though I might run into a trainer who asks me to work a horse."

Morning life at the track is not always fair, especially for beginning riders and even over-the-hill veterans. It's not unusual for financially pressed trainers, trying to cut exercise costs, to take advantage of the less successful riders by having them work their horses for free in the morning under the false expectation that they will then get to ride them in the afternoon races. Kaenel, a fellow with a strong sense of justice, said, "Basically the unwritten rule is that when you work horses in the morning you ride them in the afternoon races down the line. Sometimes you don't ride a horse you've worked because you've already got another mount in the same race. Or maybe the trainer changes his mind. That's okay, once in a while, because a jock don't mind doin' a trainer a favor. But no one likes to be used. I'd rather have a guy tell me, 'Jack, someone else is gonna ride this horse for me next Wednesday, but can you do me a favor and work him for me? I need to get him out.' In that situation I don't hesitate at all. But if a guy comes up to me three times in one week telling me to work his horses, and I don't ride any of them in a race, then I feel like I'm being used and don't care about helping that guy out anymore."

Between morning works and afternoon races a jockey's day is a full one. That's why all the regular riders have agents. A good agent makes it his business to know which horses are ready to run and have a good shot at winning. He gets the live mounts for his jockey. For his efforts an agent gets a hefty twenty-five percent of his jockey's earnings. When I raised my eyebrows about the size of an agent's cut, Jack said, "Hey, seventy-five percent of something is better than a hundred percent of nothing. But you have to have a good agent, otherwise they're a total drain."

Since even the best jockeys win only one out of every four to six races, I've often wondered if a jockey and his agent know when their horse isn't going to win and when it is merely being prepped by its trainer for another race. Kaenel didn't think it was that simple. "For example, if my agent gets me on a horse coming off a layoff, who knows, maybe the layoff did him good and he'll win fresh. But if he was injured, the layoff might not have helped him to heal and he may run lousy. With horses you just don't know what's gonna happen, and you can't get into a trainer's mind because a lot of times he's guessing too. Handicappers get their pick from *all* the horses, and even when they pick the favorite they're only gonna be right three out of nine times. So, if you're the jock or an agent, how are you gonna pick the best mount in every race? The truth is there's no set rule that works in racing, except that in any particular race, on a given day, the fastest horse wins."

Jockeys are paid to help horses *win*, and that is reflected in their pay scale. At Golden Gate Fields, jockeys are paid a minimum $40 fee for simply riding a horse. But the real money is in riding well, especially in stakes races. Jockeys get 10 percent of the owner's purse money as a bonus for coming in first, and 5 percent for finishing second or third. In California, for example, the owner's win share of a typical $10,000 purse is 55 percent, or $5,500, and a jockey's 10 percent cut of that is worth $550. The jockey's 5 percent cut for finishing second or third in the same race will be worth $100 or $75, respectively. While owners earn 7.5 percent of the total purse money for running fourth and 2.5 percent for fifth, jockeys get only the basic $40 riding fee if their mounts finish fourth or worse, which barely covers expenses.

Out of the $40 fee—regardless of whether any purse money is won—a jockey gives the agent $10, the Jockeys' Guild gets $8 for life insurance and a very modest injury fund, and a final $5 goes to the jockey's valet for organizing and repairing the riding equipment for each race. This means that a jockey's actual income for a losing mount is only $17, out of which the rider has to factor in morning exercise time as well as pay for all personal equipment— saddles, boots, pants, T-shirts, goggles, and so forth. The economic reality for jockeys (most of whom get only two or three mounts a day) is that they have to finish in the money. Jockeys who don't finish in the first three positions—especially first—don't last very long. Statistically, fewer than 20 percent of the apprentice riders survive their first year. Of those who become journeymen, the typical racing career lasts only five to seven years.

As most jockeys get older, according to John Giovanni of the Jockeys' Guild, "They give up the profession because of problems in making their riding weight, chronic physical problems caused by past injuries, and because of the constant influx of fresh young competition. In California, one of the more progressive states, injured jockeys are eligible for $100 a week Workmen's Compensation, and the Guild throws in another $50. These payments are good for up to 104 weeks. After that, jockeys are on their own."

At Jack's invitation, I arrived at the jockeys' locker room at Golden Gate Fields at eleven-thirty on a Wednesday morning and was greeted by a security guard. His job, he informed me, is to keep unauthorized personnel, especially "unsavory elements," away from the jockeys from an hour before the first post time until after the last race of the afternoon. Confirming that my name was on his approved list, he tipped his hat, and then waved me into the concrete bunker that is sited just south of the grandstand.

Once inside, I was struck by the sauna-like ambience of the locker room. Most of the sequestered jockeys were lounging by their corners, shirtless and in various stages of undress. The smell of boot polish, leather, tobacco, and talc hovered in the humid air. The only ventilation was from a small jalousie window at the top of the brick wall that faced out toward the track. In the small open spaces between the equipment and clothing racks, *Playboy* pinups and good-looking horses were juxtaposed and taped to the gray walls. Each jockey, it was evident, had a different idea of what constituted good conformation.

In Kaenel's corner were jockeys Sam Maple, Tim Doocy, and Kenny Tohill. Tohill was passing around some homemade beef jerky. Tim Doocy was flossing his teeth and Sam Maple was cracking jokes. Pointing to their valet, Maple laughed and said, "That's Ron. He's our mother. He takes care of everything for us."

Doocy told me that Kaenel, who at five feet seven is big for a jockey, was still in the box sweating away a few more ounces to get down to his 114-pound riding weight. "The box" is jockey slang for the sauna, which is located on the north end of the locker room. That's also where the massage tables are located, where the jockeys go to have their leg cramps worked on as well as the aches and pains from minor spills, and where jockeys "flip" if they have eaten anything between races. Most jockeys flip as a way of staving off hunger and yet limiting their calories. Some of them are so adept at it that they can win bets by regurgitating on cue.

Wednesdays are the toughest days for jockeys to make their riding weights. They've been away from the track for two days, pigged out a little, and often need to lose a quick four or five pounds. The use of diuretics is not uncommon. Some jockeys also pop Lasix pills, the same controversial medication that is given to horses to control pulmonary bleeding. The Lasix dehydrates their bodies. After taking one of these pills, a jock will urinate profusely and frequently over several hours. It is an effective but exacting way to lose weight quickly. But too much Lasix can drain a jockey of the strength he needs to ride well.

Kaenel returned nonchalantly from the box with a towel draped around his waist. He didn't have a mount until the third race, so we had time to talk. I asked him what an ideal riding weight is. "Well, Willie Shoemaker weighed 95 pounds for most of his career and Laffit Pincay usually comes in at 117, so you've got the number one and two riders of all time with a 22-pound difference between them. A lighter rider has an advantage because he can ride lighter-weighted horses. Other than that, it varies with the ability of the man."

At 117 pounds Pincay is the exception. Most jockeys have to keep their riding weight at 114 pounds or less. If they come in a couple of pounds over and lose a race by a nose, the trainer, the owner, and the handicapper in the grandstand are all liable to blame them for the loss. Not surprisingly, Kaenel thinks that weight considerations are overemphasized as a factor in the outcome of all but the highest-priced handicap races. "How much difference," he reasoned, "can even another ten pounds make to an animal that weighs up to twelve hundred pounds? A horse's basic ability and desire is much more important. If I ever own and train horses, I'll ride them myself and tack 128 pounds. I could lead a normal life at 128."

Jockeys weren't always required to make such light weights. The way the 114 figure evolved as the ideal weight is an interesting historical development. To understand it, you have to go all the way back to the early eighteenth century, when thoroughbreds were first bred in England. While the first thoroughbreds were bred for speed, they were even more importantly bred for strength and endurance, qualities they would need to carry their heavier "gentlemen riders" over the classic distances of two and three miles.

By the early part of the nineteenth century, however, "flat" racing—the shorter five- and six-furlong sprint races where speed is at a premium—and handicap races, where less capable horses are given weight allowances to help them compete, came into vogue. Both of these developments favored lighter-weighted riders. English trainers, motivated by a mixture of greed and genuine concern, began to recruit their supply of light riders from the "common" ranks of orphaned rural adolescent boys. The best riders from this somewhat indentured lot lived on the premises under the trainer's paternalistic authority and became the forebears of the modern jockey, who to this day is often still condescendingly referred to as a boy. Meanwhile, many of these same trainers, who were themselves of humble origins and who previously were in the exclusive employ of aristocrats, began forming public stables and increasingly took on nouveau riche owners from the emergent mercantile class who had the wherewithal to pay them day rates for conditioning and managing their horses.

In the twentieth century the increased racing of physically immature two-year-old horses, whose fragile bones often can't handle the heavier weights, also served to increase the demand for lighter riders. In England, horse lovers and animal rights advocates were instrumental in requiring lighter weights on younger horses. When all of those factors are added up, it isn't surprising that a premium is now put on lighter riders. The daily racing card at most racetracks, especially during the fall, is dominated by short sprints, two-year-old races, and handicap races.

As jockeys get older, anywhere from twenty-four to thirty years of age, most of them, in spite of starving themselves, begin losing their adolescent bodies and slowly put on the dreaded weight. They begin their losing battle with diet and water pills, alcohol, and other drugs. Most quit, though a few, like Steve Cauthen, brave the cultural shock and move their tack to the European turf circuit, where higher riding weights prevail.

Jack Kaenel is tough-minded about the weight problem that he faces every day. "Jockeys have to develop the discipline to keep their weight down. They basically have to decide they want to ride more than they want to eat. Weight problems are partly genetic, but a lot of it has to do with mind. The mental part is important. I'll give you an example. Let's say I was a jockey that wasn't having much luck and starving myself most of the time. Well, after a while I might decide that it wasn't worth it. I've seen a number of jocks make that decision and I don't blame them a bit. It might even happen to me. But as long as you want to ride more than eat, you'll find a way to keep your weight down. Most jocks put on weight after they've made the mental decision to try something else. It's not the other way around. Each jockey has to look at his career and decide whether or not it's worth it to him to keep his weight down."

During the week Kaenel's riding diet consists of one cup of black coffee in the morning and then two egg yolks plus dry toast, or a small amount of lean meat and a little salad for roughage in the evening. At the track he sometimes will eat as many as fifteen sliced tomatoes (mixed with a little olive oil and spices) between races, then flip this up before his next mount. Given his meager diet, I wondered about vitamins. Jack said he's tried them. "But all they do is increase my appetite. Every jock's got to find what works for him."

The first race had just ended and the jockeys filed back into the locker room. Their faces were lined with the dirt kicked up from the track, with a gritty outline where the edges of their goggles had been. Like matadors, they carefully took off the silks, which belong to the owners of the horses, and splashed water on their faces from a bucket provided by their valets. Hand towels were also nearby. After cleaning up, they congregated around a closed-circuit television set to watch the video replay of the race. Their valets and the rest of the jockeys in the room joined in. Kaenel turned to me and said, "You can learn more things in the jock's room watching the replay than out on the track—because it's the second time around. You get a whole picture of everything, the way the race develops and what you should or shouldn't have done at various stages of the race. If you've screwed up"—he laughed— "the other jocks will let you know."

Within the jockey room there is an efficient and methodical division of labor to prepare a jockey for each race. First there is the colors man, whose job is to organize, wash, and repair the various silks or "colors" that jockeys wear for each race. The jockey's valet is responsible for getting the correct silk to each of the jockeys in his corner before each race. Often a valet will set up several races in advance, arranged in order, so his jockeys can go from one silk to another without waiting. The valet also sets out the right saddle, pommel pad, girth, stirrups, whip, and any leaded pads necessary to meet the jockey's stipulated weight for the race. He then takes all this equipment and puts it in a numbered box that corresponds to the number of the horse the jockey will be riding in the next race. The boxes are at the very front of the locker room, next to the entrance/exit.

From there another valet will take the equipment out to the paddock area, where the trainer is waiting to saddle his horse. Only the reins and bridle are provided by the trainer. When the race is over, both the winning jockey and his equipment are weighed to make sure he has raced at his assigned weight. If he is underweight, his horse can be disqualified. On really hot or cold days riders are given a little leeway, because they can lose a pound or two during the course of a strenuous race.

When valets aren't organizing a jockey's equipment for a race, they're busy polishing and repairing it. They shine boots, clean goggles, and replace frayed straps. I noticed numerous rolls of duct tape. On rainy days jockeys wrap it around the bottoms of their pants to keep the mud from getting into their boots. Jockeys wear both leather and plastic boots. They use the leather boots when it's hot because they breathe and the plastic ones when it's cold because they keep the heat in. The thin-skinned boots cost $150 a pair and last anywhere from twenty to forty rides.

Goggles need to be replaced frequently, too. They cost $3.50 a pair. On sunny days a jockey will normally use only one pair during a race. But on muddy days he will ride with three or four perched on his forehead and pull them successively down as the pair he's using becomes covered by the mud being kicked back in his face. About goggles Kaenel joked, "They last forever if you're in front. You don't have any pebbles or dirt being kicked up into your face to scratch or break the lenses. But if I've been layin' back in the field on a muddy track, there are times when I've gone through all my goggles and had to ride without them. When that happens you get a lot of mud in your eyes and have to squint out of the corner, with your head ducked sideways, so you can see where you're going and keep away from trouble."

Perhaps closest to a jockey's heart are his saddles and the way they fit. Jockeys basically use two types, soft-backed and hard-backed. "All saddles have a tree," Jack explained, "but soft-backed ones have a shorter tree and a 'floppy-tailed' foam rubber backing that moves. Your hard-backed saddles are heavier—there's a full tree around the whole area that you sit on that's hard. Which saddle you use in a race depends upon how much weight you have to tack. If you're tacking 124 pounds, you can use either a heavy saddle or a lighter one with leaded pads. It all depends on how smooth it feels to you when you ride."

The second race was about to go off, and Jack had a mount coming up in the third. I asked him how he would prepare for it. "I'll look at the *Racing Form* and try to figure out which are the speed horses and where my horse is likely to be layin'. Of course, I may have what looks like the fifth fastest horse in the field and still wind up in front if the other horses get bumped or step in a hole and break stride. Basically, I try to get a general idea of how the race is gonna set up, even though when the gates come open I may have to throw my guess out the window."

An important variable is that horses don't always run the same. "Coming up to a race," Jack emphasized, "you never know for sure what they're gonna do. Horses are just like people: some days they feel good, some days they don't. You can have an idea, if they've been training better in the morning. But you can still be wrong. The trainer may have put them in over their head where they can't win."

What are some of the signs Kaenel looks for that a horse is ready to win? "I like a horse that seems alert or attentive when he's in the post parade or going to the gate and that takes a strong hold of the bit. I don't like horses that are real washed out or nervous before a race. Usually that takes too much out of them."

Jack stressed the importance of post position, especially for younger horses. "I think the one hole is the kiss of death, especially for first-time starters. That's because if a young horse is in the one hole, in a race with other first-time starters, he gets loaded in first and has to wait while all the other horses, who are nervous too, get loaded in after him. Sometimes the horse in the one hole will get tired of waiting and get too relaxed in there and won't break good. And that's a real disadvantage, because most races for young horses are sprints, where they run six furlongs or less and need to break good. I also think being in the one hole bothers young horses because they don't have the same thing on each side of them. Most of them will react to that difference by ducking in toward the rail or out toward the other horses and get bumped and break their stride. I basically hate the one hole for first-time starters or any horse—unless I'm on a pushbutton horse that will get out and fly."

With distance races Kaenel is partial to an outside post position, "because, if you're inside and on a horse with no early speed or you get away a little bit bad, you're going to have a whole wall of horses in front of you because everyone is trying to get the lead on the rail. What often happens is you're locked in, there's no way to get out, because everyone has already settled into position. Then, if a couple of horses in front of you start coming back to you,

you have to pull your horse back too, and lose even more ground."

An outside post gives a jockey more tactical choices in distance races. "If you've got enough horse, you can send him to the lead and ask him to get on over. If you don't, you can take ahold of him, tuck in behind the leaders, and make your move later. Sometimes you're gonna get stuck raw on the deal, regardless of what you do. But other times the fact you can adjust from the outside can make a big difference in whether you can get up as you head for the wire. In a race going a distance, if you break bad from the one hole you may lose ten lengths, whereas on the outside you might only lose three."

With year-round racing Kaenel thinks horses coming off a layoff have a better shot at winning than they used to. "With so many claiming horses and claiming races on the card these days, a lot of the horses that have been campaigning all year are worn out and feeling sour. I think a horse that hasn't been running is going to be fresher and has an advantage over the others. Especially if he's got decent works that are far enough, say a couple of three-quarter-mile works. That horse can definitely be fit enough to win off works alone."

Kaenel also likes inside speed horses on a muddy track. "The early speed horses, in the first three or four positions, percentagewise win a higher number of the races on a real muddy track. That's because it's not unusual for the horses in back and their riders to pick up four or five pounds of mud. The extra weight has to be a disadvantage when you add to it not being able to see where you're going. The only time that those plodding closers have a real advantage is on a slow, tiring track. In that case, the speed will burn itself out. The horses that come from ten lengths out of it will win, because all they're doing throughout the race is just galloping at a steady pace like they do in their morning works."

Kaenel has a jaundiced view of the *Daily Racing Form*. Waving his copy in front of me, Jack laughed. "This is one of the most lying sons of bitches there is. The most deceiving thing about the *Racing Form* is when you see a horse that's been off six months and runs a good third the first time back and gets beat only three lengths. Well, you think, now that he's had a good race underneath him, he'll come back and run real good. I'll guarantee that nine times out of ten that kind of horse bounces—it doesn't come back and run good his next race. I don't know why that is, but it seems to work that way. Maybe it's because, even though they were fresh, they weren't quite ready for that first race, they wore themselves out trying to win, and it took too much out of them. I'd rather ride a horse his second race back, if it's running at the same class level and not dropping drastically down, that ran an even eight lengths back his first time than the horse that tried real hard and came in third."

About horses that "bounce" their second race back, Kaenel observed, "Usually, he'll be rested a couple of weeks by the trainer and then come back the third time and run a bang-up race. I've seen that happen for years all over the country, in both sprints and distance races."

Kaenel gave me another example of how he tries to overcome the deceiving nature of the *Racing Form*. "If I look up and see a horse that's made two moves, that's been laying, say, six lengths coming into the turn and moves up three lengths and then moves back eight lengths and then comes back on and gets beat a couple lengths, I like to see that. Because you can't tell for sure what happened in the race from the *Form*. Maybe the horse run up in a jam and got slowed down, or had to go wide and lost ground. So the horse made up three lengths, lost five lengths and made up three lengths more, and got beat two or three lengths. That's about the best thing I could see in the *Form* for a horse that wouldn't otherwise figure. That's the reason why I would figure him. I like that kind of horse a lot better than the horse that's in front, and in front, and then stops and gets beat by ten lengths. Everybody can see that he went too fast or can't run that far. If you can see a change in there, in the middle of the race, where a horse showed some run and stopped and then made another run, that's what I like to see looking at the *Form*."

Jack also likes a speed horse that stumbles out of the gate, is rushed up by his jockey, and then quits for his next race back. "That's something I never do, is rush a horse up to the lead when he breaks poor. Because you use all the horse you have getting back up there and don't have anything left to finish with. I'd rather ease my way up, though a lot of times that won't work because the horse is used to running on the front end. But if you see a horse that breaks poor and runs up to the lead and stops, he might be a good bet back if he can break good."

Another pattern handicappers see is one in which a horse that's been off shows early speed in its first race back. Typically it will be within three or four lengths of the lead and then finish ten or more lengths back. But in its next race this same horse will carry its speed all the way and win. Jack explained what goes on: "If I'm on a horse that's been off for a while and know I'm beat, that I can't finish in the money, then there's no sense in beating him so he can finish sixth by seven lengths as opposed to tenth by thirteen lengths. There's no money difference there. You're better off easing back on the horse because he's tired anyway. You can beat him all you want and it won't make him run that much faster. But it will take something out of him for his next race that he might have a shot at winning. So a horse showing early speed that's quitting will often be eased up on, if it doesn't have a shot at the money. That's kind of an unwritten rule with riders, trainers, and everything: If you're on a tired horse, don't beat him up. On the other hand, if you got a horse that's stopping on you because he's sulking and 'common' [refuses to try] you can't give a horse like that a break. You beat him half to death and try and adjust his attitude."

People in the grandstand think a trainer is always trying to set a horse up for his next race. "What they forget," Kaenel explained, "is that a lot of times a trainer can't get a horse in to where he wants him. Maybe the horse is a week short of being ready, but the next race won't be for another four weeks. So the horse is entered and runs evenly to get it ready for that next race. But a horse can surprise you. The trainer might not think he's ready, but the horse wakes up and runs the race of his life."

Jack emphasized that the outcome of most races is determined by a fraction of a second. That's where the physical skills and judgment of an astute jockey come in. Kaenel puts particular emphasis on the mental side of riding. "The main thing in ridin' any race, whether it's a six-furlong sprint on the dirt or a two-mile race on the turf, is that I have to judge how much horse I have under me. Whether I go :22 and change [a fraction of a second] for the first quarter mile or 25 seconds flat depends on how the race develops. I have to feel not only how much horse I have, but also guess how much horse the other jocks have . . . so I know when to make my move. I may go slower sometimes if I'm on the front end, but that's okay if I make the other jocks go slower than me. It's tough to explain how I judge what's going on, but it's all timing. Good jockeys have that sense of timing. In my opinion a racetrack changes every time the tractor's harrows go across the top of it. So just time doesn't mean anything. You have to be able to judge how a horse is handling the track given the speed at which he's going. Pace, not just time, makes a race. Also, a horse can go a quarter mile in 25 seconds and it can take more out of him, if you're holding him back, than if you let him run freely in :22 flat. It just depends on the horse."

Racetrack professionals talk about how a jockey like Willie Shoemaker had good hands. As Jack puts it, "Shoemaker knew how to rate a horse without strangling him. If you take too hard a hold of a horse with the reins you wind up choking him. Good hands is really having a feel for a horse and taking ahold of it, rating it, in a way that gets it to relax, without doing it so hard that you throw the horse off its stride or tire it too much. You can tell when a horse is relaxed by the way it feels to you. Shoemaker knew how to ride chilly and not be flopping all over the horse. If a rider can't sit still and relax, how can the horse relax? They definitely pick up on that. A lot of times when a horse's ears are pinned back you can tell they're getting tired or don't like what you're doing to them. But horses are different. Another horse will have its ears pinned back and be all business coming down the lane."

Kaenel emphasized there are different ways to rate a horse. "Some horses rate easy. Others you have to take a hard hold of for a little while, to get them to the position and speed you want them, then turn them loose a little bit and they'll stay at that speed and position. Other horses you have to take hold and keep it there until you're ready to run. Still others you can't take ahold of at all; you just have to turn them loose. You're better off doing that than taking ahold of them, because the more hold you take of them the more they want to run, and they just wear themselves out. With that kind of horse you sometimes have to just let them run, and then when you want them to try harder you take ahold of them for a second and they'll respond by trying to run even harder. It just depends on the horse. You have to feel what will get the most out of your horse. If you can get your horse to relax while the jocks in front of you are pushing their horses or fighting them to slow down, then you know, percentagewise, that's gonna take more out of theirs than you're taking out of yours, and you'll have more horse to finish with."

Though good jockeys are supposed to have clocks inside their heads that tell them how fast they're going, Kaenel thinks the notion is too simple. "There's an old racetrack saying, 'Time only means something if you're in jail.' I don't really worry about how fast the horse is going, say, every eighth of a mile. It's how much it's taking out of him to go as fast as he's going that I pay attention to. You really can't gauge the splits in every race exactly anyway, because the track surface changes with every race."

If having good hands and being able to rate a horse is important to a jockey's finesse, having strong legs is no less important when it comes to riding fitness. "For a normal person," Kaenel explained, "to crouch halfway down and have their weight on their ankles for a minute to a minute and forty seconds and just hold it there is pretty tough. It's pretty tough for me, fit as I am. When a jock's standing in the irons and bending down on a horse, some of his weight is on his knees, but for the most part it's on his feet in the stirrups with the horse moving underneath him at forty miles an hour. So your main ridin' strength comes from your legs. When your legs get tired, that's what changes a jockey's style.

"The first part of a race you see every rider sitting even, whether they ride high or low. As the race develops it's tougher to keep your stance even. But that's important, because if your legs get weak, and your stance uneven, that gets in the way of your hand ride in the stretch. During a race a jockey's rear end should never touch the saddle. From the time you break out of the gate until the race is over and your horse is stopped and about to come back, you never touch the saddle. It's just strictly on your legs. When a race is over a jockey will stand up in the stirrups and bend over the horse. It's called 'cockin' your legs' and is a way of slowing your horse down. You unbend your knees and stand straight up so that the pressure is off your leg muscles and your weight is just on your bones."

The only time that a jockey will stand straight up in the stirrups during a race, other than when his horse breaks down, is when another horse bears in sharply in front of him and he has to steady his horse to avoid a collision. In that situation, Kaenel said, "You've got to put all the pressure you can to slow your horse down. In order to do that it's like being a weight lifter. You lift with your arms first and then use your legs to pick it on up. On a horse you pull back with your hands and then use your legs for the leverage to move your whole body back and take hold of the horse."

While the general public doesn't think of jockeys as athletes, as Jack talked I began to appreciate the argument that pound for pound they are the most skilled and coordinated in all sports. It's a statistical fact, according to John Giovanni of the Jockeys' Guild, that minute for minute, being a jockey is also the most dangerous athletic profession in the world. "Over the past thirty years," he told me over the phone, "an average of two jockeys have died each year, and we currently have forty-six riders who are permanently paralyzed as a result of racing injuries. Racing thoroughbreds is dangerous because, unlike racecar drivers, jockeys have little protection. They don't have seat belts, adequate helmets, or any of the protections that car drivers have. A racecar driver can hit a wall at 150 miles per hour and walk away without serious injury. Jockeys, when they're thrown from their mounts, can hit the ground or the rail with no protection at speeds exceeding 40 miles per hour. It's difficult to protect them because of the weight limitations on their gear and because of the unsolved problem of maintaining their peripheral vision in the design of safer helmets."

While death and paralysis are the most extreme examples of danger, jockeys regularly incur a number of other injuries. The most common nonfatal injury is a broken collarbone, because jockeys are usually pitched forward, headfirst, when their horses break down or fall during the course of a race. Broken arms, legs, and ribs are also not uncommon. Then, too, internal injuries— damaged kidneys, spleens, livers, and cracked vertebrae—are part of a jockey's daily risk. Injuries occur because of hitting the ground wrong, getting kicked by a passing horse, or being crushed against the gate or rail.

The guard rails along the inside of a racetrack, according to Giovanni, are the most dangerous obstacles to falling jockeys. "Straight rails that are directly connected to posts are the most dangerous. Slant-back rails, which have the posts set back, are safer but jockeys can and do still hit them. The safest rail is the Fontana, which is goosenecked and has the posts set back, with the actual rail having a plastic cover that the jockey can land on and 'cushion' off of. A Fontana rail acts like a shock absorber and helps to break the velocity of a rider's fall. Del Mar in southern California has one, and its presence probably saved Lafitt Pincay from serious injury, if not death, when he took a bad spill there this past summer. At Del Mar and elsewhere there have been numerous spills on the rail since its installation without a permanently disabling injury. Every racetrack in America should have a Fontana rail installed for the protection of the jockeys."

Bad running surfaces are also dangerous to jockeys. It amazes Giovanni that no racing association has ever paid for a study of what the best racing surface for thoroughbreds and jockeys should be. "Owners will pay $2 million for a horse, then run him on a two-dollar track. It's crazy. And another thing: Two-year-old horses are breaking down because they are being raced while physically immature. The purses are so big for two-year-olds, though, that owners ignore the danger. If two-year-olds were only raced late in the fall of their second year, and then very lightly, it would be better for both horses and jockeys in terms of avoiding injuries."

Since races begin at the starting gate, I asked Jack to talk about the confusion that often goes on there. "Most horses don't want to load into the gate because the adrenaline gets into their system when they know it's time to run. It's not that they're scared so much as that they get excited. The starting gate is just wide enough for the horse plus four to eight inches on each side. So when they start into the gate they sometimes hit the side, and that makes them balk and want to back off. Sometimes they do that on purpose. There are bad horses that back off or flip in the gate. But mainly the horses are just pumped up. They know it's time to run, and the gate just seems like an obstacle to them."

A horse flipping in or near the gate creates one of the most dangerous situations for a jockey, in which the horse's back legs go out from underneath it as it is backing up. This can happen even when the back gate is shut behind the horse. There is enough room for an excited horse to move up a step and then back a step and flip over. The jockey risks being crushed between the falling horse and the gate. The smartest thing a jockey can do in that situation, according to Kaenel: "Stay with your horse. You shouldn't take hold of the safety bars on the gate or anything else. That's when you get hurt. If you get half off, with one foot in the stirrups, and your horse goes ahead and flips, you can get pinned between the horse and the bars and be crushed."

Kaenel has a special approach that has worked for him in avoiding injuries around the starting gate. "First off," he explained, "when a horse begins to rear up, you don't pull on the reins, because that's what pulls the horse up over you. That's what an inexperienced rider's first reaction would be. I have what I call a 'sissy strap' on all of my saddles. It's just a nylon loop that goes from one side of the saddle's tree to the other. I can loop my finger in there when a horse goes to rear, instead of grabbing hold of the reins and pulling him over on top of me. I actually learned to ride with it and without stirrups when I was a young boy. My dad didn't want my little feet tangled up in the stirrups, so he took them off, and the sissy loop was all I had to hang on to. It's the best insurance policy I ever bought. Grabbing a handhold on a sissy strap has saved me quite a few times from potential injury in races."

Since we were talking about potential injury, I asked Jack what it's like to hit the ground at thirty-five to forty miles an hour when a horse falls or breaks down. "Well, it's pretty hairy. If you want an example, you could get on the front end of my pickup and let

me rev it up on a dirt road to thirty-five or forty and then, when
I hit the brakes, you can dive off headfirst. Then imagine there's
eight to ten horses running right behind you that you have to avoid
getting trampled by."

Jockeys are sometimes blamed for not avoiding fallen horses
and riders. "But the public doesn't understand," Jack observed,
"how quick things happen, that a horse runs a length every fifth
of a second. So if a horse goes down in front of you and you're only
a length behind it, you only have a fifth of a second to react. If
you're five lengths behind, you only have one second. That isn't a
very long time to react. You've got to decide to guide your horse
inside or outside of the fallen horse or rider in that one second.
Maybe you make the right decision but your horse don't. Your
horse only has that one second to react, too. So it depends on each
individual horse as much as or more than it does on the jockey. I
would definitely rather depend on my horse's reaction more than
my own. There isn't time enough to tell the horse what to do and
then have him do it. I would rather trust my horse's reaction than
to try and fight him in that split second. I think the reason there
aren't worse spills is because the horses generally know how to
react to obstacles. If you let them, they'll usually jump over or
skirt around them."

What about when Kaenel is the rider on a horse that is going
down? "Your best protection is in knowing how to fall. The first
time I had a bad injury, I didn't know how to fall. I went off a
horse that was my father's. She really didn't do much of anything
wrong—she just ducked out, and I went off. I'd rode for quite a
few years and could ride real good, but it became a disadvantage
because I didn't go off much and didn't know how to hit the ground
rolling. What I did was stick my leg out as I came off, and the
impact snapped both bones in my leg. I've gone down tons worse
since then and not hurt myself, because I learned how to fall. I
learned by getting in a sand arena and bailing off a horse so that I
hit the ground rolling. That's what protects you. Most of the time,
when you break an arm or leg it's because you haven't overcome
that natural tendency to stick that arm or leg out there to help
break your fall. That's what snaps your bones.

"Nobody wants to come off a horse going forty miles an hour," Jack emphasized. "It's not something you expect to do, because you can't have that in your mind when you're ridin'. But you still have to hit the ground rolling. If you do that and ball yourself up, the horses going over you won't step in the middle of you and break a rib or kick a kidney. A lot of times they'll graze you and any injury will be a lot less severe. When you go off headfirst in a spill, you tuck your head and shoulder as you roll—ball yourself up more or less—and your momentum will carry you and keep you rollin'. It's when you're spraddled out that you get stepped on and hurt, because you're a bigger target. Basically the idea is to keep the target area small and keep moving when you fall."

Apart from falling or breaking down, there are other troublesome things horses can do during a race. They can lug in or bear out; they can panic and bolt. In most cases a jockey isn't helpless. There are different bits and blinkers a trainer may add to help a horse run straighter during a race. A jockey can use his reins and stick to guide a horse. As an example, Kaenel says, "Let's take a horse that starts off on the inside and suddenly bolts out to the right. Who knows why? Maybe that horse saw something, or thought he saw something, that scared him. It might have been a scrap of paper or a flashbulb. Unchecked, that horse is gonna run into the outside fence or wall, and there will be a collision. In that situation, rather than keep turning the horse's head to the left if he's going to the right, what I've done is to keep trying to pull them to the left up to the point where I know a collision is about to happen. At that point, if I've been unsuccessful in changing the horse's course back to the left, I'll turn its head sharply to the right, in the direction of the fence, so it can see it. If the horse will look at the fence in that moment, it will often have the last-second sense to veer back to the left. Most horses aren't out to deliberately hurt themselves. They don't want to crash into a fence or go over it. They've bolted because maybe they're sore on one side or something scared them and they panicked. In that situation their mind is in a half-blank and they don't actually know that wall or fence is there. So when you pull their heads to the right and give them that shot to see the fence, they'll straighten out for you."

· · ·

Once horses have broken out of the gate and headed into the first turn, in fact any turn of a race, they tend to drift out as they change leads from their right to their left front leg. This means that most jockeys hit their horses on the right side coming into a turn to keep their horses from drifting too far out and to keep from bumping into another horse. The natural progression for a horse is to lead with its right foot on the straightaways and with its left foot on the turns.

Some horses naturally switch leads; others have to be nudged. When a horse is running on the wrong lead during a race, jockeys will shift their weight in what Kaenel calls a hesitatin' action. If a rider wants a horse to change from a left lead to a right one, this involves shifting his weight to the left side of the horse, then quickly shifting all of it over to the right. The change in weight and balance forces the horse to change leads in the direction the jockey wants.

Experience, however, has made Kaenel leery of forcing a horse to change leads if it really doesn't want to. When he was racing at Aqueduct he had two horses at the tail end of one card and a horse in the first race the next day all break down and throw him as a result of his forcing them to change leads. "If a horse doesn't want to change lead, there's probably a good reason for it. It may be running with a sore foot or leg. It knows better than me what it can and can't do."

During the running of a race, jockeys can get into trouble in a number of ways. Sometimes, when they're on the lead with a tiring horse, they'll try to save ground by moving toward the rail and inadvertently cut off an approaching horse, forcing it to steady and lose ground or, more dangerously, to clip heels and tumble. A jockey may try to scoot through a narrow, closing hole and bump another horse. Or two horses may be running head and head, a jockey hits his horse on the wrong side, and it drifts into the adjacent horse. In those instances the inquiry sign will invariably light up on the tote board, and the stewards will review the video of the race to determine whether or not the transgression was severe enough to have affected the outcome of the race. If so, the horse will be disqualified and "have its number taken down."

About bumping, Kaenel reflected, "If you do it, they have to take your number down. Because there is no way a human can judge how much a bump will take out of a horse. Say you're on the inside and you bump the horse next to you and that one bumps a third one on the outside. You've caused a chain reaction, where maybe the third horse would have gotten up for second or even won the race. Some horses can be bumped and recover real quick, others get untracked and never get back in the race. A little bump might totally spook one horse and a bigger bump might not really affect another one. Each horse is different."

Often, when one horse impedes another, the jockey isn't at fault. Thoroughbreds are high-strung animals and will veer in or lug out of their own accord. It isn't always possible for a 110-pound jockey to control a 1,000-pound horse. Besides disqualifying a horse for a racing infraction, the stewards have to decide if the jockey was at fault and should be suspended or "given days."

Regarding suspensions, Kaenel explained, "In California it's usually for five days, which is the same as a week, because there are two dark days when we don't race. Typically, the jockey goes before the stewards the next day and tells his side of the story. If he's suspended, it usually starts the day after the overnight listings so as not to interfere with the next day's racing schedule. Now if a jockey does something really malicious, like grab your reins during a race, the stewards can hand out six months, a year . . . whatever they want. There's a rules book as thick as my leg that guides the stewards, but the last rule in it is that the stewards have the final discretion."

Elaborating on the subject of suspensions and competitive riding, Kaenel said, "There's an adage around the track, 'If a rider doesn't get any days, then he's not trying hard enough.' But there's also another saying that I was raised on: 'When you're on the best horse, you don't get yourself beat.' When you're on the best horse, why take a chance? Your job is to just get your horse around there and don't get him in trouble or bother someone to get your number taken down."

In judging how aggressively to ride, jockeys have to know the predilections of various trainers. Some trainers want a jockey to take a chance; others don't. Some horses are willing to shoot through a gap and others won't. "It's really a tossup as to how trainers feel if you take a chance and go inside and get stopped or have your number taken down. Some trainers will blame you for not going around, and others will say, 'The jock tried, and that's horse racing that he got stopped and had his number taken down.' "

Since trainers often give jockeys riding instructions, I asked Kaenel to talk about them. "Instructions depend upon whether or not you've ridden the horse before, and the trainer. For example, let's take Chuck Jenda, who I've done quite a bit of ridin' for this past year and had quite a bit of luck. We talk about a race, but I can't remember the last time he gave me specific instructions on how to ride a race. The owners were in the paddock one day at Golden Gate Fields and I was on a horse that I had ridden two seconds and a third on that should have won all three of them. But the horse, called Mean Cuisine, just didn't want to win. It didn't want to try hard enough. I said, 'Chuck, I'd like to try—' and he cut me off and said, 'Hey, you ride your race and I'll criticize you after.' Well, Jenda rides me because he has confidence in my riding. So he lets me ride a horse the way I want to ride him, and it makes my job ten times easier. I'd a whole lot rather blame myself than any trainer for getting beat on a horse. I think I've lost more races by following instructions than I have by an error in my judgment during a race. Now, don't get me wrong. I've messed up, too. But if you never mess up, you ain't trying very hard. 'Cause if you rode a horse twice and it didn't work, and don't try something different, nothing's gonna change. And sometimes you might want to try something new, but the race doesn't let you. Maybe you want to try for the lead earlier, but your horse stumbles from the gate or gets blocked by another horse. My point is that it makes it a whole lot easier if you have the trainer's confidence in your judgment."

Kaenel feels jockeys are often unfairly second-guessed by people in the grandstand. "It's such a different view when you're actually riding, as opposed to sitting in the trainer's box or the grandstand," he emphasized. "I realized that when I broke my leg and started watching races from the grandstand for the first time. I'd never realized that you don't see the same thing from the grandstand or from them TVs. Let me give you an example. You drive a car all the time, right? Now watching a car race on TV, you can say, 'Yeah, they're close there to the bumpers, they're going in and out'—a little bit hairy, right? Now, remember that they're going 150 miles an hour. Suppose now you're driving fast, say 80 miles an hour on the freeway, weaving in and out of traffic—see if your hair don't stand up a little on the back of your neck. Now, if you're in that car with a driver going 150 miles an hour, you're gonna get a whole different view of things about timing, what's developing, and when to make a move during the race. It just looks so much simpler from the grandstands—there's just a mass of horses moving there. But that's just not the way it is when you're on a horse in the middle of a race. You're in your own world out there with the horses. For instance, I can't normally hear the P.A. system that you can hear in the grandstand. But I can hear the riders hollering behind me, the snap of a whip, the horse's hooves hitting the ground, and the way they're breathing. There's like a pocket of air that carries all that for you during a race. But you can't hear the whole crowd screaming; at least I can't."

I was curious what kinds of things jockeys holler to each other during a race. "Most of it's stuff like, 'Hey, watch out, pick your head up,' and some swearing if somebody is getting shut off. You holler to get another jockey's attention and let him know you're there. Basically, the hollering is to protect yourself. If you're coming into the stretch and really smoking and another horse is tiring and drifting out, you yell out, 'Hey, pick your horse up.' Because it's real dangerous when two horses are going at different speeds for them to get tripped up. Everybody's got their own vocabulary as far as hollering, and we usually know who's who."

There are also some jockeys who have a reputation for crying wolf when they're not in trouble. "They're gonna pay for that, because no one is gonna believe them when they might really need some help. There is this one rider that starts screaming and hollering when things get just a little bit tight. That can be irritating, especially when you're finishing second, you know you can't beat the lead horse, but you slow down to help a rider and then they beat you for second. It makes you look stupid for letting them through."

Kaenel elaborated about the difference in perspective between being in the grandstand and riding in a race. "When horses are running up the backside, a fan can't tell from the grandstand how far the horse laying third is off the rail. When he sees his horse coming up the backside and says, 'Well, here he comes, he's gonna run good,' well, he can't see from the grandstand how far apart the three front horses are or if there's a place to go through. He can't tell from the grandstand if that horse in front, who's been in the lead by a length and a half the whole way, is tiring like you can when you're in the race."

Fans in the grandstand are often critical of jockeys even when they're not at fault. Jack gave an example of a ride a jockey can be unfairly criticized for. "A jock doesn't always know what's gonna develop," he emphasized. "Say, if I'm moving up on the inside with a lot of ground to make up and there's no way I can win if I go to the outside. And the horse in front of me on the inside is showing lots of speed, but all of a sudden the horse in front of him stops and forces the horse in front of me to slow down and there's two horses outside of me not going nowhere. Now, I'm stopped right there. I can lose five or six lengths easy, and there ain't nothin' I can do about it. At the time I went to the inside, the horse in front of me was moving the fastest of all—how could I know the horse in front of him was gonna stop? When a jock gets blocked it gives the impression to the public that he's not letting his horse run. Well, he's not because there ain't no place to run. The jock's got to take hold of his horse and steady him. Otherwise he'll run into the horse in front and cause a bad spill. The public may think you're stiffing their horse, but shit, unless you want to be suicidal what you're doin' is saving your life."

Jack described some of the body-language cues he looks for during a race to tell him a horse is tiring. "You can tell by a horse's ears and by his head. His head will usually drop when he's getting tired, or come way up. A horse that is in front with his ears pricked is usually doing it easy. If you see a horse's ears coming back, laying flat, that's a good indication that it's starting to tire. I watch its stride too. If you're right behind it you can usually tell a horse is getting tired when it starts to wobble. Its stride gets shorter and its whole body starts moving rather than maintaining that free-flowing stride. This is stuff a rider can pick up on that you don't immediately see from the stands or on television."

A lot of horses drift out as they come down the stretch. I've often wondered if that's because of fatigue or some deeper physical problem. "Usually, it's just fatigue. More often than not horses will drift out to the right because the right front leg takes more pressure than any other thing on a horse. That's because horses in America all run counterclockwise. They're trained going left, they run going left, they do everything to the left. When they hit the turns all the pressure is on their right front leg, and that's the one that gets tired, regardless of what lead they're in. When that happens their left leg is gonna be stronger, and that usually causes their back ends to drift out to the right. Another reason that horses drift out when they're getting tired in a race is that they know 'out' is where they go to slow down and pull up in the mornings after their workouts. They know fast speed is down on the inside. That's where they're trained to run as fast as they can. So if a horse wants to quit, it's going to drift to the outside, more often than not."

Horses get tired, but what about jockeys? I asked Jack what the most exhausting kind of ride is for a jockey. "Riding a horse that's not trying, that you have to keep after the whole way, is the most tiring. There are a lot of horses that will be ten lengths out of it that you have to keep after or they'd be fifteen lengths out. Those horses you have to ride the whole way, whether it's three-quarters of a mile or a distance. It's a lot less tiring to be riding for a win, head and head and switching sticks, than it is to be on a horse that refuses to take the bit and is trailing the field twenty-five lengths. Those kinds of horses feel like you've been on them forever. That's not only because you've got to crouch on those stirrups longer and fatigue your legs more, but also because a slow horse isn't moving under you easy like one that's running good is. The 4½-furlong races for two-year-olds are actually the most tiring of all the races to ride. That's because they're greener, and you have to keep their minds on business the whole way. You have to break them quickly out of the gate to get position, and once you have position you have to keep it and keep on ridin'. You basically have to ride them from the gate to the wire with no letup, and that's the most exertion there is. The longer the race is, percentagewise, the easier it is for me to ride. Usually horses that can run 1⅜ miles aren't common or cheatin' horses that you have to beat half to death. Sure you've got to cluck to them and get them into position. But after that, basically you just sit there on them. You don't do any real hard riding until the stretch, that last quarter of a mile to the wire. A six-furlong race is almost always more tiring to ride than a mile-and-a-quarter race."

I asked Kaenel what goes through his mind once he has broken his horse out of the gate, established his position, and arrived at the top of the stretch headed for home. "If you're coming from off the pace, the shortest way home is definitely the rail. But once you're lined up around the turn, it's the same distance home for everyone, and generally horses will run better in the stretch if they are on the outside and in the clear. Most horses would rather be on the outside. Even if there is a hole on the inside, a lot of horses won't try as hard because they just don't want to go in next to the rail.

"If I'm on the rail coming for home and blocked, the main thing I try to do is get my horse outside as smoothly as possible without having to stop its momentum. The main thing in finding a hole to go through is predicting what's gonna happen in front of you. If the outside horse in front of you is dying, where say there are three horses in front of you, then sometimes you have to wait for it to come back to you before you make your move to the outside. If you go too soon, then you'll get stuck behind the outside horse and have to pull your horse up and break his momentum.

"If you're in front it depends upon the horse as much as any-thing. A lot of times you'll want to let your horse drift out from along the fence and take a chance on a horse coming through on the rail, because most horses don't want to come through on the rail. Generally, I'd rather have a guy come up inside of me, if he's on the horse to beat, than on the outside of me. That's because I can put pressure on him and make the hole smaller that he has to go through between the rail and me. His horse may want to lug out and not come in there as good. All this depends upon being on the lead. When you're on the lead you can dictate everyone else's position a lot easier."

While most jockeys ride the first part of a race with their butts sticking six inches or so above the saddle, when they hit the stretch and start to hand ride they lean farther forward and begin to move their hands up and down a horse's neck. Kaenel elaborated. "In the first part of a race, especially a distance one, I've got a little more hold of a horse, and my knees are even with my shoulders and my heels are down. But when you go to hand ridin' a horse in the stretch you actually start pushing on the horse, which changes the position of your legs. Your knees then go forward and your heels come up so you can push and scrub with your hands."

Good jockeys time their movements with the stride of their horse. "In the stride of a horse," Kaenel continued, "most all the time they only have one leg on the ground at a time. The other three legs are various distances off the ground. What you have is a pattern where in their stride the horse is pushing off their back end and pulling with their front feet. That's their stride. When their head is going out, that's when you're pushing. The scrubbing is when you're coming back with the rhythm of the horse as it's pulling with its front legs. The reason that term 'pushing and scrubbing' is used is because the jockey's hands are going up and down the horse's neck. As the horse is reaching out, your hands are going up their neck. And as the horse's head comes back up, your hands come back too. While you're hand riding you also have to vary your control, your pressure on the reins. Some horses like you to keep their heads picked up while they're pulling with their front legs. It builds confidence in them. It gives them a little more support when they're coming back up off their front stride. Even though you're pushing forward with them, you still keep their heads picked up by having a fairly strong hold of the reins. Some riders, when they're hand riding, have their reins loose all the time. It's partly a matter of style. I usually keep all my horses' heads picked up. I can have my reins where there's no slack in them, but not necessarily have a real hold of them either."

A horse, in Kaenel's opinion, does eighty percent of its running off its front legs. "They push off with their hind legs, but it's the reaching out with their front legs that gives them their momentum, their speed. When the horse in its natural stride is reaching out with its front legs, a jockey is pushing with it so that maybe the horse will get six more inches out of each stride to pull itself forward with. Normally, their left front foot hits the ground first and their heads go down as their right front foot follows, hitting the ground. That's when they're pulling. When both of their front feet have hit the ground in that stride, a horse's head tends to be closest to the ground. As they start pushing with their hind legs, their heads start to come back up. When a horse is really trying for you and beginning to tire or founder, you can help a horse out by picking it back up a little just before their head reaches that lowest point in the front stride. You don't interfere with the natural movement and stride of the horse, you just try and time your own movement in a way that gives a horse its best balance and efficiency in its stride. When a horse is trying for you but beginning to get a little leg-weary and doesn't have quite as much control, the weight of their head tends to overcarry them in their front momentum. What you're trying to do by picking a horse's head up is allow their front legs to catch up and extend in front of their neck and head. That way they can have a longer reach in their front stride and run faster. You're encouraging them to stay with it. But each horse is different, and a jockey has to feel what's right with each particular horse. With some horses, picking them up too soon will interfere with their stride."

As Kaenel talked I became more fascinated with the precise detail involved in hand riding a horse to the wire. I told him, "Jack, as you guys are coming to the wire, head and head, it appears to me that you're riding totally on balance, giving it everything you have, with the horse going full bore too. It seems like a real delicate athletic skill to be doing that, going forty miles an hour and not falling off. How do you guys do that?"

Kaenel looked at me with an appreciative twinkle in his eyes and said, "You're right, it *is* a balancing act. In the stretch a rider's body is forward and his heels are up. At that point he's pushing off his heels, and his weight is more on his hands and on the horse's neck. That's why, when a horse breaks down in the stretch, the rider will go off headfirst—because he's so far forward. Earlier in the race, when a jockey is ridin' more upright and a horse breaks down, he can pull back on the reins using his feet for leverage, and pick the horse's head up, and keep himself and the horse from going down. The worst spills usually don't happen during the middle or end of a race. If a horse has made it to the wire, he's usually okay. It's at the head of the stretch, when the horse switches leads and lands on it wrong, that he's most likely to break down. That's the time when he's most likely to get leg-weary, take a misstep, and break a leg. I guarantee you that the ambulance comes and picks up the horse and rider more from the quarter pole to the eighth pole than anywhere else."

Kaenel extolled the value of knowing when to ride absolutely still or chilly, coming down the stretch. "There comes a point in every race, especially for a young rider, where he gets worried about maybe losing the race and gets tempted to do something extra that might actually get in the way of the horse's best stride. A jockey should be doing whatever he can to get to the wire, but he should also know when to ride chilly."

Jack learned to ride chilly on a mare called Jamilla by watching how other people rode her. "She would lay third or fourth on the outside, behind the leaders, and look like she was gonna win easy. The jocks who were riding her would go to hitting her in the stretch, and she would stay close but never win. I rode her eight times and won eight stakes races on her and never hit her once. During that time she beat the best mares in the country and even beat the boys once. Zany Tactics was the same way, except I could hand ride him hard. With Jamilla I didn't even do that. I could get the most out of her by never moving on her, never asking anything of her."

When a jockey does resort to the whip, he must time his hit to the horse's stride. "The time you want to hit a horse," Kaenel emphasized, "is when it's pushing off its hind legs and beginning to reach out with its front legs. That will often make a horse reach out a little farther. An inexperienced rider will often look like he's slapping a horse rather than hittin' him because his timing is off. You don't want to hit a horse while it's trying to collect itself off its front stride. You have to wait until the horse has already done that and is beginning to push off its hind legs. It's also important that, while you're hitting a horse, you're still hand ridin' with the other hand. Trainers will sometimes ask me why I didn't hit the horse because they can't see that I've hit him with my left hand while I'm still hand ridin' with my right hand. A jock's rhythm has to work with the rhythm of the horse, although that's not to say there aren't split seconds where a jockey has to lean back a tad to help balance a horse who's foundering in its stride. A jockey has to be able to switch sticks from one hand to the other while keeping control of his reins and maintaining the rhythm of his hand ride. It has to be done real quick, without making a mistake and without dropping the reins or the whip."

Laffit Pincay is famous for "muscling" a horse down the stretch. "That's basically about hand riding and not doing a lot of whipping," Jack explained. "The reason Pincay has that reputation for being a great hand rider is that he's got a good sense and feeling with the horse underneath him and the strength to pick a horse up when it gets tired. He knows how much horse he's got and if the horse is really trying for him or not. If I could cut out the public, the owners, and trainers, I would hand ride a lot more races than I do now, and never hit a horse, and win by a nose or get beat by a nose. Everybody thinks a jockey's not trying if he don't hit his horse. But that's not necessarily true. At some point you've got to trust a jockey's judgment."

When I suggested that Kaenel could fake it and hit the horse easy, he laughed and said, "Yep. That's what I do to make up for it. In Pincay's case, he's been around for so long that people trust his judgment, and he can do pretty much what he wants to do. Not taking anything away from Pincay, but there are other riders just as strong as he is physically, who aren't given the freedom to hand ride their horses like he is."

If Pincay has a reputation for muscle, Willie Shoemaker is the epitome of a jockey who knew how to coax the best ride out of a horse. I asked Jack to compare the two. "Well, Shoemaker weighed ninety-five pounds for most of his career—he's definitely not 'muscle' like Pincay. He had to carry all that 'dead' weight, and yet he's the winningest jockey of all time. He won over eighty-eight hundred races. It's a known fact that he didn't hit horses hard, didn't have the strength to do it. Still, he won more races than anyone else. Pincay is number two on the all-time list. The only thing similar between Shoemaker and Pincay, when they were riding against each other, is that they both owned saddles and boots and jockey pants. Shoemaker was the lightest jockey in America, and Pincay one of the heaviest."

It was a lazy Monday afternoon the next time I saw Jack, who with his family was now at their ranch in Martinez. Jack was in front of his tack shack fixing up some gear so a bunch of us could go mule riding. Somehow it made sense that a man who races thoroughbreds at forty miles per hour for a living would enjoy riding a mule for pleasure. But I was there to talk about fast horses, especially Zany Tactics, who holds the world record for the fastest six furlongs ever run.

"Zany Tactics is definitely the fastest horse I've ever ridden," Jack reminisced. "I would break in front with him and then take ahold of him, because he was a horse that would rate easy. I didn't have to choke him to slow him down. I would take him back one horse off the pace until a horse came up behind me trying to catch the lead or the front horse made its move. Zany was a horse you didn't want to make a move on between the half-mile and quarter pole. Early in his career he lost some races because he made his move too soon and would stop halfway down the lane. I believe there was rapport between Zany and me. When I asked of him, he knew what I wanted. When I set the world record on him on the dirt at Turf Paradise, I never even uncocked my stick. I just hand rode him the whole way."

In fact, hitting Zany Tactics actually slowed the horse down. "If a horse is giving you all he's got, how is beatin' on him gonna make him run faster?" The first few times Kaenel rode Zany Tactics he did whip him in the stretch, and the horse lost. Trusting his intuition, he asked the trainer to let him hand ride the horse. The trainer initially hesitated, because it's a dicey situation not to hit a horse in a close race. If the horse loses, owners and the public will often think the jockey isn't trying if he doesn't go to the whip. With Zany Tactics, however, the trainer's willingness to listen to Kaenel's advice paid off. The horse ran 1:06.3, the fastest six furlongs in history.

Unfortunately Zany Tactics dropped dead after a workout a few months later. Lamenting the loss, Kaenel said, "It just seems that it's the horses with a lot of heart that always go early. There was Landaluce, Zany Tactics, and Bedside Promise. They're the type of horse that gives you all they've got, and then their hearts go on them."

Moving to Kaenel's best current mount, I asked him about Brown Bess, the sensational older turf mare from Chuck Jenda's barn that was challenging for an Eclipse Award. Even though she's a little mare, I'd heard she needs a strong rider. "Brown Bess definitely wants to run off when she's running," Jack confirmed. "She wants to go as fast and as hard as she can, and it takes some strength to slow her down. But it also takes patience to ride her. I've won all my races with her by coming from just off the pace. I keep her close and then just let her run that last eighth of a mile. To me, she's the easiest horse that I ever ride. When I say that Brown Bess is an easy horse to ride, I mean she is the same type of horse as Zany Tactics was. When I first started riding him, he would always go to the front, run for a half mile, stop, and then get caught. When I got him to rating, to pick it up from off the pace and put that energy into the last quarter of a mile, he ended up setting two world records. It's the same thing with Brown Bess.

My key to her is to get her to relax in the first part of the race and then to come from off the pace."

Kaenel basically hand rides Brown Bess. "She don't take a lot of stick. In the Ramona stakes down at Del Mar, I hit her real lightly, just showed her the stick is all, because she's so willing. She gives you all that she has when you ask her. Of course, you have to have a good sense of pace to use that ability that she's got right. It's tougher mentally than it is physically to ride Brown Bess. In the Ramona, we laid second most of the way and I just let her drag me up until I was head and head for the lead. When we turned down the lane every horse was within two and a half lengths of the lead, and I just let her run the last eighth of a mile. Even though she won by less than a length, she actually won that race easy. She's not the kind of horse that opens up a big lead. She just does what she has to do down the lane. As soon as that other horse got to her on the inside, she moved away from it and back out in front a half a length. We could have gone all day that way. Of course, I couldn't have got her to win by more than she did, either."

Chuck Jenda had been quoted in the *Racing Form* as saying that Kaenel had given Brown Bess more courage since he had been riding her. I asked Jack how a jockey can give a horse courage. "Everybody's got their own style. One thing I do, even when they're running relaxed on the front end, is keep their heads picked up. I have a tighter hold than having the reins completely loose. I think that gives them more confidence to start with. Keeping the reins gathered up also helps a horse because it gives them better balance, especially toward the end of a race when they start to get tired and weary-legged. Another way to build confidence in a horse that doesn't have much, is not to put them in a situation where they're gonna get scared. You try and do everything smooth and steady, so you don't have to snatch the reins too abruptly when you make your move. Sometimes when a horse runs three or four races and nothing bad happens to them—maybe they're scared of running on the inside or going between a hole—they get braver and try harder. It's just like a fighter. Once he wins four or five fights, I don't care who he beats, he's gonna have more confidence than he had right after he got beat. It's the same way with horses, winning races or just having everything go good.

"Brown Bess is such a gutsy, hard-trying horse that maybe she didn't do as well before I rode her because someone was using too much stick on her. When a horse is trying as hard as it can and you're whipping and beating on it, that's not a confidence builder. So, what you *don't* do to a horse is sometimes as important, maybe even more so, than what you do."

It's always surprising that a little horse like Brown Bess can carry its speed and high weight over a distance better than a bigger horse. Kaenel drew an interesting analogy. "Well, look at your track runners, ones that run marathons. What are they? They're thin, skinny people, most all of them. You don't see no bulky big-thighed football players running distance races. They're all sprint-ers. With horses, a lot of the smaller ones are more agile. They can be more athletic, quicker as far as being able to adjust. Also, because they weigh less they're not as hard on themselves as far as their legs go. They have four hundred pounds less pressure coming on their legs every time they take a stride. That's got to be a little bit of an advantage going a distance."

Still, if a horse like Brown Bess, who weighs only 850 pounds, has 122 pounds on her back, that's a higher percent of her body weight to carry than if she weighed 950 pounds. "That's true," Kaenel acknowledged, "but there's also 250-pound guys that aren't very good fighters. You have to be athletic to begin with. I wasn't meant to be a football player when I was born. There's some big horses that can't carry the weight, just like some big people aren't that strong. The coordination and athletic agility of a horse, how free-running they are, determines how well they carry their weight. When they're free-moving horses and they have a nice stride on them, the weight doesn't seem to bother them nearly as much as it does a big lumbering horse that's got an up-and-down stride."

On the flip side of horses like Brown Bess and Zany Tactics are those like Lejoli, a faint-hearted horse that Jack rode and grew to dislike. "Lejoli was a horse that as a three-year-old ran against all the best horses in the country. He actually earned quite a bit of money. But he never did anything except break his maiden. He kept running second, third, and fourth against all the best horses in the country. His problem was he never wanted to win. He'd run up to within a length or two of the lead but would never pass the winners. He didn't win his second race until his fourth year, when the owners put him in a sprint and he got through on the inside and won. Horses like that most jocks call common because they don't really want to win. They aren't nearly as enjoyable to ride as, say, a cheap $6,250 claiming horse that tries real hard every time. Some horses just aren't meant to be racehorses as far as their competitiveness. Lejoli was like that. You can see some two-year-olds training out here that as soon as they get near another horse they're very competitive. They have that desire to win that can't really be trained into them. It's just something that has to come natural. Some horses are racehorses and some aren't."

Jack described his favorite kind of ride. "There's nothing easier than a horse that will break out of the gate hard, go to the lead, and that you can sit on and he will kind of relax himself, then try as hard as he can when the other horses come up to him at the three-eighths. I don't think any jockey would disagree with me on that. That's an easy race to ride, because you don't have to worry about getting through traffic. Any time you've got speed, you're dangerous over a horse that comes from out of it—because something can happen to a horse that is closing to get him in trouble. A horse can be stopping in front of the closer and cost him just enough distance to lose the race."

Horseplayers talk about a horse getting a perfect trip around the track. For Jack the perfect trip is "Ridin' a horse that's got enough speed to get out of the gate going a distance, gets himself in position, and lays third on the outside. Because any horse making a late run, if I'm third on the outside, is gonna run into a trap on the inside unless the horses in front come off the rail. At the top of the stretch it's important not to let another horse get the jump on you. Now, I'm talking about a race where I know I have enough horse left to beat the front-runners, where I've judged the pace right. If that's true, any horse that's going to beat me is gonna have to come around me on the outside and lose two or three lengths doing it. In this kind of race, I put a lot of pressure on the horses coming from out of it because they have to take a definite chance of getting stopped, if they go to the inside, or of losing too much ground if they go to the outside."

Jack emphasized the importance of position, of being at the right place at the right time during the course of a race. I asked him what he does when he doesn't have a favorable position and can't dictate what the other riders have to do. "That's when the importance of experience comes in. If I'm the guy laying fourth or fifth off the lead horses, I have to make the same decision to go inside and risk getting shut off or going outside and risk losing too much ground. For one thing, not all horses will go through a small hole. If I've ridden a horse and know he'll go through a small hole, sometimes I'll take the chance and go to the inside. I'll hope that one or two of the tiring horses will drop back enough so that I can catty-corner through without bothering anybody. If I have a horse I've never ridden before, and nowhere do I have a feeling for what he'll do in tight quarters, a lot of times I'll take the outside chance and make sure I have clear sailing. It really comes down to whether you have enough horse and have the right feeling as to whether you go inside or out. It's the same thing if there's a jock on your outside who has a whole lot of horse and you know you can't go around him. Then, you better go inside and try to cut some ground between you. Sometimes in a close race you can beat the best horse, depending on what you and your horse can do to save some ground."

Jack's comment about saving ground reminded me of his ride on Big Conviction when he was disqualified against Rob An Plunder. I mentioned Frisco's assertion that it was the worst ride he'd seen the whole meet and asked Jack for his view of the race. "I know the press was saying the rail was dead all week," he acknowledged. "But I get paid to pay attention to things like track conditions. I went out, like I always do, and walked the track that morning and it wasn't any deeper on the rail than the outside. Also, you have to realize that early in a card there are usually a lot of cheap horses running who can't carry their speed. Fans will mistakenly think the rail's dead, when what's happening is jockeys are moving their horses to the rail because they're tiring. It's a self-selection deal. Jockeys are trying to save ground and hold on long enough to win. When the horses don't win running on the inside, the fans think that proves the rail is dead. They're always surprised when later in the card a good horse closes on the rail and wins. I went to the inside in that race with Big Conviction because I knew Rob An Plunder was coming after me and my horse was tiring. I wanted to save some ground. As far as being disqualified, if I hadn't used the stick left-handed, Big Conviction wouldn't have won the race. Don't forget he did win the race. Unfortunately, he drifted out the last time I hit him and we got disqualified. I don't think it was a bad ride—I wasn't on the best horse. It was just bad racing luck we had our number taken down."

The afternoon sun was beginning to wane, and it was time to do some riding. Dale Kaenel and his middle son, Willie, came up to help saddle our four mules. We decided to head up to the top of the Martinez hills, which overlook the Sacramento River Delta and San Pablo Bay, for what promised to be a spectacular sunset. While Jack filled up a goatskin pouch with a little Jim Beam, I asked him what the hardest thing is for a jockey to learn. "It doesn't matter," he observed, "whether you're starting out, a year into your career, or five years into your career: the hardest thing to learn is not to let yourself get caught up on those high and low points. You have to train yourself to know that they're gonna come. It doesn't matter where you are. If you're starting out, there'll be times when you can't even get a job galloping for people in the morning. Three weeks later, you may be winning three races a week. Or you may not get a mount for eight months and then turn around and win three races in a week. Nobody knows, nobody can predict when that will come. The basic thing is to train yourself to do the best you can with whatever comes. Don't let yourself get down when times are tough, and don't get high-headed when times are good."

Well, that afternoon, times were surely good. We ambled up the hillside on our mules. Jack was riding with only a bareback rigging. I bumped along beside him laughing, not quite yet an adept. "Hey, Jack," I called out, "how come you ride so smooth?" He grinned back at me and said, "Easy. You got to move your hips with the rhythm. Just like, you know, when you're makin' love."

5

AT THE RAIL
An Insider's Analysis

*I*t was a little after six in the morning and the sky was still dark. I was in the middle of the backstretch near the half-mile pole, with trainer Chuck Jenda, watching his horses work. He had his stopwatch with him as well as an expensive-looking set of binoculars that was small enough to slip into the side pocket of his parka. A couple of his older horses had just completed their works.

Jenda called out to one of his exercise riders, "How'd it go— did he take much of a hold?" The rider said no, that the new bit they had added was working. Jenda turned to me and said, "This colt had a night out on the town last night. Broke through the doors. We found him a couple of hours later. I guess he was out cruising for babes or something."

Though the grandstand part of the track was brilliantly lit with floodlights, it was much darker where we stood, and I could almost hear the horses better than see them as they galloped by. Behind us the quarter moon still hung brightly in the starry night. If Frisco had been with us he would have made some cynical comment about what was going on. Jenda was training by moonlight, though not because he was trying to slip in an unrecorded work but because as winter approaches and the days shorten at Bay Meadows, there isn't enough time to exercise all his horses and wait for the natural light.

At forty-three, Jenda was on a roll. He was training Brown Bess, his turf sensation, to what looked like a possible Eclipse Award. Jenda is a trim, medium-sized man with intense, alert eyes and a droll sense of humor. He also sports a full, though well-trimmed, peppery beard that runs up into a black shock of hair, which cumulatively gives him something of the appearance of a riverboat gambler. There is a bouncy yet controlled sense to the way he moves and squares himself off from shoulder to shoulder that is reminiscent of the moves of a tennis player; in fact, Jenda plays the sport to keep himself in shape. Being a bit of an athlete, Jenda later tells me, makes him appreciate how important regular exercise and conditioning is to the success of his horses. "When I don't play tennis or jog for a week, I can feel how much that takes away from my game. It's the same with horses. Most of them aren't going to run worth a damn if they're locked up in the barn."

Jenda is a shrewd judge of horseflesh and has the reputation of working patiently with what he has. He generally limits his stable to around thirty horses, and in recent years his winning percentage has hovered close to twenty percent. His barn consists of a nice mix of younger and older horses, and he enjoys recognition among northern California handicappers for running them fit. While most trainers have a lot of sprinters in their barns, Jenda is partial to horses going a distance. "Routers are a little more predictable," he explained. "They can have problems during a race and still overcome them. The best horse will usually win—whereas sprinting is a little more unpredictable in terms of the trip that they can get. Routers also tend to be more durable and stay a little sounder. Routing is not as stressful on the horse."

．　．　．

It was beginning to get light by now, and Jenda had a couple of unraced younger horses on the track ready to work. One was a filly and the other a colt. "There they go right now," he exclaimed as he set his stopwatch. He had instructed his riders to break the horses from the quarter-mile pole. When they galloped past us he stopped his watch, looked at it, and told me he was a little disappointed in the six-furlong work. "I would have liked them to go a little faster than 1:16. Of course, we don't know how fast the track is running yet. It changes from day to day. Sometimes 1:16 is a pretty good work. You also have to look how easily they ran. These two did it pretty easily. But when you breeze them in company like that, even though they're going easy and under a hold, you like to see them do it in 1:14. But like I said, we have to see how the racetrack is before we start crying in our beer."

Like most handicappers, I've found interpreting the works listed in the *Daily Racing Form* perplexing. On more than one occasion, after betting on a horse with bullet drills, I've wondered why it didn't run to its works. I asked Jenda if that was simply a case of a trainer working his horse too hard. "Not necessarily. A lot of horses you just can't control. They have two gears, first and fifth. But they're not like cars. I mean, I would love to be able to tell a rider, go the first eighth in thirteen seconds and then pick it up to twelve and change, but they're not like that."

Slow works can be deceptive too. "You have to consider who's riding in judging a work," Jenda cautioned. "Is it someone like Victor, my exercise rider, who weighs 135 pounds, that's breezing the horse? And is he keeping the horse under a real tight hold? Or do I have Ron Hansen at 112 pounds working the horse, and is he beating the shit out of him every jump? So when you see workouts in the *Form*, unless you really know how the horse was worked, you have to take them with a grain of salt."

Jenda believes the *Racing Form* should provide some kind of notation on the work tabs. "I wish they'd use *breezing* more. A lot of these horses are just breezing, which means 'under a hold.' You watch Victor ride this next horse, Rakish Cavalier. He's just gonna breeze him. He'll probably breeze in 1:13 or 1:14, whereas those horses that just worked, even though they went in 1:16, I would say they went *handily*. They were in hand the first part, but the last part we were kind of asking them a little. They should also have something like *all out*, because a lot of these trainers work their horses as fast as they can go."

Jenda advises handicappers to try and pick up on the workout patterns of various trainers. "If Hector Palma at Santa Anita has a horse that works five furlongs in :58.4, that's as fast as that horse can go. He's a real 'Let's work these mothers, hang them on the wood' kind of trainer. So a fast work for him isn't very significant. If you see one of my horses go :58 and change, jump up and down, because my horse can go faster than that."

I asked Jenda how he handles a horse that tends to be speed crazy. Does he avoid working the horse close to a race for fear of taking too much out of him? "Not necessarily. Those kind of horses I prefer to work long and slow. The trick is to get them to relax so they can carry their speed farther. I try not to even breeze them, because they're lunatics and breezing normally just rattles their cage. So I space their works out, and I try and space their races out too. You just can't work speed-crazy horses every five days."

Jenda seemed to be saying if a speed horse quit in its last race, and the trainer has been working it long and slow for the current one, the horse might just be relaxed enough to win this time out. While I was making a note of this for my handicapping file, jockey Tim Doocy pulled up in front of us on SayItAintSo Joe—a young colt that Jenda partly owns and is high on. "He had a lot more gas than what he showed," he told Jenda.

Victor Trujillo, Jenda's main exercise rider, came onto the track with Rakish Cavalier. Jenda had instructed him to work the horse breezing for three-quarters of a mile. "He's a runner and has won some races. I would expect that Rakish Cavalier on a fast track could breeze in 1:12 and change and do it pretty easily. I should be able to tell how fast the track is running this morning by his time."

In anticipation of wet weather they had been adding sand to the Bay Meadows track, and I asked Jenda if he thought that was slowing the times down. "Not necessarily. If they put a lot of water on it, it could get faster. Like at Portland Meadows—the more water they put on it, the faster it is. The drier it is, the more laboring it is. It's like running at the beach. It's a lot easier to run along the shoreline where it's wet than farther back where it's totally dry. So sand, on its own merit, isn't essentially a slow track. But if you're a handicapper and come out in the morning and see a lot of water on a sandy track, that probably means it will run fast. This track right now, I wouldn't say it's sandy. There's a lot of clay, you can see it balling up. They might have to add even more sand than they have right now to deal with the coming rains."

Jenda talked about his training philosophy. He said he trains his horses harder than most. He likes to gallop them a mile or two almost every day—though he does give them a day off after a work and three days off after a race. If a horse isn't up to a regular exercise schedule, Jenda turns it out for some rest.

Victor was about to break Rakish Cavalier on the rail, and Jenda clicked his stopwatch. As the horse came around the first turn Jenda remarked on how impressive he looked. When I asked who he was out of, Jenda surprised me by saying, "Hell, I don't know. I tell you what, I'm not a big pedigree freak. For me, beauty is what beauty does."

As Rakish Cavalier galloped past us I could see that Victor was just sitting on him and not moving his hands. Jenda looked at his watch and said, "He went three quarters in sixteen, so this course is pretty dull. Normally he would be going about fourteen, so I would suspect the track is gonna be at least a second off."

While we waited for the next set of his horses to work their way past us, Jenda asked me who I liked in the World Series. The third game between the Giants and the A's was set to go off at Candlestick Park later that afternoon. Jenda had a hundred bucks on the A's to sweep at ten to one. "Good pitching beats good hitting," he said, "and the A's have both over the Giants. I liked the odds."

Aha, I thought to myself, a fellow gambler! I had also heard that Jenda had an unusual past—that he hadn't, like most track people, grown up around horses. Various accounts had described him as having been everything from an ex-hippie to a graduate student at the University of California in Berkeley in the early seventies. I asked him about it and learned that he had grown up in Arizona and graduated from the state university there with a degree in business management. He followed that up by working a year for a small firm in the Phoenix area, but was not happy with it. Then a friend who was living in Berkeley encouraged him to visit.

Like thousands of other young Americans in the late sixties and early seventies, Jenda was attracted by the excitement the San Francisco Bay Area was generating. It was where the action was. While opposition to the Vietnam War was an important part of the spirit of the times, so too was the hedonistic lure of sex, drugs, and rock 'n' roll. It was the time of Big Brother and the Holding Company, Santana, Credence Clearwater, Country Joe and the Fish, ten-dollar lids, cheap rents, and lots of liberated young women with flowers in their hair. I asked Jenda if that was part of the attraction for him.

"Well, hey, you bet your sweet ass." He laughed. "I wanted to party. I was a young buck, and I came up here and fell in love with the area. I moved in with my friend and took a couple of classes at Cal. But I also needed some income. Somebody told me that I could take classes in the afternoon and go down to the racetrack and walk hots in the morning and be done by ten-thirty. I thought, well, what the hell. I already knew I liked the track. I had gone to the races quite a bit at Turf Paradise, and I was a handicapper and a gambler."

Jenda, who at the time barely knew which end of the horse to put the bridle on, was also intrigued by the social milieu of the track. "I'll never forget an incident when we were hippies with long hair and sharing a box with a Marine Corps drill sergeant and a business guy. We were all in the same box. This is in the early seventies, when I couldn't go to dinner with my parents or out anywhere without getting into a knock-down-drag-out fight about the Vietnam War, or my hair, or whatever. And it was kind of refreshing, I noticed, that you could go to the racetrack and be stark naked and nobody would give a damn. You could literally go through the grandstand naked and nobody would care. I mean we're talking about a career Marine Corps drill instructor from Camp Pendleton beside me, and we're getting along and talking: 'Hey, who do you have in the third, you wanna bet the exacta? I'll go in with you.' I mean, you couldn't do that in the outside world. All this political turmoil was put aside at the track, and that was intriguing to me. There was a certain camaraderie between people of different backgrounds that captured me. And once I got around the horses, I fell in love with them and never left. That was it."

Two more horses galloped past the quarter pole, then—in accordance with track etiquette for departing horses—turned around clockwise and came back toward us along the outer rail. One of them was a young colt that Victor was riding. Jenda called out to him and said, "He looked like he was struggling. Maybe we ought to space his works a little further out."

Jenda turned and began walking briskly back toward his barn. "You're just gonna have to keep up with me," he cautioned. "I've got eight more horses to get out." As I watched the efficiency with which he worked, I could see that his degree in business management hadn't been wasted. Everything was one, two, three. Back in the barn area Jenda looked over a couple of young horses, Gaelic Intuition and Curragh View, that were already saddled and ready to be worked. He wanted to make sure nothing was wrong. He talked with Bill Patterson, his assistant, and gave some instructions to a stablehand.

On our way back to the rail Jenda filled me in on more of his past. It hadn't taken him long walking hots to realize he wanted to take a shot at training horses. He worked with several veteran horsemen, including Mort Lipton, Charlie Comiskey, and Olen Battles, in order to pick up on the basics. "Battles was kind of my mentor," Jenda reflected.

Like Bill Morey's, Chuck Jenda's initiation into the business came with a leased horse. He didn't have any better results. "She was a maiden filly." Jenda shook his head. "I went in with a friend. I don't think she ever broke her maiden. She was third the first time out, but she was one of those horses that is just about five lengths not good enough." Operating on a shoestring, Jenda won his first race with a horse he got from "a friend who had a friend who knew a friend in Oregon." The horse's name was Patient Ellen. Since Jenda has a reputation for being an extremely patient trainer, I asked him if getting his first win with a horse called Patient Ellen was not perhaps prophetic.

"I'll tell you what," Jenda emphasized, "you gotta be patient in this racket. It teaches you patience or it will bury you. Anyone that's in a hurry has ulcers and they're going crazy. You see these people around here who try and push these horses and they pay the price. Unless you're like Wayne Lucas and you have so many horses coming through. I don't get that many good horses. When a good horse comes through this barn, I don't want to fuck 'em up. Lucas gets fifty or a hundred good horses coming through his barn and he can afford to mess up fifty of them, because there'll be fifty more right behind them. Well, that's not the way I work. That's not what I'm here for."

Jenda emphasized that every day there is a decision to be made about whether or not to run a horse. "Maybe a horse has a little puffy ankle, not hitting the ground quite right. Now, obviously there's some damage there, right? It's the fork in the road. It's shit-or-get-off-the-pot time. Do we inject the ankle and make the big race, with the risk that we're gonna hurt this horse and he might not ever run again? Or do we give the horse three months off and start all over again? Here, we give them the three months off, kick them out. I mean it's a bitter pill to swallow, especially when a horse is doing great and looking in the peak of condition— but you've got that one little sprained ankle."

Jenda followed up his initial success with Patient Ellen by claiming two more runners, a filly called Win Big and a colt, Doctor's Intern. He won several races with both of them. About his modest beginning, Jenda reflected, "That's the way everyone gets started in this business. You claim a few cheap horses, do good with them, and hope you get noticed."

Jenda began to get noticed when he claimed Time to Stare for $8,000 and won five races in a row, including his first stakes, the

Sacramento Derby. Winning the Sacramento Derby might not seem like much, but as Jenda explained, there are lots of angles to consider in the horse business. "Prior to the Sacramento Derby I knew Time to Stare had a big shot to win the race, and he was the foal of a mare that W.T. Pascoe III—one of the biggest breeders in the state at the time—owned. So I went down to their ranch in Los Cerritos and tried to buy the mare. This was when the brood mare market was unbelievably volatile, and black type [a stakes win] of any kind would almost triple a mare's value. I figured, 'I'll buy this mare for ten. Her foal, Time to Stare, wins the Sacramento Derby and is now a stakes winner—bingo. Hey, I'm hitting a home run on all fronts.' But the guy didn't want to sell at any price, didn't even come up with a price."

Jenda didn't get the mare, but he did make an impression. A couple of weeks later the ranch manager at Los Cerritos called and asked him if he wanted to take a couple of horses for W. T. Pascoe III. Jenda jumped right in. "I got a couple of horses from him and did a little good, had some rapport with both him and the ranch manager. They sent me a couple of more, and we did good, and the thing just snowballed. That's basically how I started, that's how Jerry Hollendorfer or anybody starts in this game. You're young and aggressive and you have to do good. Nobody is gonna walk up to you and say, 'Hey, you look like a nice guy, maybe you know what you're doing. I'm gonna put a quarter of a million dollars in the office for you to claim some horses and pay you forty dollars a day to train them.' Well, that shit doesn't happen."

What does happen is that aspiring trainers have to put up some of their own money. "That's what my wife and I did," Jenda recalled. "We saved, and the first couple of horses we claimed, we claimed with partially our own money to give clients some confidence. So the guy thinks, 'Hey, this guy knows what he's doing, he's got some of his own money on the table too.' And with the first couple of horses we got half-assed lucky and made some money. And then friends that had some money heard about it, and pretty soon we could come up with enough money to claim a horse like Time to Stare and get lucky with him, and he wins five in a row.

"This business," Jenda reflected, "is 'What have you done

lately?' I swear to God. Hey, you've gotta be happening *now*, and the minute you get cold you begin to lose clients and horses. Fortunately, the people I train for have taken the big right hand more than once and I haven't been able to stagger them. They've taken a loss more than once and they're still in the game."

Then there are the owners who come into the game with unrealistic expectations. Jenda recalled a heart surgeon who was making over $1.5 million a year and wanted to put some of his cash into horses. "So I told him, 'We'll start out real easy. We'll claim a couple of horses, maybe one for $12,500, another for $20,000. Then maybe we'll buy a two-year-old and maybe a couple of yearlings so you can get a feel for this business.' He looked me in the eye, and after a while he said, 'You know, I don't really want any claiming horses. Basically, what I want is Breeders' Cup and Kentucky Derby horses.' I thought to myself, 'Good fucking luck.'"

Jenda said that the surgeon had actually done all right. "But he's one of those guys that always has to blame somebody for problems. He just couldn't accept that this is a tough business and you're gonna take a certain amount of casualties no matter who you're with. He couldn't attribute those injuries to just the nature of the business. He had the attitude, 'This horse would have been fine except somebody fucked up.' That's just not the case. And now that guy is in the business on just a very limited basis."

We were back at the rail, and Jenda had his binoculars out. He was watching a filly gallop around the far turn. I asked him what he was looking for. "Just the way she's traveling. Whether she's doing it easy or hard. When you're training you're always fine-tuning. Depending on the horse you might have to back off on its training or increase its training. She's one I have to watch that she's not doing too much."

By "doing too much" did Jenda mean he was afraid the horse might hurt itself? "Yeah, that's definitely part of it. Because I'd love to train them as hard as I possibly could. But the governor here is failure. That's where the art of training comes in. You want to train a horse as hard as you possibly can without having something go wrong."

Jenda emphasized that it's a mistake to train all horses the same way. How hard you train a horse varies with its constitution and character. "Some horses take a lot of training, they actually thrive on it. Other horses don't like to work, or you can't gallop them too much because they're frail. You're limited by that. And there are a lot of horses that are impossible to train. Either they want to go 5 miles an hour or 150 miles an hour, and it's very difficult to train those kinds of horses."

Jenda talked about the challenge of developing young horses. Most of his horses these days come from either breeders or from two-year-old-in-training sales in southern California. Typically, he will get a young horse late in its second year or early in its third. Most of them have already been trained to go up to half a mile, and it's Jenda's job to stretch them out from there.

Jenda explained how he brings a young horse up to its first race. "First time out, I usually work them an easy three-eighths of a mile. What I try to do is usually double up on their works. I work them twice at each distance up to an easy three-quarters of a mile in 1:15 or 1:16 then drop them back and ask them for some speed. But up to that, I try to not ask them for much unless they're just really dogging it, then maybe I'll have the rider get after them a little bit. With young horses you generally need to work them in company. They need someone to lead them around the track, and you want to give them that experience of breaking off next to another horse. You basically want to get them comfortable with what's gonna happen in the afternoon.

"Some young horses come along real quickly," he elaborated, "while others are almost shell-shocked when they get here. You can see what's going on around here in the mornings. There's a lot of confusion—horses and equipment all over the place, the loudspeaker blaring. It's different from home, where they were only with a couple of other horses and grazing on a hundred and sixty acres."

It's not unusual for Jenda to gallop a young horse around the track in the mornings for thirty or sixty days just to settle it down. When confronted with the reality of racetrack life, some horses go through a difficult period of adjustment, while others never adjust and simply aren't meant to be racehorses.

Jenda emphasized the importance of a horse's appetite as a gauge for evaluating its training program. "There are some fillies that you'll race or train in the morning and they won't eat for three days. They're telling you that they're not happy campers. They don't like the stress, they don't want to be here. Obviously you have to space the works for those horses out a little further."

I thought about the way Panama, Ronnie Beau, and I usually read the *Daily Racing Form*. If a horse doesn't show a recent work, we seldom play it. Jenda seemed to be saying that just because a horse doesn't have a recent work, that doesn't mean it isn't fit or ready to run. Maybe it just hates to work in the morning. "Win Big was like that," he explained. "She was a frail filly, but she was very competitive in those marathon starter races. You'd think that horses like that would require a lot of training to prepare them for a race like that. We would run her once a month, once every six weeks. Between races she might have the saddle on her back two or three times, I swear to God. The rest of the time all we would do is lead her around with the pony or walk her. Basically, it was just a matter of feeding her and taking care of her."

Jenda recalled an instance when Win Big hadn't met the rule that says a horse has to have at least one work thirty days before a race. "She was entered in a six-horse field at Golden Gate Fields. The stewards called me up and said, 'Chuck, Win Big hasn't had a work in thirty days. We don't want to scratch her, can you work the filly this morning?' I said, 'Well, sure, but normally she runs well without recent works. She's doing well, and I see no reason why she shouldn't run her race. But I'll go ahead and work her for you. So Tony Diaz is riding the horse, and we break her off with the pony, and she refuses to work. She says, 'I ain't working.' I mean, we cut her a couple of times and really got after her, and she was just not going to work. I called the stewards back and told them Diaz had tried to break her off three times and she just refused to run. The steward asked, 'Well, how's she doing?' I said, 'Great, she shows me no sign that she's not going to run her race. She's acting just the same as she has for the past dozen times prior to this.' So only because it was a six-horse field and they'd have to scratch down to five and lose part of the betting handle, did they let her run. And of course, she won!"

Jenda's point was that a fan who wasn't aware that Win Big had won off of light workouts in the past would be at a real disadvantage. They'd look at their *Racing Form* and think, "Oh, man, she hasn't worked in thirty days. No way she can win a marathon race." Of course, Win Big was the exception to the rule. "But there are horses," Jenda explained, "usually light-framed fillies, who don't require that much training. Basically you just have to chase them around the stall and they're ready to run. And then there are other horses that every five or six days you had better do something with them, or they're gonna come up short in their race. When you train a horse you have to see how much enthusiasm it shows and use a little common sense. I think the psychological thing with horses is really underplayed on the racetrack."

The psychological aspect intrigued me. Jenda said it starts with the way young horses are broken and handled early. "If you put too much pressure on them early, sometimes it will fry their brain. You just have to be careful about all those things, about attitude and how willing they are. Some young horses are too willing. They don't know how to relax and can burn themselves out. It seems like some people have that *simpático* for the horse and other people never get it. I see people working here twenty hours a day, who have been around for fifty years, and never get that feeling. Not that I have it—that's for sure. But there are certain things you shouldn't do with horses, and you see people doing them all the time. You see some trainers working nervous fillies together or working them too fast. Or other trainers who take a fast horse and try to route him, but keep his works restricted to short, fast breezes. That doesn't make a lot of sense."

Good trainers also listen to their horses. "If you go up to a horse in the morning and show them the saddle, and they're hiding in the back of the stall, shaking like a leaf, they're trying to tell you something. When you have to kick one in the belly all the way to the racetrack and all the way around to make them train, maybe you should adjust your training style and not be locked into the idea that you're gonna work them every five or six days, come hell or high water."

Most horseplayers' knowledge of how a horse is trained is limited to the clichés they read in the *Racing Form*. Trainers will say things like, "We've been working the horse long and slow, trying to put some air into it and build its endurance." Or, "We blew her out three days ago to put some speed in her for this race." On a base level, Jenda said, the clichés were true: short, fast works generally put more speed into a horse, and long, slow ones develop its endurance. "But I don't think you can change a horse's intrinsic style of running. You can't take a closer like Yeah Me Do and put him on the lead and expect him to run a good race. His style is to drop back fifteen lengths and make one big charge. You aren't going to change that. If you beat him up early in the race and force him to run, he won't finish. By the same token, if you take a speed horse and try to water-ski him at the start and hold him back, that's not going to work. You're taking all the energy out of him by fighting him. So you can't totally change a horse's running style. But you can refine it, by maybe putting blinkers on and training him a little differently. Instead of long, slow gallops, you might give a closer like Yeah Me Do short little breezes in :34 and change and put blinkers on him. With that pattern, obviously what you're trying to do is put a little more early speed into your horse, so he can lay a little closer to the pace."

Conversely, by taking a nervous, front-running horse and galloping it two miles or breezing it an easy mile, a trainer is trying to get the horse to relax so it can carry its speed over a greater distance. "It never ceases to amaze me when you see a trainer say, 'Well, we're trying to get this horse to relax,' and you'll see a :57.3 five-furlong workout four days before its race. That's not going to relax a horse. Wouldn't it be better to work that horse three-quarters of a mile in 1:14, take ahold of him, and then just gradually get him to pick it up?"

One of the problems all handicappers face is trying to guess when a horse coming off a layoff is ready to win. Some horses seem to need three or four races; others come back at first asking. Jenda indicated that some horses are reluctant when they come back into training. "They're real slow and lazy to work in the mornings, and the rider is constantly trying to get the horse to get with it. Other horses, like Brown Bess, are just locked on that bit and trying to rip that rider's arms literally out of their sockets. Those kind of horses, when they're coming off a layoff, are usually real fit. The fan in the grandstand, of course, wouldn't know that. The only thing they can go by is the appearance of the horse: Does he look thrifty? Can you see the rib cage? Does he have good works? Is he trained by a good trainer, a Bill Morey or a Jerry Hollendorfer? Or does he have a belly on him, his sides are all filled up, and he doesn't have any good works? I'd stay away from those kinds of horses."

Jenda's comment about seeing the rib cage confused me. Wouldn't a prominent rib cage suggest that a horse had lost too much weight and was maybe off its feed? Jenda elaborated. "I definitely want to see some ribs when a horse turns its head to the side. I don't mean it's gotta be like a xylophone where you can count every single rib. But I want to see a little outline of that rib cage. I go by that little water mark, that little indentation at the back of the ribs. I want to see that. I think weight is very important, very crucial, and a lot of trainers overlook it. I starve horses to death in this barn. If they come in big and fat and overweight, they literally don't get any grain. We put them on the old weight-watchers' diet until we get their body fat down, and then we can start hammering on them. You see some of these porkers around here two hundred to three hundred pounds overweight, and they're asking them for their lives out there—that's crazy. Why risk an injury to a horse by asking it to carry three hundred pounds that don't have to be on those joints and tendons? When a horse has any kind of extra body weight, it's like handing it dead weight to carry around. It can't help but slow them down."

Since we were talking about weight, it seemed an appropriate time to talk about jockeys. What is the trade-off for a trainer between using a light apprentice and a more experienced but heavier rider? Jenda feels it all depends upon the horse, how small it is, and how far it will be running. "If the horse weighs eight hundred pounds, a lighter-weight jockey is a little more significant than if it weighs twelve hundred pounds. A lot also depends on what kind of rider the horse needs. Does the horse need a dominant, stronger kind of rider? Does it need a Laffit Pincay or a Jack Kaenel? Well then, maybe you'd go with a heavier rider. Or is the horse the kind that says, 'Just stay out of my way, I'll do it.' The idea that so many extra pounds translate into so many extra lengths lost, I don't know about that. That's probably too simple. On the other hand, I don't think you can totally ignore weight."

The next time I hooked up with Jenda was three days after the October 7, 1989, earthquake. Things were still chaotic around the Bay Area. The World Series had been postponed. Part of San Francisco's Marina district had been leveled, the Bay Bridge was down, and the Cypress Street overpass in Oakland, not far from where I live, had been pancaked. Though the track was temporarily closed to check for structural damage to the grandstand, the horses still had to be exercised and fed. I'd had visions, during the earthquake, of the two thousand horses at Bay Meadows stampeding. But Bill Patterson, who had been working around Jenda's barn during the quake, told me the horses hardly flinched. They were in a secure environment and had simply bent their legs and swayed with the tremors.

I walked out to the rail where Jenda was watching his horses and learned the Friday night card had just been canceled. The jockeys had voted not to ride. They were concerned that, because of earthquake-related problems and power shortages, the lights might go out in the middle of a race. Jenda agreed with their decision and said he wouldn't want to be riding down the stretch at forty miles an hour and be blacked out in the midst of a dozen frightened horses, either.

Though I had come to talk about Brown Bess, Jenda had another horse that also fascinated me, named Roving Free. He was a lightly raced four-year-old that Jenda had run against Simply Majestic the previous spring at Golden Gate Fields, in what was perhaps the most dramatic race I have ever seen. Panama, The Stone, and I had been intrigued by the race because it was a classic situation where a talented but still relatively green horse comes up against a proven monster. It was definitely, as the *Racing Form* likes to say, a test of class. The two horses were going a mile and one-sixteenth. When they broke evenly from the gate and ran the half in :44.3 and followed that, head and head, with six furlongs of 1:08 flat, Panama and I looked at the timer on the tote board and nudged each other incredulously. To appreciate the fractions, you have to understand that the track record for sprinters at Golden Gate Fields is 1:07.3. Both of us knew something had to give. It was a question of which horse would collapse first from the pace. At the top of the stretch it was Roving Free, the younger horse on the inside, who suddenly began to quaver and fall apart. He had tried his best and it was just not good enough. He ended up a well-beaten third. I asked Jenda his thoughts about that race.

"Well, hindsight," he reflected. "We made a mistake. We shouldn't have run the horse in that race against Simply Majestic. However, going into it, there were a couple of things that tempted us. First, Simply Majestic had not been out for a while, and it was only a $50,000 race. His condition was suspect. I mean, what was a graded stakes horse like him doing in a $50,000 race? I thought maybe there's a hole in Simply Majestic, a little chink in the armor, and that's the reason he's at Golden Gate Fields and in a $50,000 race. Meanwhile, our horse is training brilliantly. He's won three straight races on the dirt and is running as fast as horses run. If Simply Majestic is going to beat our horse, he's going to have to run the mile and one-sixteenth in one-forty and change. And if there's a horse on the planet that can run one-forty and change, I want to see him.

"Then the race came up and Jack Kaenel was trapped down inside, and the two horses just lapped on each other. I'll tell you what, it was just an awesome display. It was the most impressive race I've ever seen since I've been training horses—a horse that could run that fast and then find another gear and kick it in and keep going. I thought it was an absolutely incredible race."

Jenda wasn't exaggerating. Simply Majestic finished the mile and one-sixteenth in 1:39.3, which was a new track record. Jenda next ran Roving Free back on the turf, where he put in a very mediocre performance. I wondered whether Simply Majestic hadn't put a chink in his confidence. "Well, the turf isn't his best surface," Jenda reflected. "But I'm not sure that answers your question. First of all, Roving Free doesn't always play with a full deck. He's a goofy horse that's hard to train. He's also a bleeder. How that affects him and how that plays in his psyche, I don't know. I don't think God knows. But we do know that when a horse bleeds, the alveoli in the lungs rupture and there's blood sprayed all over the place, and that interferes with that oxygen/CO_2 exchange and a horse's breathing shuts down."

Interestingly, Roving Free had been on Lasix but had bled through it. "Nobody knows how much that scares them or what the stress is. Roving Free didn't bleed outwardly. Only one or two percent of the horses that bleed, bleed out the nostrils. In all the years I've been training, I've only had a couple where blood trickled out their nostrils. Most of them you run the endoscope up in there and you'll see little streaks of blood in the trachea and farther up. In the old days we used to call horses that suddenly quit 'dirty, no-good, cheatin' sonuva bitches.' But now, with the fibrostic scope, they've got an excuse. It explains why up to the quarter pole you've got a handful of horse and then all of a sudden you wonder where did they go. People used to think that they just quit for no good reason."

So what does a trainer do when he has a good horse, like Roving Free, that has tried really hard and been beaten—does he back off, drop him down into an easier spot, or give him some time off to help restore his confidence? "Basically, you try to evaluate the psychological damage," Jenda explained. "You have to watch the way he trains, the way he eats, the way he acts. If you think he didn't take that big of a hit, then you can go ahead and run him back. If it really rattled his cage and he's not doing everything that you would hope, then you give him more time to recover."

In Roving Free's second race after meeting Simply Majestic, Jenda brought him back on the dirt against easier competition, in a race where he was the only speed in the field. Rather than have to run fractions of :44 and 1:08, as he had had to against Simply Majestic, he got the lead with fractions of :46.3 and 1:10.2. "I love those kinds of races where they go the half in forty-six and change,"

Jenda beamed. "But he ran two stinkers after that and we had to turn him out. He'll be five when we bring him back."

Jenda's patient approach toward training explains why he has such a high percentage of older horses in his barn that are still running. By way of contrast, I wondered what he thought about the proliferation of two-year-old racing. "It's my opinion," Jenda said, without pulling any punches, "that they should ban two-year-old racing, because horses aren't ready to run at two. The baby races should be the three-year-olds, and the classic Derby races should be the four-year-olds, and then they should race five-year-olds and up. You brutalize them when you run them at two. Any other part of this racket, they don't even want a horse until they're three or four years old. A lot of the problems two-year-olds face are problems of immaturity. Those same horses, if you give them some time and train them a year later, you're not going to have those problems. Shin bucks and splints are problems of immaturity. One out of a thousand two-year-olds is ready to take the kind of punishment we're dishing out at the racetrack. It destroys a lot of horses. How many older horses do you see D. Wayne Lukas train?"

Ah yes, the specter of D. Wayne Lukas. The shadow the man has cast on thoroughbred racing over the past decade doesn't bother just Jenda, it troubles a lot of horsemen. Though there's no denying Lukas's eight straight training titles and financial success, to many he is the Elmer Gantry of thoroughbred racing: a high-priced hustler who, with his wraparound glasses and bottom-line rap, has learned how to sweet-talk owners and parlay a cynical numbers game into a lot of money soaked in the blood of broken-down horses. Though his critics acknowledge Lukas knows how to read a Conditions Book and is a good judge of horseflesh, they don't think it's accidental that a great horse like Grand Canyon was a winner at two and dead at three. Still, with the advent of year-round racing and its institutionalization, Lukas's approach was probably inevitable. And, in fairness, he certainly isn't the only fast-buck operator. Given the financial pressures that face horsemen, the temptation to run them younger and harder becomes ever more difficult to resist, and patience almost seems like a quaint luxury.

The danger of pushing young horses was further confirmed in the tragic breakdown and death of Go For Wand, the three-year-old filly who was courageously challenging the six-year-old mare Bayakoa in the 1990 Breeders' Cup Distaff.

For trainers like Chuck Jenda, the horses might still have the final say. Even in terms of bottom-line economics, it might turn out to be more profitable to wait on your horses and extend their racing lives.

Since we were talking about what was good for young horses, I wondered what Jenda thought about the decision by Bob Umphrey, Racing Secretary at Golden Gate Fields, to write some distance races for two-year-olds in the belief that they are easier on young horses than the speed-oriented 4½-furlong sprints. Umphrey argued that a longer race is more interesting for the fans to watch and also allows younger horses to develop their lung capacity in a more controlled way. They could gallop the first mile or so and then, when they were warmed up, they would have to run only the last eighth. Jenda wasn't convinced by this logic. "Maybe Bob would like to come here and train these fuckers to go a mile and a half," he snorted. "Running two-year-olds a mile and a half is the most ridiculous thing I've ever heard. At that distance the ligaments and tendons get so tired that they can't support their weight anymore and start stretching. They wind up tearing all those ligaments and tendons, that's what happens. Speed hurts, too, but when you try to go that far with a two-year-old, that's ridiculous. But I know what Bob's trying to say. Routes aren't as stressful, and that's one reason why I prefer to train horses that go a route of ground. They're more durable. I think for the time and money invested in a horse you get a better payback with a router."

We walked back to the barn where Brown Bess was being saddled. Victor was about to give her a light gallop. As I looked at her, I was surprised by how small the nearly eight-year-old bay mare actually is. The last time they had weighed her, right after a race, she had tipped the scales at 838 pounds. I asked Jenda if there was anything particularly noteworthy about her conformation. "First off, she's very nicely balanced," he explained. "That's her long suit.

She's got a wonderful leg on her, too. You couldn't draw a better-looking leg on a horse. Nice flat joints, perfect angles. Nothing's crooked. A lot of horses will have one or both feet pointing out, or a knee will be crooked, putting excessive stress on that particular joint. Brown Bess is nicely balanced where everything is taking the shock equally. She's got a beautiful shoulder and her hip matches everything else. When she runs she just hits the ground effortlessly. You can go out and see other horses train, and it seems they work hard for every foot that they move forward."

Jenda emphasized the importance of speed in American racing. He said it was a big advantage that Brown Bess had enough speed either to be on the lead or to lay close to the early pace. I had noticed in going over her pedigree that on the Petrone side she had quite a bit of French blood in her breeding and wondered if that had given her any extra stamina. "A of lot people think that we need that European influence to give a little more stamina to our bloodlines," Jenda reflected. "Certainly the Nijinsky, the Nureyev, and the Be My Guest bloodlines seem to give the stamina for the 1¼- and 1½-mile distances. As opposed to some of the American stallions like Fleet Nasrullah and Bold Ruler who are fast but generally can't carry their speed. What a lot of breeders strive for is to mix those two and get something that can at least lay close to a fast pace and finish well. Apparently that was accomplished with Brown Bess."

Jenda's training pattern for Brown Bess has been pretty straightforward. He spaces her races a month to six weeks apart and then gives her a couple of months off during the winter when there aren't many turf races. When in training, Brown Bess is generally breezed a mile once or twice a week and then given an easy half-mile just before a race. In between works she is lightly galloped almost every morning and ponied or walked some more on the side. Jenda's goal is to keep her sharp without wearing her out.

In looking up Brown Bess's record, I noticed she had been raced only once as a three-year-old and seven times at four. I wondered if that was by design or if she had had some problems. "Early on," Jenda explained, "she just wasn't hitting the ground right. We gave her some time off because of a 'checked ligament' problem, which is basically a euphemism vets use when they don't know what's wrong. Then she had an abscess and we gave her time off for that. Then it was the dead of winter and a lot of rain, so we decided to wait until spring. So there were lots of complications. Suzanne Pashayan, the owner, never really starts on her horses until the spring or summer of their third year, anyway. So with Brown Bess that's just the way things worked out."

The Brown Bess story may be the ultimate illustration of the virtue of patience, of waiting for a horse to develop. At first Jenda and Pashayan weren't sure what they had; certainly there was nothing to suggest a future Eclipse Award winner. In her fifth race at Bay Meadows, they even risked losing her for a $50,000 tag. But when Brown Bess got nipped by a nose at fifty-three to one in her first turf try, that alerted them that they might have something special. Accordingly, Jenda and Pashayan continued to take the long view with her. They rested Brown Bess when she needed it and spaced her races. By the end of her fifth year she had still been raced a total of only twelve times.

Then, at six, when most racehorses have been burned out or retired, Brown Bess blossomed. She won six of nine races, including five stakes. At seven, after several preps on the dirt, she won four more graded turf races. Coming up to her Yellow Ribbon confrontation at Santa Anita with Claire Marine, Nikishka, and Colorado Dancer, she had not been defeated on the turf by another female horse in nearly fifteen months. During that time Brown Bess's only turf loss had been when she tried the boys on the front end at a mile and three-eighths. Without her regular rider, "Cowboy" Jack Kaenel, who had broken his leg, she tired and was caught in deep stretch by Charlie Whittingham's Frankly Perfect.

It seemed ironic to me that in a speed game like thoroughbred horse racing, patience would wind up being the most important virtue. I put the question to Jenda. "Well, like I said before, you have to be patient. You don't really have any other choice, unless you want to plow through and ruin them. But that's not real smart. Waiting on Brown Bess has certainly paid off. But that's also true with some of my other horses, like Casa Petrone, Dublin O'Baron, and Love Boat Champ. We've got a lot of older horses in the barn that are still running at a reasonably lucrative level, and I think part of the reason is that we gave them time when they needed it."

I asked Jenda what his strategy was going to be for the Yellow Ribbon, the race Brown Bess had to win to have a shot at the Eclipse Award. He said she was working great and he saw no need to change anything. Surprisingly, Jenda didn't plan to work Brown Bess over Santa Anita's new turf track prior to the race. He said he wasn't worried about it. "She isn't a real fussy horse. She's handled every kind of turf we've thrown at her. She was never on the course at Del Mar and won the Grade I Ramona Stakes there. I would only worry about giving her a work if she was going to be running on a real sandy kind of track. When you go from a California to an eastern track, then I think it's important to work a horse, because those tracks are aerobically tiring, and they need to get used to them."

We headed back to the barn and were met by a couple who wanted to talk to Jenda about his training a young horse of theirs that was "doing real well at Pleasanton." Jenda told them he'd had horses that trained well at Pleasanton before, and usually they didn't measure up at Bay Meadows. But he agreed to let them bring their horse over and that he would work it in the morning in company with a horse he knew could run and see what happened.

After the couple left, we talked about where Jenda gets his good young horses. While breeders like Golden Eagle Farm and Sunflower Farm provide some of them, he also likes to buy a half dozen or so for different clients. Jenda's approach is to go to the two-year-old-in-training sales and look for bargains he can develop into successful three-year-olds. Jenda shies away from yearling sales. "When I was training for W. T. Pascoe, the southern California trainer, the ranch manager and I would go down every year and evaluate the yearlings and see what the hell we had. But horses that I thought were muskrats—oh, man, if it was a choice between that horse and my German shepherd, I'd take my German shepherd—you'd get those horses six months or a year later and they didn't even look like the same horse. They'd have taken a quantum leap. When horses are two, you have a little better idea of what you have. You can see them train and see how they move."

In past years Jenda has primarily gone to the Hollywood two-year-old-in-training sales in March, but that sale has now moved to Del Mar. "That's the premier sale in California, in my opinion. The better horses are there, so we have a better chance of coming up with a big one. I'm willing to give up a couple of things to get a good value. If you want pedigree, conformation, performance, and a horse you can go on with, you're gonna pay six figures and up. I'll give up pedigree and horses that you can go on with [that are sound enough to put into training immediately] in order to get a bargain. Basically, I go down there and try to find something that looks like an athlete, that's maybe a little big and gangly, like a sixteen-year-old kid who's trying to play basketball but who's gonna require some time. What I primarily look for is good conformation. I don't give a shit about pedigree. It's okay if their shins are bothering them or maybe they have a hot ankle. We'll X-ray the ankle to make sure it's okay. If all that is needed is to give the horse six months off, we'll go ahead and do it and then bring the horse back. Buying horses this way lets you buy a horse at a reasonable price. You can buy a decent horse down there for anywhere between $15,000 and $30,000. But if you want all of the above, the pedigree, conformation, performance, and soundness, you're talking big numbers. The horse that just worked out in twenty-two flat and he's by Nijinsky and so on, Lord knows what you're gonna pay."

Bill Patterson, Jenda's right-hand man, joined us and gave a graphic illustration of what Jenda was talking about. "It's like the story two years ago, when Chuck went down to the Hollywood sale for Al Hoffman and he calls me up here and says, 'I've seen this tremendous-looking filly out of Marfa. There's not a lot of black type. It's her first foal. I love her. She's just as good looking a two-year-old filly as I've ever seen. She's got no pedigree. She's probably gonna go for thirty or thirty-five. I'm gonna call Al and say we oughta go fifty thousand or sixty just on looks and we'll get her.' The day before the sale they worked her. She goes :33.2. It was like the eighteenth hole at the Masters. Everyone is following her back to the barn. Chuck went to seventy-five and Wayne Lucas just kept going bam, bam, bam. Lucas got her for a hundred grand. That horse turned out to be Imaginary Lady, who won five of her first six races and turned out to be one of the top five three-year-old fillies."

Jenda pointed to a big red colt, Gaelic Intuition, that was on the hot walker and said, "He was bought out of the Hollywood sale. We turned him out and he's been back in training about sixty days. He's by Vigors, who was a big closer. But his offspring don't seem to be coming back to that. He's had speed horses instead, horses that can lay close to the pace. It's interesting, if we ever figure that pedigree thing out: Some of the horses that I thought were gonna be just outstanding sires never turned out to be worth a shit, and some that I thought would never get a good horse, turned out to be successful sires. Hoedown's Day is an example. I never thought he would throw a horse that would run that much, I swear to God. He was kind of weak, just another horse, and here he's had some runners. A horse like Rising Market is a contrary example. He was one of my favorite horses. A tremendous-looking individual—a huge, macho, strapping-looking thing, big old jowls on him like a pizza pan. He traveled all over the country and beat the best of his generation and had a strong pedigree. He threw one horse that could run, and after that he didn't get anything that was worth a shit. So breeding is interesting."

I caught up with Jenda again a couple of weeks later. He was at the rail, watching Rakish Cavalier work. He'd just run his third race back from his layoff, and Jenda was getting him ready to run on the turf. It was time to ask Jenda the $64,000 question. Rumors were flying around the track about the alleged fixing of races. Two casinos in Las Vegas had even stopped taking bets on northern California races because of what they called the Bay Meadows steam. "You know," I told him, "a lot of gamblers in the grandstand are suspicious about whether or not the horses they bet on are well meant. When they lose, rather than accept that they bet on the wrong horse, you'll hear them say things like, 'The game is crooked . . . the jockey stiffed me . . . the trainer just had the horse in for the exercise and was trying to darken his form.' I'd say the prevailing attitude in the grandstands right now is that the trainers on the backstretch are in control of the situation, cynically manipulating a race's outcome."

Jenda took the bit and ran with it. "I'll tell you what. I should be able to give you a decent idea of how my horse is going to run, because I'm involved with the horse. I know what the horse is doing. Hopefully, I know what's happened in the last few races. Maybe, through circumstances, he didn't get the best trip. But I sure don't have any idea of how Jerry Hollendorfer's horse, Bobby Martin's horse, or anybody else's horse is gonna run. So how can I possibly predict the outcome of a race? I can tell you that most of the time 1:11 flat will win the race and my horse will run 1:11. But I don't know what Hollendorfer's horse is going to do. Maybe he's changed something, put blinkers on. Maybe he's trained his horse a little harder, maybe his horse was short for his last few races. Maybe he's changing jockeys. So there's no way I can control those eleven other horses in a race. That's why any horse can get beat. That's why they call it gambling. Hell, what about the situation where all of a sudden at the quarter pole your horse starts to bleed and dies a horrible death? The horse has been training good, looking good, and all of a sudden at the quarter pole he stops like someone shot him in the head with a rifle. How much control does a trainer have there?"

Jenda had raised some interesting points. Racing is probably a much cleaner game than the public gives it credit for. Compared to inside trading on Wall Street and the savings and loan fiasco, racing seems almost pristine.

Nevertheless, when a trainer changes equipment on a horse it perplexes handicappers and raises suspicions. As Ronnie Beau has often lamented, "It's easy enough to figure a horse has a shot if its trainer switches from an apprentice to the leading rider. Or if a horse is given Lasix after it died its last time out. But blinkers and front wraps confuse me. And what the hell am I supposed to do when I'm told a horse has been gelded since its last race?"

Jenda explained how a handicapper in the grandstand might interpret these changes and started off with blinkers. "Normally, adding blinkers will intensify a horse's speed, get him into it a bit more. He won't be as distracted. It's not always true. Usually a horse that's dropping back fifteen to twenty lengths in a race, if you put blinkers on him, the next time he'll lay a little closer to the pace. If a horse is running too fast in a route and is wearing blinkers, taking them off normally will get him to relax a little bit more. It still depends upon the horse. If you have a slow horse routing and put blinks on, it will intensify their speed. If you take a fast horse going short, you'd probably want to take the blinkers off because maybe he's opening up too much. Maybe he's going the first quarter in :21 flat and not having anything left. So distance doesn't have much to do with using or not using blinkers—it's their style of running. If you've got a horse that is always wanting to bolt toward the outside, you might put blinkers on him because that's the only way you can keep him between the fences. So if you see that big cup on the outside of a horse's head, that's primarily to keep him from bearing out. You use that in combination with different kinds of bits—whether it's a runout bit, a James bit, a ring bit, or prong bit to control the horse. Changing bits in combination with adding the one cup on the outside is primarily a steering mechanism to keep the horse running straight. A lot of times there will be a little hole in the cup so the horse can see if another horse is coming up to him and be able to respond to it. There's all kinds of little tricks. But for a handicapper I think that with blinkers on for the first time, you ought to take a good look at the horse before you throw him out. Because blinkers can make a dramatic change in a horse's behavior.

"With wraps," Jenda explained, "some horses are having tendon and suspensory problems. Other horses just need some protection. Maybe they hit themselves, or their pasterns are so long, they get so much flex, that they run down a bit and burn the back of their ankles on the racetrack. Bandages will actually help those kinds of horses. But the ones with the tendon and suspensory problems that are front-bandaged, I'd stay away from as a bettor. If a horse has front and rear bandages it probably means the trainer is trying to protect him from rundown problems. But just two on the front would worry me."

What about a recently gelded horse—how should this change

in a horse's racing condition be interpreted? "Well, it could mean a major behavioral change," Jenda said. "A lot of times when you geld a horse, they're not as aggressive. They're putting more of their mind into work as opposed to pussy. It's a significant change. I wouldn't make a big bet on a horse just because he's been gelded, but I'd take a closer look at him. If I was making a bet in a particular race, I would look at him as the mystery horse, because I have seen significant changes after a horse has been gelded. I mean, they say John Henry never ran much prior to being gelded. We have a colt in the barn that was almost unmanageable. We gelded him and he's much nicer to be around now. It focuses their attention on their work. They're not as distracted."

I asked Jenda if he ever put front bandages on a horse he didn't want to lose to scare away other trainers from claiming it. "Sure, I've done that," he admitted. "If you're playing the claiming game, you have to protect yourself. It's just like baseball, you can't throw fast balls at the hitter all the time. Occasionally you're gonna lose a good horse, occasionally you're gonna get rid of some bad ones. The main thing is that you just can't be too predictable. There was a trainer around here who would almost never take a shot, never drop a horse down, never take a chance. And he would never lose a horse to the claiming box. Of course he never won any races either. It got to be a joke around here because when he did drop a horse down, everyone knew the horse had to be close to death."

On the other hand, trainers from bigger stables, like perennial leading trainer Jerry Hollendorfer, sometimes drop a horse down from, say, twenty to eight grand and get away with it. If you're a trainer in that position, Jenda explained, "Just by sheer numbers, you can afford to drop a good horse down every once in a while to win a race. A lot of times it works big-time, because everyone stays away from the horse like the plague, figuring it's bad. Only you know the horse isn't bad, and bingo! You can win three or four races coming back up the ladder before anyone figures out what you've done. So that's all part of it. It's a big poker game, and some people know how to play it to a T.

"They talk about what a good trainer Hollendorfer is, but his strength as far as I'm concerned is they claim the bad ones from him and he keeps the good ones. How he does it, I have no idea. But I've never seen anyone on such a roll as far as losing the bad ones and keeping the good ones. When he does drop those good ones down, they stay away from them. When he drops the bad ones down, they're standing in line for them. Although, the last couple horses that he claimed down south, I think he got stung. But hey, this is a risky business. It's like shooting craps."

I asked Jenda if he was much of a gambler. "I was for a while. I was almost possessed with it. Now, I don't bet hardly at all. I don't make more than four or five bets all year long. I'll bet maybe two hundred to win on them. Usually it's a horse that I think should be five to one and he goes off at twenty to one, due to circumstances. The kind of horse that maybe had a bruised foot that's been haunting him, and we finally figured it out and got the problem rectified. Or maybe he's had so much trouble in his last three races—either bad rides or working against a post or track bias. There are all kinds of ways a horse can get beat. If you get that three times in a row and you continually drop the horse down, now you're in a situation where you're running a $20,000 horse for $12,500 and only you know it. The horse is doing fine, but due to circumstances he's got his ass kicked three times. Those are the kind of horses I'll bet. And hell, even those horses will get beat occasionally. They'll rip a shoe off at the start or stumble. So they're certainly not Michael Jordan going to the hoop."

Jockey Chris Hummel, who had just finished working Rakish Cavalier, paused in front of us. Jenda, who had been timing the horse while we talked, asked him, "Whaddya think, Chris? I caught him in :49.2. How'd he feel underneath to ya?" Hummel answered, "Pretty good, 'bout the same as before."

Jenda thought for a moment and added, "Maybe, we should have a tongue-tie on him. It looked like he was having a little trouble breathing." Hummel rode off, and Jenda explained to me that some horses have a tendency to swallow their tongues when they're racing, and tongue-ties can help them out dramatically.

The more time I spent with Jenda, the more I realized how many factors can affect a horse, and that, more often than not, the people on the backside are guessing, right along with the fans, about who will win a race. When I asked Jenda about this he said, "I learned a valuable lesson out here early on in my career. One of the horses was Tragic Isle. It was a maiden allowance race at Golden Gate Fields. Tragic Isle ran once and got beat an inch in 1:09.2. So on the program he's six to five. The other horse, who would turn out to be a pretty good horse, was ten to one and had some decent works. Well, two minutes before post the second horse plunges to eight to five. Now you have two horses in the race, one at eight to five and another at six to five. They end up running 1:09.1, and the two of them are just smoking a sixteenth of a mile in front of the third horse. Here's a perfect example where you think you've got a world-beater in a race, and all of a sudden you catch a Secretariat breaking his maiden. I swear to God you have to be careful, you've got to be aware of what the other guy is doing. In maiden races you've always got that mystery horse—one that's only started a couple of times and needed that extra seasoning, or maybe they're putting blinkers on or stretching him out."

I noticed that every race on the card that afternoon except one was for claiming horses. Even though Jenda had started out as a claiming trainer, he hardly ever claims a horse now. I asked him why. "Well, you have to be here all day long. You have to watch every single race, watch them go to the racetrack and come off the racetrack—or pick them off the *Form*, which I think is suicidal. A lot of guys do that, look at the *Form* and say 'Oh, he looks good, let's claim him.' But if you really want to be in the claiming business, you should watch them pull up. Take a look at their legs, try to identify them in the morning, and really play that game. Hey, it's tough enough just trying to keep track of the thirty horses that I have, let alone be worried about the other two thousand head on the grounds."

Since most of the races are claiming races, Jenda still has the problem of worrying about someone claiming a horse off of him. How does he decide where to run a horse so that it can win and not get claimed? "It's fairly easy. If you run a horse for twenty-five grand and he gets beat, you drop him down to twenty. If he gets beat for twenty you drop him down to sixteen. When you start out with a maiden, you generally put him in for twelve-five, sixteen, or twenty, depending on how fast the horse is training or if the horse has a pedigree and you want to protect him. That's how you place them. That part isn't that difficult. I've had horses that I knew couldn't run. But due to their pedigree their owners would never agree to run them for a tag, in which case I'm willing to try them a couple of times. But I'm not going to run them a dozen times and have them get crushed each time by twenty-five lengths."

So what does Jenda do in that case? Does he call up the owner and tell him to come get his horse? "I'm a bit more diplomatic"— Jenda laughed—"but, in so many words, yes. We had a maiden filly out of Secretariat that was maybe a maiden $12,500 horse, but the owners paid a quarter of a million bucks for her. It's pretty hard to tell them that you want to run that kind of a horse for a twelve-five tag. And that makes sense. They might as well take a shot and breed her for that kind of money and see what they get."

Most breeders want a trainer to try their horses a number of times. "If you don't go the extra mile," Jenda explained, "if you don't try their horses short, long, with blinkers, then you're not trying. For some reason they think you don't believe in their program. They take it like I'm a teacher telling them, 'Little Julie ain't gonna fuckin' make it to first grade.' Their first reaction, of course, is 'This bastard can't teach worth a shit.' So you kind of have to read the owner, especially if they're good clients and sending you good horses."

Fortunately, Jenda has some savvy clients. "I can call them up after I've had a horse a week and say, 'This horse is not going to make it. Send him to a cheaper track. And bingo, the horse is gone to Turf Paradise, Caliente, whatever. I personally prefer the owners that I don't have to pull any punches with. When one of their horses walks off the van I can say, 'Hey, give me a break. This one's outa here.' That's great."

Then there are the people who ask Jenda to try training their horse as a personal favor. Jenda shook his head and said, "These are the cases where I know the horse isn't worth a shit. I give them my 'give me your wallet' story. 'Let me take all the money out of your wallet—at least one of us will be happy.' And that doesn't work. They're convinced they've got Secretariat and don't see that they're just burning their money up."

We talked some more about the typical daily racing card. I told Jenda that as a fan and even as a handicapper, I prefer watching and betting on maiden races than cheap claiming ones where the same tired and half-broken-down horses are constantly run. He surprised me by saying, "I do, too. I don't know why in so many cases they would prefer to card a cheap claimer than a maiden $12,500, which I think is a little more interesting from a handicapper's point of view."

In bottom-level, maiden claiming races, where the horses with records are proven plodders, I often scratch all of them out and wheel all the first-time starters that have decent trainers. In those kinds of races, Jenda added, "You also get some horses that have been beaten ten or twelve times. I just cross those horses out."

The other interesting thing about maiden races is that it's fun to catch a young horse that wins and follow it through its career. "Sure, absolutely," Jenda agreed. "I remember I jumped on Gold Seal, a Greg Gilchrist horse, years ago when he broke his maiden. I think I bet him every time he ran and made a lot of money on that horse. I just loved him. It's like Brown Bess. Had you jumped on her early on in her career, a guy would have been way up."

We discussed racing strategy. Jenda said he generally liked front-running speed. "Going a route of ground, I like a horse like Time to Stare. He was the kind of horse that would open up a length or two and relax. If he was on a clear lead, boy, his ears would come up and he'd relax for the rider and run easy. Then, if someone came to him, he'd take off again. That's the ideal horse. The ones that open up five or ten lengths, just running crazy, that's the worst kind of horse you can have, because all they're doing is running on nerves."

I wondered what other signs, besides pricked ears, indicate that a horse is running easy. "Usually, when a horse is running relaxed, it's kind of goofing around, looking for something to do." But pricked ears, Jenda warned, can also signal something else. "A rider, when he sees a horse's ears are pricked, is very cautious. He's aware they might make a sudden right-hand turn, a left-hand turn, do something silly. When a horse sees something, the first thing they'll do is prick their ears, then they'll kick or bolt or whatever. So you have to be very aware of that when you're around horses."

As we were talking, a couple of horses galloped by. One of them appeared to be compensating for a bad case of crooked legs. Its front legs were paddling out in the midst of its stride. I asked Jenda how dangerous it was to ride that kind of horse. "I remember a good filly, I forget her name, who down the lane, if you saw a head-on view, her legs would be paddling out. It's the worst case I've ever seen. When she was on the rail, her legs would almost be hitting the posts. Looking down on her, she had to be absolutely frightening to ride."

What about riders? I was particularly curious whether Jenda had any preference when it comes to a jockey's style. "I like the Laffit Pincay, Jack Kaenel, Marco Castaneda style," he said, "where you get down and your back is level with the horse and you have a good hold of them early on. You watch some riders, and they look like they're standing up on a horse and pitching them the lines. They're almost erect when they hit a horse. They just look like shit as far as I'm concerned. You watch Jack—his back is down, his knees are bent, he's pushing on a horse, he's helping him with his hands, and when he reaches back to hit one, it's almost like he doesn't even turn around. All his motion is still going forward. He's just smooth."

I had noticed on that day's racing program that Jenda had replaced apprentice jockey Nate Hubbard on Loveboat Champ with Jack Kaenel. Hubbard had won on the horse last time out, and the switch surprised me. Jenda said he had no choice because Hubbard had disappeared after he learned he was going to be called before the stewards on a substance-abuse problem. About the temptations facing a young jockey, Jenda reflected, "You're eighteen, you're running on hormones, you've never made any money; now you're making more money than God, and you can't handle it. I don't know that I could. A lot of it also has to do with trying to make weight. Hell, look at Laffit Pincay. Did you read that story in *Sports Illustrated* a few years back? He was drinking, flipping, popping

Lasix, using drugs, doing all kinds of crazy stuff—things that would kill a normal human being. Now, he's got it down to where he eats a few mouthfuls of granola a day and a steak once a week. You've got to admire a guy that's got that much money and, because he still loves riding so much, is willing to forsake one of life's great pleasures—eating some prime rib or lobster when you feel like it."

It was time to broach another dicey subject: the illegal drugging of horses. I asked Jenda what he thought. "Nowadays we can't use hardly anything," he insisted. "I mean, they test for everything. I'm just speculating here, but if they would test football players the way they test horses, about half of them wouldn't be playing football. I mean they're on uppers, downers, steroids, injections of cortisone, all that stuff."

Still, the California chapter of the Horsemen's Protective and Benevolent Association had been sufficiently concerned about the use of illegal drugs that it had commissioned a study to look into the problem. The results had not been encouraging. Out of 1,024 urine samples taken from winning horses in California races, 109 had tested positive for trace elements of one or more of twenty-one prohibited substances, including cocaine. Whether these trace elements were actually injected into the horses by unscrupulous horsemen or were part of a contaminated testing process was the subject of hot dispute—as well as the question of whether or not any of the trace elements were sufficiently potent to have affected the outcome of any of the races.

One upshot of the whole investigation had been that such prominent trainers as D. Wayne Lukas and Laz Barrera in southern California and Bryan Webb in the north had been charged with giving their horses cocaine. Though the charges were subsequently dropped for insufficient evidence, the suspicion of a possible whitewash still lingered in many people's minds. Jenda felt strongly about what had come down. "The recent charges of cocaine against those trainers, when they didn't really know what they had—to release that information as if some horse had been found with two ounces of cocaine in him was absolutely ridiculous. I mean we're talking about billionths of a gram here. I read a statistic in *Playboy* that if you checked out hundred-dollar bills, over thirty percent of them would have larger traces of cocaine on them than was found in those horses."

A related scenario for how cocaine might inadvertently get into a horse's system has been suggested by a number of trainers. A groom could roll up a dollar bill to snort a line and then, when he unrolls it, get some cocaine on his hands. If he puts a bridle on a horse a few minutes later, the cocaine could be transferred from his hands to the horse's mouth. With the sophisticated tests now available, it wouldn't take much to have the horse test positive after a race. "Right on," Jenda agreed and then added, "About those charges, I never heard that anybody was convicted. I never heard what these substances were. But I'll tell you what. If someone is abusing the rules, then I say hang the motherfuckers, because they're not playing with the same deck that I am and most of my colleagues are. I mean, if they were injecting horses' joints with a solution of cocaine, I say hang the motherfuckers. But as long as I've been in this business it's been pretty legit. Everyone makes a pretty decent living, and there's too much at stake to lose."

Jenda speculated that there was no incentive for a trainer to drug a horse deliberately and risk losing his license unless he was going to cash a big bet. Even then an unscrupulous horseman would have a problem. "I mean, how can you cash the big bet? Have you ever tried to get down ten thousand or twenty thousand dollars, let alone fifty or a hundred grand—have you ever tried to bet that kind of money? You can't do it. I know one or two people who can go to Vegas and bet ten or twenty thousand, and they don't bat an eye. But I mean, these are real heavy, heavy players. Most people go there and want to bet two hundred dollars on a maiden at Golden Gate and they're calling over the manager. It's just hard to get down a lot of money, unless you bet it at the track. And if you bet it here, you get crushed. Maybe at Santa Anita or Del Mar you could bet fifty grand on a Saturday or Sunday and not have it show that much on the board. But otherwise it's ridiculous to even try."

Whenever a drugging scandal comes up, racing officialdom and the state close ranks behind the rubric of "protecting the integrity of racing." But what's really meant is that a lot of bucks are involved. Nationally, racing is a $10 billion-a-year business. In California over $2.6 billion was wagered last year, and horsemen, track operators, and the state took over $140 million apiece out of the roughly eighteen percent vigorish that is taken out of the betting handle. The entire industry, they correctly argue, is dependent upon maintaining trust with the gambling public. If the public stops coming because they don't think the game is clean, the industry will collapse. The kingpin in their strategy for protecting against drugged horses is what racing officials call the Trainer Insurer Rule. This rule makes every trainer absolutely responsible for the condition of each of his horses when they are entered into a race. Trainers are absolutely responsible, not only for their own acts, but for anyone else's who might come into contact with their horses.

Trainers, for their part, are understandably touchy about bearing the brunt of the responsibility for racing's honesty. Chuck Jenda was no different. When I queried him about the Trainer Insurer Rule, his voice rose an octave. "It's ridiculous, absolutely ridiculous. How can I control the behavior of everyone around my barn twenty-four hours a day!"

Then what does Jenda see as an alternative? "The truth. How about trying to find out the truth. To be held accountable and responsible for a disgruntled employee, that's every trainer's worst nightmare. You know, an employee that's pissed off at you, somebody who has a grudge against you. It's very easy to sabotage a horse and just ruin a trainer's career. To hold somebody responsible until proven guilty for an act that he didn't commit is a little ridiculous, isn't it? I don't know what the alternative is, but that sure isn't the way to go."

Illegally drugged horses make the most sensational headlines. But what about what many consider the abuse of legal drugs in racing? Drugs like phenylbutazone, Lasix, and cortisone. In racing's fast claiming lane, which in northern California falls between the $8,000 and $16,000 level, fans often see dramatic improvements in a horse's form after it is claimed. A lot of people in the grandstand say about one particularly successful trainer in this bracket, "What is this guy, a genius?" Then answer, "No, man, he just claims these sore horses, shoots them up with 'Bute' and cortisone, and runs them till they drop. He doesn't care about the welfare of the horses—they're money machines. He just wants to get five or six good races out of them. You don't see many of the other trainers claiming horses off of him, so obviously they know what he's doing."

I asked Jenda if the fans' belief had any basis. "That's not too far from the truth," he said. "So, how about the morality issue. Obviously, he's reconciled that with himself. His average vet bill— I know this for a fact—is like $500 per horse. My average vet bill is $50 to a $100, which is significantly different. Of course, our goals are different. I'm trying to develop better horses, he's trying to get what he can right now with claiming horses. A lot of times a horse may have something like a bone spur that's not going to go away. It's going to bother them, and you either rest them or drop them down and live within those boundaries. But let's say a horse has a stress fracture on his cannon bone, and you're risking something catastrophic. That's the kind of situation where you hope the guy makes the right call. You know, his vet comes in and says, 'Whoa, we just can't run this horse. We're risking too much if we do that.' Not only breaking the horse down, but also endangering the jockeys' lives if there's a spill out there. I mean how would you sleep with yourself if something like that happened?"

Jenda had a meeting with one of his clients coming up at ten o'clock, so I moseyed over to see how Bill Morey was doing. I hadn't seen him since the Golden Gate meet, and I wanted to ask him some more questions about the claiming game and a gelding named Lisa's Score he had recently claimed out of a $10,000 race and double-jumped to a $16,000 win.

When I knocked on his barn door, Morey seemed relieved to be able to take a few moments away from his books. It was getting near the end of the month, and there was a mass of ledgers and invoices on his desk large enough to daunt an accountant. Whatever else they are, the paperwork reminded me, successful trainers also have to be good businessmen.

Settling in, I asked Morey if, when a fan sees a trainer jumping a horse up a couple of notches off a claim, that should instill confidence in it as a good bet. Morey thought for a moment and said, "Whenever you see a double jump up on a horse, I think that's an encouraging sign. I don't like to see a double jump going down. If I was gambling and knew a trainer's pattern and saw a double jump, I think that tells you the connections like their horse. You never know if a horse is going to win, but when a good trainer double-jumps one it means he thinks he's got a healthy horse and a good shot to win."

I asked him where Lisa's Score would run next time, now that he'd won for $16,000. Morey said what he does depends upon the owner. "The fella that picked Lisa's Score and asked me to claim him is a real close friend and business associate. We'll talk it over together, and if he favors a certain race, I'll probably lean toward him in this situation."

Morey thinks owners generally tend to be more optimistic than he is about where to run their horses because they are in the business to take some chances and have fun. They don't have to make a living from it. If Morey owned a horse like Lisa's Score, he conjectured, "I'd probably run him back at an attractive figure, try to win the race and make some money. I'd let the horse be claimed for $20,000 and wish the new guy good luck. Since I claimed the horse for $10,000, I'd wind up with a twenty-thousand-dollar bill in my pocket by 'losing' the horse for $20,000 plus keeping the purse money from two wins. That's not too shabby for a month's investment. Put it this way: a guy like myself and most other trainers would probably handle a horse just a tad different than an outside owner. We'd try to win some money from the purse and sell the horse at the same time. Now, don't get me wrong, I'm not in a hurry to sell Lisa's Score—but I do like to make a profit with my own horses."

One of the hazards of being a claiming trainer is to lose a horse like Lisa's Score for $20,000 and watch with chagrin as it moves up the ladder and becomes an allowance or stakes horse. But Morey has a practical view of the matter. "One of the things you learn is that you can't run scared in this business," he explained. "If you run scared you don't do good. You also have to be willing to not be greedy. When you can make a profit, take it. That's my viewpoint. Now, there's some owners we train for who don't want just a small profit. They don't need a small profit. They'd rather risk running a horse over its head. So we'll try it."

In general, Morey said he preferred to claim horses that run in the $25,000 to $50,000 bracket. One of the advantages of claiming a more expensive horse is that at a higher claiming level, you have a shot at moving him into stakes company. That is what Morey and one of his principal clients, Bart Heller, had recently done with a horse called Big Chill, by It's Freezing. "Even if you don't move your horse up," Morey reflected, "you've got a $50,000 horse and in thirty days—that's the amount of time you have to spend in jail if you don't bump your horse up twenty percent off a claim—you can run him back for fifty and the purses are pretty good. I claimed a horse here for twenty-five grand and entered him several times for fifty, but none of the races filled. So I shipped him down south. At Santa Anita the purses for $50,000 claiming races are $30,000 for three-year-olds. That's a nice purse he's running for. If he wins a couple of races and places a couple of times, he'll earn back close to forty grand. Then if someone claims him for fifty, you've made thirty or forty grand. What's wrong with that?"

The actual process of deciding to claim a particular horse intrigued me. How did Morey and Bart Heller decide they wanted Big Chill? "What caught our eye was that Big Chill raced against another of our horses, Quick Twist, here at Bay Meadows. And the horse was in a world of trouble. We watched the race and then looked at the reruns. Reruns are great for gamblers, too. They show you more sometimes than what you see in a race, because the tendency is to watch your own horse or the one you bet on, and you don't see what else is going on in the race. Sometimes you'll see things that will help you. In Big Chill's case we watched the race and saw that he was in a lot of trouble, but we didn't know who the horse was until we watched the rerun and saw that it was Big Chill. Bart and I decided that if the horse ran back in the neighborhood of $40,000 to $50,000 we were gonna take a chance and claim him.

"Big Chill didn't reappear for close to four months. Then my owner, being on top of the game, called me and said, 'Hey, that horse we looked at four months ago is in today.' And I said, 'Gee whiz, I got a fishing trip lined up.' I didn't have any horses running and was gonna go up to the Delta and go fishing. I had worked the morning but was gonna take the afternoon off. Bart said, 'Well, don't worry about it. It's not necessary for you to stay here. We'll take care of it. How much do you want of him?' I said, 'I'll take a third of him if he looks okay to you.' Now, you have to understand that I have a lot of trust with this owner. He knows his horses pretty good, and my foreman can look at a horse pretty good, too."

Morey said that if he'd never seen the horse before, just seen him in the *Racing Form*, he would have canceled his fishing trip to see what he looked like. "But as far as their legs go, nowadays it's hard to see anything with the paddock bandages or 'boots' on, as we call them. The horses all go through a physical in the morning with a licensed vet and are examined again at the receiving barn. So therefore, what do you see? An individual that you like or don't like and you kind of go from there. And we did like Big Chill."

Big Chill went on to win the Tanforan Handicap, a Grade III stakes race. But the race that really interested me was an overnight handicap that Morey had used as a prep two weeks before. The Stone and I had been in the grandstand that day and wondered if the entry was well meant. Gamblers in the grandstands are always trying to figure a trainer's intentions when a class horse is entered in a cheaper race. I asked Morey what his strategy was in that race. "Well, we ran Big Chill in that overnight handicap on October seventh, which was a race restricted to horses on the grounds, as a stepping-stone to the big stakes race. It gave us a nice two-week gap between races. We were hoping that Big Chill would win the race on the seventh, which he didn't—he ran second and got in a little trouble. But we thought he was gonna be running with some easier horses on the seventh than he was on the twenty-first for that $150,000 stakes. We certainly didn't want to be racing him against top horses like Variety Road and Mr. Wonderful two weeks apart. So, we were using the overnight handicap as a real strong prep, hoping to win, but also trying to avoid the real killers. Of course, what happened was that there was a real tough horse in there that beat us, Hardrock Hank, and he came back in the stakes too and ran a helluva race."

What kind of instructions would a trainer tell a jockey in a prep kind of situation, where he really doesn't want to extend his horse? Would he tell the jockey not to beat up on the horse in the stretch? "The old days of taking ahold of your horse are kind of gone. The jockeys are just watched too heavily by the stewards. As a trainer, what you're trying to do is do it naturally. You're trying to get your horse into a spot where he doesn't have to give 110 percent to beat the other horses. When horses run in a big stakes, they have to give 110 percent in order to be competitive. That much is gonna be demanded out of your horse to win. In the overnight handicap that we lost, we were hoping Big Chill would only have to use 90 to 95 percent of his power to win. So he would have a little extra left in the tank for the next race. And it worked out good. The only downside was we didn't win the earlier race. Hardrock Hank ran a helluva race and beat us."

Still, there are numerous situations where a stakes horse coming off a layoff is entered in a cheap allowance race as a prep and doesn't win. I've torn up enough tickets on odds-on class horses in that situation, so that now I tend either to bet another horse or stay out of the race. Morey agreed that sometimes races are used to get a top horse into shape. "But once again, the horse is not in there with the thought of 'anchoring' him. They're trying to use that race to build him back up, so that when he goes in with the big boys he's ready. It's a lot like boxers—they start in by slapping around bums. What they're doing is building their confidence. Then when it's time for the championship bout, they know they're gonna have to really put out in order to win it. It's the same with these horses. You try to get easier fields, easier opponents, to use them as good conditioning before you step into the championship bout."

Morey said trainers do the same thing with younger horses in the morning. They build up certain horses by working them with other horses they can outrun, to build their confidence. "Sometimes you keep them head and head, sometimes one horse back a little bit. Sometimes you put one on the inside, one on the outside, and one in the middle. You change it around. Occasionally, if you have a horse you really like and want to get him pumped up, you'll use a rabbit, a horse that runs as fast as it can, and then the horse you like will tag him at the end and just go whoom! That really builds them up."

Morey extended his boxing metaphor. "It all goes back to preparation. A fighter can't give 110 percent every time or he'd be all dragged out. He has to have some fights that he can damn near win using only 90 percent of his strength, because he's got a fight two weeks down the road where he's gonna need everything. If he uses up too much in the first fight, it might tax him in the big one. That was the strategy we used with Big Chill and it worked. The same strategy might blow up next time. Horses beat horses out here. We don't have any horses out here that don't get beat, that's for sure."

Why horses beat each other, Morey reflected, is really a hard thing to put your finger on. But he had an interesting observation about one of the differences between winning and losing a race. "You have to remember, when these horses are running a mile or more and get beat a length, that's not very far. So if another horse comes back the next race and beats the previous winner, that's no big surprise. Because things happen out there. As many strides as they take, as many times as they jump, and you end up with a one-length difference, that's not much. Maybe, for some reason, your horse's stride is cut down an inch each jump for a sixteenth or an eighth of a mile during the race. Maybe there just wasn't enough room for him, and the dirt was flying into his face, and he just flinched a little bit. Well, it doesn't take too many jumps where you've lost that length that cost you the race."

I was curious what had happened with Morey's involvement with the breeding side of the business. Young Commander, the stud he was hoping would throw some runners, hadn't had much luck. When I mentioned the subject, Morey flinched. "As soon as we got into breeding, the market started to nosedive. I probably lost a helluva lot of money, and I'm afraid to even go back through it and see how much I've lost. It would probably make me ill. We were breeding to race, but I haven't produced a good one yet. I think breeding your own horses is the toughest way to go. If I was a person getting into the business right now, I wouldn't recommend it at all. You can go to a sale and buy a racehorse a helluva lot cheaper than you can raise one. Most of the people I work for are breeders, but we've kind of slowed down because the homebreds haven't come up with a heck of a lot. The hardest thing about breeding is that it takes years to know if your mare is any good. I haven't been active at sales. I don't have those kinds of owners. In all the years I've been training, the most I've ever had an owner pay for a horse at a sale is $10,000. That was a horse called Day Rullah. I'd rather go to the sales than claim horses, but I just don't have the people who want to go to the sales. My owners right now are breeders. So if they're breeding their own, they aren't gonna go out and buy a bunch from some other breeder. They know they should, but they're into a lane they can't just get out of."

Given his experience with breeding, what would Morey advise a first-time owner to do? "If a guy comes up to me and says he only has enough money for one horse, I'd claim him a horse. If a guy comes up and says, 'Here's $200,000. Build me up a small stable,' I'd try and balance it so the guy would get a two-year-old in training, maybe two of them, and claim him two. The claiming horses maybe could help support the two-year-olds as they were developing. I'd go in that direction rather than going and getting a brood mare and breeding her and dragging it on. I think the name of the game is to try to get into action as soon as possible."

Morey's comment about action reminded me about what he had called the fast claiming lane, the $8,000 to $16,000 bracket. Fans in the grandstand often feel that owners and trainers in that lane drop a relatively sound horse down primarily to cash a big ticket. About the gambling factor The Stone has often quipped, "Hey, don't tell me these guys aren't cashing some big tickets when they drop their horses down off of wins. They know enough people will get scared off that they'll still get a good price on the board. They don't care if they lose a thousand dollars in purse money or even have the horse claimed, because they're gonna make two or three times that on their bets."

Morey was inclined to see that as just part of the business. "Those guys," he observed, "train for a different type of people. They work for owners who want action. They like action. A horse like Big Chill only runs once a month or once every two months. That's not enough action for some people. I'm not saying what's right or wrong. Some individuals just want the action. They like to have horses running every day. I'm sure they like to gamble some too. There's nothing wrong with that. After all, that's the backbone of our business."

The next time I saw Jenda he was in a stall looking at a quarter crack on one of his horses. It was a minor split in the hoof, he told me, and could be reinforced with a bar shoe. "But it might get worse. Racehorses are fragile creatures, and keeping them sound is a constant challenge. You never know when you're gonna lose one. Charlie Whittingham said it best when he said, 'Horses are like strawberries. They can spoil overnight.' One day you can have a $100,000 horse and the next day, due to an injury, it might not be worth a thousand."

As we walked down his shed row, I could see the feed tubs were out. Jenda explained he generally uses cold feed but occasionally cooks up a hot mash for a horse that isn't eating well, in the hope that trying something different will stimulate its appetite. In addition to hay, molasses, corn oil, and grain, he gives his horses apples, carrots, and red apple vinegar. The vinegar surprised me, and I asked him if horses really liked to slurp that stuff up. "Not all of them," he said. "It's just one of the tricks you use. Some of them develop a taste for vinegar for some reason. We feed them a lot of soybean meal, which is real high in protein and has all the enzymes that a horse naturally needs. But it tastes a little bitter, and it's hard to get them to eat it. So we've found that brown sugar and molasses mask it nicely. But on some horses you need more than that to get them to eat it, and you keep trying different formulas until you hit on something they might like. Vinegar sometimes does the trick. Hell, I'd pour A-1 steak sauce on their feed if I thought they'd eat it. Years ago we used to give one horse, Doctor's Intern, beer all the time. Obviously you couldn't give it to him on race day, but other times it would take the edge off."

A horse that liked to drink beer and was named after a doctor? I could already see the commercial with a talking horse. "Yes, sir, folks, a six-pack a day keeps the Doctor in shape." I asked Jenda what Doctor's Intern's brand was. "Actually," he laughed, "I was giving him Mickey's. He'd drink the cheapest stuff. He'd drink it right out of the bottle. He was the cheapest claimer I had. We fed him donuts, too. He wasn't on our weight-watcher diet. I tell you what, we feed them anything to make their existence a little brighter than the other guys'. I think you're helping them out. They're also herd animals so we try to walk them together in the afternoon—anything to get them out of the stall. But it's kind of a miserable existence, and anything you can do to brighten their day, I think you're better off."

The herd animal aspect of horses has always interested me. I've often wondered how the pecking order gets played out on the track. Is it possible the outcome of some races is psychologically established in the paddock area prior to the actual running? Jenda wasn't so sure. "I think, in racehorses anyway, there is a real thin line between fear and courage. I mean, are they running because they're brave or because they're scared shitless? You tell me. If they run like a jackrabbit maybe they're scared shitless, and maybe those that come from the back of the pack are a little bit braver. I don't know."

We talked a little about the business side of running a barn. Forty or more dollars a day to train a horse seems like a lot of money. Where, besides feed, I asked him, does the money go? "Just guessing," he replied, "I'd say seventy percent to labor. You've got hot walkers, grooms, foremen, exercise riders. And every dollar that I pay an employee I have to pay twenty-nine cents for Workmen's Compensation Insurance. Our rates are way up there. There must be a lot of claims, because our rates are higher than for tightrope walkers. I don't think the rates for firemen or policemen are any higher than twenty-nine percent. Then you also have to have liability insurance. It used to be about five grand a year, but now through the HBPA it's around a grand."

I hadn't seen any invoices or accounting paraphernalia on Jenda's desk and asked him about it. He said his wife, Sue, handled all the billing and was the bookkeeper. When it comes to dealing with clients, he considers himself doubly blessed. "I'm blessed in that not very much of my time is spent talking with clients. Most of my clients know what's going on. They've been around the block a few times and I can't really tell them anything new. Clients like Sunflower Farm, Al Hoffman, Golden Eagle Farm have been in the business for a long time. When I call them they know what I mean when I say a horse has a bowed tendon or quarter crack. I don't have to go back and get out the vet manual and explain to them what they're up against. They already know all that. Explaining that stuff can take up a helluva lot of time.

"When you have somebody who just gets in the business, they're the absolute worst. They don't know anything. They've been a success in everything and think that this is one more thing they're going to conquer. Learning about horses is a humbling experience for most people. It's a lot easier working with knowledgeable people. They're the ones who know that no news is good news. If I call them up at seven o'clock in the morning, they can guess that we have some trouble."

Since my last visit with Jenda I had been in the grandstand several times and had even bet on Rakish Cavalier at thirteen to one. Apparently a combination of conditioning and that tongue-tie had helped, because he won easily, stealing the race on the front end. I asked Jenda if he was surprised. "Not really," he said. "We had only run him three times since his layoff, and he hadn't run that bad. He finished third in an allowance race against American Patriot that wasn't a bad race. I don't know why they let him go off at thirteen to one. In the program, I think he was nine to two. It was a hell of an overlay, an unbelievable one, because he had run a decent race on the turf last time out and the competition wasn't nearly American Patriot. From a handicapping point of view I thought the horse looked pretty solid in there. I didn't think he was slam-dunk. Everything just came together. Competition, fitness, and a lot of the contenders were coming off bad races."

Since Jenda considers himself a decent handicapper, I asked him what he looked for in the *Racing Form* as a good bet. "I like horses coming off good races. That last race is a key race, in my opinion. I don't like horses sixth beaten fifteen lengths, seventh beaten fifteen and down. I like horses third beaten two, second beaten a length. Or ones that maybe got into some trouble their last race and are running back at the same price or maybe bumping up. I don't like horses dropping down off of good races. One thing I've learned in this business is that nobody gives anything away. Those big droppers, ninety-nine times out of a hundred they've got a big hole in them. And it might not show up in this race, but somewhere down the line in the next few races it's gonna show up. Very few people are caught with their hand in the cookie jar in this business, because the worst thing, the absolutely worst thing, that can happen to a trainer is to lose a horse like Novel Sprite—the one that Hollendorfer claimed—and have it step right up the ladder. You'd rather run the horse over his head until you know what you've got. I don't like very much to give up on young horses. I like to make sure I know what I have before I tell that owner we've got to run the horse for a tag. I like to try them short and long, maybe give them a shot on the turf. I may be wrong, but the worst thing you can do is lose a nice young horse, trying to take a chance or break their maiden."

Once a horse breaks its maiden, a trainer has to decide where next to place it. Unless the horse looks like a world-beater, its next start is going to be somewhere in the claiming ranks. How does Jenda decide? "Horses afer they break their maiden take a quantum leap. In a maiden race, if you run against twelve horses, six of them are probably never going to break their maiden. They aren't worth a shit. So you're running against six horses that might be okay somewhere down the road. Now, after a horse has broken its maiden, all of a sudden they're running against twelve horses all of whom have proven themselves by winning at least one race. Going from a nonwinners to an all-winners race is the most difficult jump for a young horse to make. A lot of times a horse will win in a maiden race with an easy pace. The time will look good, but the next time they'll be running with horses that will put a little early heat on them for a quarter mile, make them go a little faster, and they don't finish quite as well. So time is a real relative kind of thing. Until they've proven they can take the heat and still run fast, I would reserve judgment on a horse."

Jenda elaborated on the importance of pace. "You see some horse sprinting that goes the quarter in :23, the half in :45 and change, and then finishes in 1:10 flat in its maiden race. Now it's running against winners, and those boys are going down in :21 and change, :44 and change. Can it still finish in ten flat? More often than not the answer is no. The other horses just went too fast, too early, put too much pressure on the maiden winner. It's interesting how that works. In judging how good a maiden win is you have to look at time: how easy was the pace, did he steal the race, did he have a lot of trouble and still get the job done? You try to evaluate the race on its merits compared to the rest of the times for the day."

Jenda illustrated his point with a classic example. "A guy had a horse at Santa Anita, this was years ago, that broke her maiden for $32,000 by five lengths her first start. He thought she was a stakes horse, right? He sent her to me and we were gonna run her in this stakes race. So I looked up the race and saw that everybody else on that particular day had run 1:09.1 or better—even $12,500 claimers were running 1:09 and change. And this horse broke its maiden by five, but it ran in twelve flat, driving. So anyone who is a reasonable person, other than the owner of this horse, could read into the situation that she didn't beat a thing, a bunch of bad horses. And when I looked at her race, there was nothing in it, just a bunch of professional maidens. If I had to pick eleven horses to run against, these are probably the eleven I would pick, they were so bad."

A lot of successful handicappers save all their *Daily Racing Forms* to refer to. I asked Jenda if he kept his. "I keep them for the last meet. But basically, with the computers and all the access you have, there's no need for me to keep all that information. The racing office has it. But I'm a real recency addict. That's my deal. I like good recent races. I'm not one of those who say, 'Whoa, back in 1985 he ran 1:09 flat and won for $50,000. Well, hey, that was 1985, it's 1990 now and he's been getting crushed for $6,250. I mean, gone are those years. McEnroe used to beat Lendl and Becker, but he can't do it anymore. Let's evaluate him the way he is now."

I've seen a number of horses that have just broken their maidens, run a good race their first time out against winners and then, maybe because of the added seasoning, win the next time out. Jenda was dubious about jumping to any quick conclusions about this as a winning pattern. "You're asking me a question God can't answer, because there's different cases for every race and every horse. You're asking me to make a general rule. Some horses, it takes them a dozen races before they even think of running their best race. Other horses run their best race the first time, and it blows their mind and they'll never run another good race. After that first race they find out what they're here for and they hate it—they don't like racing, they don't want to be here, it stresses them, they won't eat, they'll hide in the back of the stall, they'll shake like a leaf in the paddock and sweat like hell in their second start, and the more starts they have, the worse they'll get. So I don't think you can come up with any kind of pattern off a maiden win."

Jenda's allusion to sweating and shaking brought up another subject that fascinates racing fans, the meaning of a horse's body language. Horses aren't paraded in front of the grandstand before a race simply for the exercise. Obviously, gamblers over the years have insisted on being able to see a horse and how it moves before they put their money on it. I asked Jenda if there were any particular signs to look for in the paddock or post parade that would tell a fan whether a horse is ready to run or not?

"I'll tell you what, I've seen them sweating and shaking—obviously telling you they didn't want to run, but they still ran big races. But those are exceptions. Unless I know that a horse has run well before when he was dripping wet and shaking like a leaf, I wouldn't bet on a horse in that condition. You generally don't want to see them with their ears pinned or looking back at the barn area, either, as they're walking in. What you generally want is their ears pricked, their head erect, maybe even getting on their toes a little bit. You want a confident demeanor. It's like the horse is telling you, 'Hey, I know what I'm supposed to do and I'm ready to do it. I'm a little anxious, but I want to get on with it.' It's like a prize fighter, getting ready just before a fight."

Jenda was dubious about another of my prejudices, a horse with its neck bowed that is kind of digging in the dirt in the post parade. "I think you're trying to read too much into a specific sign, unless you know the history of a horse—maybe then you can put some credence in it. But just because you see a particular horse doing a particular thing on a particular day, I don't know that you can translate that into this horse is going to run big today."

Okay, then how about a horse that is kicking the stall in the paddock? Is that a sign the horse is nervous and out of control? "No, I kind of like that aggressive behavior. But Brown Bess will walk around in the paddock with her head down like an old pony. She's real mechanical. She doesn't make a move, she's real quiet. You'll find that the more times a horse has started, the longer they've been around, the older they are, the quieter they get in the paddock."

What about post position, especially with young horses? Suppose they draw the rail, is that a disadvantage? "Yes, because if they break just a half-step slow, they've got eleven other horses breaking on top of them, heading for the rail. If they have an outside post, even if they break slow, they have a quarter of a mile run into the first turn to find a spot where they can drop over. The rail is not a disadvantage if you've got an experienced horse that breaks cleanly and rockets away from the rail. For a young horse it is a little bit intimidating to be pinned into the rail with eleven other horses outside you. It's not real comfortable. Although a lot of the good horses I've had drew the inside post the first time out."

While trainers will scratch a horse because they don't like the track conditions or post position, they also do it when they find an easier spot for their horse to run in. Ronnie Beau has cashed some nice tickets by keeping track of late scratches that show up in a race a day or two later. I asked Jenda how much freedom trainers have to scratch a horse without upsetting the racing secretary. "When there are horses waiting on the 'also eligible' list, the racing secretary doesn't mind. He can replace your horse with another. The only time he gets pissed off is when he has a short field, or only eight horses in an exacta race, and you're gonna scratch your horse outa there and make it a smaller field where less money will be bet."

As we were talking the racing office's loudspeaker blasted on with a request for more entries into a particular race. They were having trouble filling a starter allowance marathon race. I asked Jenda if trainers sometimes enter a horse that's a bit short to help the racing secretary out. "That does happen," he acknowledged, "but you have to understand this is an imperfect business. The problem is that there are some races, especially for an allowance horse like a Casa Petrone or Loveboat Champ, that have run through most of their conditions, that don't get written all that often. You might have your horse in the peak of condition and there won't be a race available. Many times you have to make a big concession to race your horse. A race comes up and you know your horse isn't at the top of his game, maybe running a little over his head, but hey, this is the only race. If you don't run him here, there might not be another race for another month. Most of the time it's not like running a Brown Bess, where you know she's going to run in a particular race and you can prepare her for that particular race. So you have to weigh the pluses and minuses of running them in that particular spot."

I had been in the grandstand a few days earlier and seen Jenda run one of his better horses, Happy Idiot, in an unusual spot. What intrigued me about the race was that Happy Idiot had just won two straight allowance sprints, and Jenda had dropped him into a $40,000 claiming race. Since he had previously told me that nobody gives anything away on the backside, it seemed reasonable to suspect Happy Idiot's condition. Was I right? "Welcome to the party," Jenda confirmed in a voice laced with irony, then added, "Well, obviously, since this book is going to be printed after the fact, we were trying to lose the horse. It's got a breathing problem that isn't going away. It's not surgically correctable. It's only going to get worse. And we thought someone would think the horse claimable at forty thousand."

From our previous discussions I knew that Jenda had once been possessed as a gambler, but now he hardly bets at all. I asked him what the major difference in his perception about horse racing was now that he made his living training horses on the backside as opposed to just being a gambler in the grandstand. "If you're a trainer and someone in my position and you gamble a lot," Jenda said, "it clouds your judgment. Rather than give that horse a good work that it's looking for, you're always thinking about trying to hide him, make him go slow, make sure the clockers don't see him and the horse isn't properly trained. There was a guy around here years ago that stiffed a first-time starter maiden three times in a row right out of the gate. He just had his rider anchor him right out of the gate. The fourth time they were going to bet a lot of money on him. Well, the fourth time the horse thought that was the way he was supposed to run and stopped at the gate. So the point is, you're trying to teach the horse positive things, and when you start thinking about trying to make a bet or hiding a horse, a lot of times you're sending him a mixed signal."

Another thing Jenda has learned as a trainer is how many things can go wrong in a race. "I would say, if every time you ran a horse you had the best horse, you would probably still only win maybe thirty percent. Horses can fall down, hurt themselves, get shut off, the track's too hard, the track's too soft, it isn't conducive to their style, the saddle slips, they take a clod in the eye, the rider fucked up. I mean, even if you have the best horse, there's a million ways to get beat. For example, I've got a horse that likes to run, but she gets a little dirt kicked in her face and she bails out early."

As a handicapper I've noticed some horses seem to win only when they have an outside post position. Was the horse that didn't like dirt in her face like that? Did she run her best races from the outside? "Absolutely. A horse like that, that's the post you want. It seems every time we draw into a race she gets the one hole, the two hole, or draws down into the middle between a couple of rockets on the outside of her that get in front of her, kick some dirt in her face, then she bails out and it's all over. Post positions are very important with some horses."

I checked back with Chuck Jenda a couple of days after Brown Bess had won northern California's first Eclipse Award. She had done so by beating the best female horses in the world on the turf at Santa Anita. Her time of 1:57.3 for the Yellow Ribbon was not a new world record, but the fastest 1¼ miles ever run by a filly or mare. The fact that she had done this as nearly an eight-year-old was a tribute to both Jenda's patience and skill and Jack Kaenel's savvy riding.

In managing Brown Bess's success, Jenda had made a couple of gutsy decisions. One was his faith in his rider, Jack Kaenel. The Cowboy had been seriously injured in a roping spill at his Martinez ranch in early June, when his quarter horse had reared and flipped over on him, leaving him with a compound fracture of his left leg. It's an injury that normally takes three to four months to heal, yet nine weeks later Jenda elected to ride Kaenel in the Ramona at Del Mar. If Brown Bess had lost that race by less than a length, with Kaenel in the irons, Jenda would have been open to a lot of second-guessing. A loss in the Ramona might even have led Eclipse voters to conclude that Brown Bess's Yellow Ribbon win was a fluke. Jenda explained how he made his decision. "I looked him in the eye and said, 'Jack, don't bullshit me. Are you ready to ride?' And he assured me. We have a pretty good rapport, and that was good enough for me. He had also worked a couple of horses for me in the morning. He had worked Brown Bess a mile, and he didn't come off the horse panting. He had been taking care of himself. He had been going to the gym, and swimming, and he was in pretty damn good shape, even though he wasn't getting on a lot of horses. You know, Jack has to fight a weight problem, and many jocks do insane things to fight weight. But physically, Jack looked healthier to me at that point than he ever had."

What about Suzanne Pashayan's role as an owner? Had Jenda discussed the situation with her? "We discussed it, just like we talk about which races to run," Jenda said. "But I'll tell you, Suzanne and I just kind of think along the same lines. Jack had had great success with Brown Bess. He'd given her more courage and confidence. It could have been a problem with another owner, if both of us had vehemently disagreed. But we didn't. The same goes for deciding when and where to race Brown Bess. There was never a grand plan with the mare. It was always what was best for her, what was coming up next. It was always, 'Let's save her for this race, and then when she pulls up out of this race and two weeks from now she acts like she wants to run, then we'll look for another race.' It was never, 'Hey, we want to win this race six months from now.' The D. Wayne Lukas bullshit, where he says, 'Yeah, I want to win the Kentucky Derby in 1992.' That's a crock. Because this business is a day-by-day business. You can say whatever you want, but basically, when they're training good, that's when you want to run them."

Another decision Jenda had to make involved whether or not to work Brown Bess over the new Santa Anita turf track prior to the Yellow Ribbon. Jenda had initially decided to work her exclusively up north, but modified his thinking a little bit once Brown Bess was down south. "She was actually on the Santa Anita track three days before the race. We two-minute-licked her down the lane. Kind of between a gallop and a breeze. The only really compelling reason to go on the track as far as I was concerned was that she would be coming down the hill, across the main track, and then onto the main turf course. I thought it would be helpful to have her duplicate that in the morning so she wouldn't shy or duck in the afternoon. I would have been a lot more concerned if Brown Bess was a young horse—then a couple of works would have been critical. But Brown Bess had run well on every kind of surface that God could come up with. I mean from hard turf, yielding turf, to ones that had looked like a minefield. She had run on every kind of surface and handled them well. Also, I was getting glowing reports about the turf course down there. So I wasn't concerned."

The last important decision on Brown Bess's road to the Eclipse Award involved what to do after her Yellow Ribbon win. Should he race Brown Bess again before the end of the year? And if so, with how much weight? Jenda was tempted and entered Brown Bess in the Bay Meadows Handicap against Simply Majestic, Ten

Keys, and some other tough male horses. When the weights came out, the track handicapper had given Brown Bess co-high weight of 124 pounds. Jenda was upset that she hadn't been given the three-pound weight allowance normally given female horses when they run against the boys and scratched her out of the race. Since almost all the books on handicapping minimize that kind of weight difference as a factor in the outcome of a race, I asked Jenda to explain his thinking.

"Well, somewhere down the road," he argued, "the weight is going to catch up with a horse. I don't care what handicappers say. The more weight you put on a horse, sooner or later, it's going to catch up to it. And when you're running a handicap horse like Brown Bess, if she had beaten the boys packing 124, what would they do to her next? So it wasn't just that specific race we were concerned about. We were also looking down the road to what she would get for the next one, if she won."

Jenda had put some pressure on Bay Meadows officials to adjust Brown Bess's weight by threatening to run her at Hollywood Park. But he confided, "We had no intention of running Brown Bess in the Matriarch at Hollywood Park as an alternative. We had already beaten Claire Marine. We were using the threat of that race to see if we could get some leverage as far as the weights were concerned here. The only way we were going to run Brown Bess in the Bay Meadows Handicap was if it came up a six-horse field and it was anybody she could beat. There was too much to lose and very little to gain. If you factor the Eclipse Award into the equation, maybe we went into our fourth-quarter offense and watched the clock run out. The worst-case scenario, we thought, was if Claire Marine would win the Matriarch. Which she did. Then we hoped it would go to a coin toss, which would be the head-to-head race in the Yellow Ribbon, which Brown Bess won."

And that's exactly how it went. Jenda and Pashayan's strategy paid off. The racing secretaries, turf writers, and members of the *Daily Racing Form*—who collectively comprise the Eclipse Award committee—overwhelmingly voted for Brown Bess, with Claire Marine finishing a distant second.

In anticipation of campaigning her as an eight-year-old, Jenda was giving Brown Bess some time off. "Rather than turn her out, she's resting at the racetrack. We're walking her twice a day and not feeding her much. She's not in any kind of training right now. Probably we'll pony her in a couple of weeks and then start breezing her. I think when you're only going to stop on a horse for a month or so, it's counterproductive to turn them out. That's because a lot of times it takes them a month to come back from the adjustment of being on a ranch and then back at the track again. Brown Bess is secure here. It's not a case where she's a nervous filly who doesn't like being here, is afraid of the racetrack, and doesn't want to train. In that case, I would agree and say, 'Hey, get her the hell out of here.' But Brown Bess is very comfortable here, and we decided we'll just leave her here for a month and then ease her back into the program."

After winning one Eclipse Award, Jenda and Pashayan were tempted to have Brown Bess defend her divisional title in 1990 and try for two. The mare, of course, would have to indicate if she was willing and ready. The alternative would be to commence her career as a brood mare at Calbourne Farm. In any event, a Breeders' Cup race was not in the works. As Jenda explained, "There's no female turf race, so we'd have to run her against the boys and we'd have to choose between two different distances—one at a mile and a half and the other at a mile on the turf. Obviously the mile is out. I think the mile is the toughest Breeders' Cup race, because you've got some horses that can just flat-ass smoke and others that will try to get up in time. It's just a tough race. The alternative of going a mile and a half against the best male horses in the world isn't a helluva lot more attractive. So you can forget that. But the Breeders' Cup should have a mile-and-a-quarter turf race for fillies and mares, in my opinion. Why they don't, I don't know. All they have is a race on the dirt for fillies and mares."

In training Brown Bess to an Eclipse Award, Chuck Jenda at forty-three has accomplished something few trainers at any age do. And if the success of seventy-eight-year-old Charlie Whittingham is any indication, Jenda has a potentially long career still in front of him. I asked what he thought about it. "I don't think Charlie Whittingham had a good horse until he was forty. Most people in this business don't think you know what you're doing until you're sixty-five. You don't have any credibility as far as training good horses. You can get hot and claim some good ones, but you really don't get a lot of respect until you're older. In some respects I think that's good. I can look back now a few years ago when I was doing good and see that I was making a lot of bonehead mistakes that I wouldn't make now. I was overtraining or undertraining certain horses. I just didn't have the *simpático* I have now. I think that comes with experience. It's kind of like Nolan Ryan when he was young and had this great fast ball and nothing else. When you get a little further on in your career you become a pitcher."

6

BEHIND THE HARROWS
The Trackmen

*T*he first time I met Track Superintendent Francis "Red" Lowery was just after a late spring deluge at Golden Gate Fields. The track was a quagmire, and horses that figured were fading like morning glories at the top of the stretch. A lot of handicappers in the grandstand were grumbling because they had come to play a big Pick Six carryover, and many of them felt that the track maintenance crew had been deliberately remiss in their duties. Panama typified their suspicions when he said to me, "Man, they've been messing with the surface. They didn't seal it last night, and I might as well throw my *Form* and speed figures into the trash can. They just want to screw up the Pick Six so nobody can get it until the weekend. That way they'll draw a big crowd and increase the handle."

When I voiced Panama's complaint to Red, he snorted. "Listen, I'd steal the grandstand if I thought I could get away with it. The reason the track wasn't sealed last night is because we've been in the middle of a damn drought and water is expensive. We use over 125,000 gallons a day here. We didn't roll the surface last night because some of the trainers were complaining the track was getting too hard and hurting their horses' feet. We decided to let the rain soak in to put a water cushion in it. I hear all this talk about us messing with the track, but let me tell you, if I could really influence the outcome of a race, I wouldn't be working here in the mud. I'd be rich from all the smart bets I made."

Red, a rough-and-tumble ex-rodeo rider and trainer, was tired and grouchy. He had put in three straight twenty-hour days since the rains had come, and the task of trying to maintain consistent track conditions was getting to him. As a handicapper, I'd only considered his job from one perspective. Yet from the little he'd told me, it was apparent that he had to try to reconcile an array of conflicting interests. He had to protect the jockeys and horses from injury, please the handicappers, and mollify the trainers all at the same time. When you added economic constraints and the mercurial weather changes that come in off San Francisco Bay to the mix, Red was between a rock and a hard place. Whatever decision he made, I could tell from his beleaguered look he was going to make someone unhappy. Red, who was on the way up to his ranch north of Santa Rosa to take care of some hurt horses and get some sleep, checked his exasperation a little and said, "Listen, you want to talk about track conditions, then get ahold of me next month when the meet ends. I'll have more time. If you're in a hurry, go talk to Scott Dorn. He can fill you in." With that he put the pedal to the metal of his pickup and spun out of the gravel parking lot.

A couple of mornings later I acted on Red's suggestion and looked up Scott Dorn. While as plant superintendent he is Red's nominal boss, the two of them are also longtime friends. Working together, in recent years they have made the dirt track at Golden Gate Fields one of the kindest, most consistent racing surfaces in America. Whereas Red is a crusty, "horsepatching" son of a gun in his fifties, Scott is a bearded, fast-talking, technically oriented guy who tends by position, if not temperament, to be more dip-lomatic. Between puffs on his Winstons, he told me he grew up in

Berkeley and El Cerrito and was "practically raised" at Golden Gate Fields. Both his parents worked there, his mom in the front offices and his father as plant superintendent from 1956 until he retired in 1977. Scott, who is also a journeyman carpenter, essentially inherited his father's job as a result of the experience he gained from working with him as well as on other jobs around the track.

A hands-on guy, Scott suggested we preface our discussion with a quick tour of the mile track on one of the tractors that was out working the ground. Though it was a "dark" day at the track, a number of horses had just finished their morning works, and the surface was being harrowed once again to keep it from compacting. As we walked over to the chute where the mile-and-a-quarter races are started, Scott commented that track conditions were almost back to normal. The feature race the previous afternoon, a six-furlong sprint, had run in 1:09.3. Scott explained he and Red can tell how fast the track is playing by the sound of the horses' hooves as they come around the far turn. "If it's a fast track with lots of bounce, their hooves will sound like the thumping of pillows. If it's a hard and jarring track, you'll hear a clopping noise like two bookends being slapped together."

There were two tractors, a quarter mile apart, out on the track, and Scott flagged the lead one down as it came to the head of the stretch. It was a 175-horsepower Ford tractor pulling a cutting harrow. "The cutting harrow is a heavy-duty piece of equipment," Scott explained. "It consists of nine staggered rows of metal teeth that are pitched at an angle to make it easier to plough into the ground. Most of the time we use it in the mornings to loosen the track up to a depth of 3½ inches, though sometimes, if the track has layered out too much, we'll go as deep as 5."

Scott pointed to the second tractor that was now approaching us. "That one there is pulling what we call a roller harrow. That's the harrow fans see in the afternoon. We use the roller harrow, along with the water truck, for fine tuning in between the races. It's got four components. The front section has three rows of adjustable perpendicular teeth for lightly cutting the surface of the track. That's followed by the rollers, which break the resulting clods down, and then there's another set of staggered teeth behind it to set the ground back up. At the back of the whole unit there's also a matt screen to rake the surface smooth."

We jumped onto a little platform on the back of the cutting harrow and chugged around the track. Scott said the thick, two-foot-long, adjustable harrow teeth typically wear out every three weeks from the friction of ripping into the ground. As we moved over the track I was struck by how much the freshly harrowed surface was being "set up" beneath us. You could almost see the air being mixed into the moist loam. When I mentioned this to Scott, he suggested we step off the moving platform and take a look. He stepped off more agilely than I and, as I picked myself up from off the ground, I quipped that I had definitely felt the "bounce."

Scott laughed and elaborated on what makes the bounce that horses seem to love. "The bounce is pretty good right now. But it's even better right after the first rains in the winter, when we've gone over the track with the roller harrows. The track will have a tremendous amount of bounce then, and you'll see some really fast times. What makes the bounce is getting that rainwater into the base, which gives us our cushion. You have to understand that we only deal with the top five inches. We don't care what happens below that. So if we can get rainwater in that area from two to five inches below the surface, we'll get our bounce. There are days when these heavy tractors run over the top of the track and you can watch the ground rise behind it—you can literally see the ground spring back up. There are places, where the horse or jockey ambulance has gone over the track, that you can walk over and feel the bounce. It's like walking on your carpet at home. You move over a few feet and you won't have it. And it won't last for long, because the water comes up out of the base on the cold nights and we've lost it. For us to mechanically put it back in there is almost impossible. We can't put the water back in there as evenly as mother nature does it with rain. And it's better water. We don't have acid rain here, luckily, because we're coming right off the coast. So that rainwater is pure water."

Scott's comment about rainwater interested me. I asked him if it was better than the snow melt that was piped in from the Sierra.

"That mountain water is clear when it's there, but by the time we get it from the water district, it's got chlorine in it, it's got everything in the world put in it. It's been run through filters. It's just not as good as what comes out of the sky. They've got a skating rink in Russia that gets water from a totally pure spring, and it's the fastest skating rink in the world. There's nothing in the water to add friction and slow you down. Rainwater accomplishes the same thing for us here."

Unfortunately, Scott lamented, months can go by at Golden Gate Fields without a storm. "When it's dry, we try to accomplish the same thing by ripping the ground, getting water into the base and then quickly putting it back together. We do the best we can, but it's just not as good as with the rainwater. Our primary objective is to have the track safe for the horses and the jocks. But we also think about the handicapper and fan. We try to keep the track consistent. In sprints, for example, you don't want the horses running in fourteen [1:14] and change today when they were doing it in eleven [1:11] and change a week ago. So we try to get the track back where it's reasonable, where the cheap claimers run in eleven and change and the stakes horses on the same day run in nine [1:09] and change. What we try for is to make the track a fair one where the good horses go fast and the bad horses go slower. I can build you a track where every horse in the barn will go out there in nine and change, but that's not right. The good horses should be running faster. Otherwise, why do we have different grades in the horses, if they're all gonna run the same? Of course, to get the track that way is a lot of work, and there are days you're gonna blow it."

I was curious if Scott had any explanation as to why cheaper horses will sometimes run faster times than good horses on the same day. "Well, pace can have a lot to do with that," he reflected. "We had a couple of races the other day like that. There were two races where the winners both ran it in nine and one. The first race was a pure hand ride and the horse won by twelve lengths. But in reality, if that horse had been pressed, he probably would have finished in ten and one. That's what's amazing about horse racing. A cheaper horse will run a race in nine and one and blow the suckers away. Then he'll turn right around a week later on the same kind of track against better horses, and the race will go in ten and two and that same horse will finish fifth or sixth. I have never been able to figure that one out. I mean, if a horse can go out and run nine and one against cheaper horses, why can't he do it against better horses? For some reason he won't. The race will run in ten and one and he'll be dead last. It's still unbelievable to me that horses do that. You look at the *Form* and see he's run over the same track in nine and one and say to yourself, 'That horse has got to win.' But it doesn't work out that way."

Scott had talked about how water helps makes the bounce, but what about the soil that holds it? I picked up a handful and examined it. Scott explained the formula that comprised its ingredients. "We try for a mix that is forty percent coarse sand, forty percent fine sand, and twenty percent silt and clay. In the summertime, we add another four percent fir bark to help retain moisture and some bounce in the track. Right now, I just had it tested, the track is at forty-two percent coarse sand, forty percent fine sand, and eighteen percent silt and clay. East Coast tracks, by comparison, are generally composed of pure sand, which makes them quite a bit duller. They're forced to go to one hundred percent sand tracks because of their long winters and generally inclement weather. They need something that drains quickly. If they tried to add clay, silt, and fir bark, they'd lose their tracks in the winter. I visited twenty-five tracks a couple of years ago and picked up samples from around ten of them, and they all tested almost pure sand. Arlington Park outside Chicago was the only different one—it had almost twenty-five percent silt and clay."

I wondered if the slower, more tiring sand surfaces resulted in more injuries to the horses. "They run slower, but I don't know that it's any tougher on them," Scott speculated. "I think they get used to it. If you get used to something, it usually doesn't matter where you're doing it. But it's a big problem for horses coming from the West Coast that go to the East Coast to try and win the Triple Crown. They're not used to the pure sand tracks."

Scott said it was hard to compare tracks, because "Everybody puts their sand tracks together a little bit differently. They use different-sized grains and types of sand than we do. So when I'm talking to someone back east his coarse sand may be the same as my fine sand."

A common problem when horses run on sandy tracks is that they get "rundowns" and have to be bandaged. "What happens in the winter," Scott explained, "is the track separates. The fir bark goes to the bottom and the sand stays at the top, and it rubs against the horses' legs and basically burns their legs and gives them strawberries. Our trainers always complain about rundowns in the winter. Back east the trainers put three sets of rundown bandages on their horses because they know they're gonna wear out two of them, they run in that much sand."

When it rains hard in the winter at Golden Gate Fields the texture of the track changes dramatically. "It'll really layer out," Scott elaborated as he lit another Winston. "All the fine sand, silt, and clay will settle and go to the bottom, and the coarse sand will stay on the top until Red goes out in his tractor and remixes it. When it's totally wet in a driving rain, that track can get as hard as the floor in my office. Some horses run better on it than others. But we don't like to let it get too hard because a hard track with no bounce is really tough on our horses. They're not used to it. When it's raining hard, we don't roll the track with the water trucks anymore. We'll take our chances that we might have an off-track for another day rather than make the track too hard."

The coarse sand, Scott explained, is the basic building and maintenance material for the track. At Golden Gate Fields they use a number two Felton sand, which comes out of Santa Cruz. "Actually," Scott observed, "that's all we use to maintain our formula, because the coarse sand breaks down into finer sand over time. We haven't had to add fine sand in five or six years. We add about six hundred yards of the Felton sand every winter and eight hundred yards or so of fir bark every spring. Every year when the rains come the fir gets washed away. In fact, that's what we want to happen. We want to wash away as much of the fir as we can with the first heavy rains, so we don't keep too much moisture in the track. That's what hurt Bay Meadows early in their meet this year. When the rains came they had twenty-eight percent silt, clay, and fir in the track and that was too much. It was a bog and they couldn't dry it out. Silt, clay, and fir are fine in the summer, but you can't make it with that stuff in the winter."

If maintaining a dirt course is one challenge, the upkeep on a turf course is an altogether different proposition. Scott and I slipped under the inner guardrail and moved out onto the grass course. What I found surprised me. From the perspective of the grandstand, the sod looks smooth and uniform, but the reality in front of me reminded me more of a cross between a heavily played golf course and a cow pasture. There were numerous bare spots and divots from where the horses' hooves had dug in for traction. Scott said that as the meet progresses each year some attrition on the turf course is unavoidable. Every time a race is run, some of the turf is torn up. "In Europe they run on the grass all the time. But they can do that because each meet is only for a few days, and then they move on to a different course."

The composition of the turf track interested me. Basically, it is composed of a pea gravel base that is covered with sand and then seeded with a blanket of ryegrass. Golden Gate Fields had tried to mix in some blue and fescue grass with the rye, but those grasses didn't stand up to the hard use. As it is, Scott's crew does the best it can during the racing season. They try to maintain the surface by constantly filling in the bald spots with pregerminated flats of ryegrass.

On our way back to Scott's office I checked out one of the starting gates that stood like a sentry at the edge of the infield grass. Up close, it was a massive metallic structure that glistened dully in the morning dew. I climbed into one of the stalls and was struck by how foreboding and claustrophobic it felt. Each stall is enclosed in a heavy metal frame designed to restrict the horse's movement. There is less than a foot of space on either side of the horse's flanks. While the magnetically synchronized gates are certainly more efficient than firing a pistol into the air as a means of starting a race, the stalls themselves, as Jack Kaenel had told me, are extremely dangerous. It was easy to see how a "schooling" rider in the morning or a jockey in the afternoon could be seriously injured when a thousand-pound horse flipped or crushed him against the posts or between the narrow walls.

Back in Scott's barn we sat down with a cup of coffee and discussed the conventional wisdom that the harder a racetrack is, the faster it plays. Scott scoffed at the notion. "That's totally wrong. On a hard track, if you look at the fractions, you'll see horses really drop off in that last quarter. They'll go :21 and :44 and then wind up running 1:12 and change. What we try to do here is get the fractions to run as even as possible—something like :22, :45, and 1:09 and change. They're gonna slow down a little bit at the end, all horses do. But on a hard track they'll just quit, because the concussion on their legs and feet starts to hurt them. The leader will still fly, but by the time he's gone a half mile and gets to the top of the stretch, his feet sting so bad that he gives up. He says, 'Whoa, this is too much. I quit.' When Caros Love set the mile record here, Marco Castaneda looked at the clock and saw 1:08.2 for the first six furlongs and thought to himself, 'My horse is done. He can't go on.' But he tapped the horse on the shoulder and he took off again. The cushion on the track that day was perfect. Same thing with Simply Majestic. He ran halfway decent other places, but he set track and world records here at different distances. He just loved this racetrack."

In northern California the Bay Meadows track, despite several renovations, has been the target of constant criticism. The most recent complaint among horsemen has been that the track has no "bottom." I asked Scott what that meant. "Well, they've taken their track apart so many times that they've only got four to five inches of soil left on top of a limestone base. And it's very hard, there's no resilience. The horses can't get ahold of it as well. We haven't touched the base of this track in years. It's much deeper here than at Bay Meadows. But as I mentioned before, we only play with the top four to five inches of this racetrack. We know it goes deeper because we've occasionally had to dig it up to put in pipes and stuff. What we've found is mostly fill. Most of this track used to be a marsh. The same is true at Bay Meadows. But our depth varies. It goes down about eighteen inches in front of the grandstand, before you hit solid rock. You go to the backstretch and you can go down three feet and still find sand. Golden Gate Fields was built in 1939 and opened in 1940, and they lost the track the first week they ran because it wasn't pitched. It was flat, and there was no way the water could run off, so they lost it. We actually found that old track this year when we cut through for the pipes. We could tell it was there because it was totally flat."

Scott believes the track has been kept in better condition in recent years, not so much because of changes in the soil mixture that is put into the track as simply having better equipment. "In the old days we used 100-horsepower International Harvester tractors. They were two-wheel-drive tractors with single tires, front and rear. Now we have these 175-horsepower Ford tractors that are four-wheel drive. We've also added dual tires to the rear end, because the more wheels you have on, the less weight is on the track at any one place. That helps you in the dry season as much as the wet one. More tires help spread the weight over the track surface, which is good because you don't compact and harden up the ground as much.

"Another problem with single tires is that you can't steer them in the mud. You have to steer them with your brakes. When we were using single-tire tractors, we were all over the racetrack. We were going sideways and everything else, which made for a very uneven track."

Golden Gate Fields went to four-wheel-drive tractors about five years ago and also brought in a power harrow. "I got the power harrow," Scott enthused like a kid with a new toy, "because it shakes back and forth and breaks up clods faster than a Rototiller. We bought it for the dry season, but when it rained, I said let's try it, because you can control the depth of that harrow. The old harrows were fixed, and you'd go around and keep going deeper and deeper. And the racetrack would wind up with bare spots, and humps and bumps and piles. With this new power harrow we can go out in a totally wet racetrack and keep it fairly even. When it's wet we set the harrows high and only go down into the track about an inch."

The piece of equipment fans see most often is the water truck that showers the ground between races. It is usually followed by one of the tractors pulling a set of roller harrows. The water truck is used for dust control and to try and keep a certain amount of moisture in the ground. At Golden Gate Fields between three thousand and four thousand gallons of water are used each time the water truck goes around the mile track. "We have to add water," Scott emphasized, "because on a windy day all the moisture can be totally sucked out of the track within the time span of two races. If no water is put on the track, it will lose its bounce and quickly turn hard."

Scott acknowledged that the water is often distributed unevenly around the track. This isn't, as Frisco has sometimes speculated, because of some diabolical plot by the maintenance crew to cash a bet. Rather it's because, as the grandstand shadows lengthen during the afternoon, less water is needed on the frontstretch and more on the still sunny backstretch part of the track. "If we added more water to the shaded area in front of the grandstand," Scott said in defense of his procedure, "it would quickly turn into a bog. If we added less to the backstretch it would turn hard as a rock. So the water truck speeds up in front of the grandstand and slows down on the backstretch. The ground crew's primary objective is to try and keep the overall texture of the racing surface as consistent as possible."

I was interested in what Scott and Red do to actually "seal" the track. Panama and I had always assumed some kind of gigantic steamroller was hidden in one of the maintenance barns to do the job. But Scott laughed and said, "No. We seal the track with those roller harrows. You just pick the three rows of teeth up. They're hydraulic. The teeth come up out of the dirt, and the rollers that are on there, which weigh a good seven to eight tons, you just roll over the track. We can actually adjust the depth of the teeth during the middle of a race. If it starts to rain, we can just pick the teeth up and roll it down. We don't have to get it as hard as we used to because of the power harrows. I'd say that having the right equipment gets us out of ninety percent of the trouble we used to get into. With more experience we also guess better about what to do and when to do it. Still, we guess wrong when the weather is different than we expect. Red is the guy actually out there in the tractor. He can tell you some interesting stories about dealing with old mother nature."

By the time I tracked Red Lowery down, he was at Tatiana Farms, the thoroughbred rehabilitation ranch he runs with some friends just outside of Healdsburg. When I pulled into his driveway, I could see a half dozen convalescing horses grazing in a fenced pasture, several more sticking their heads out of their barn stalls, and a couple horses in a special exercise area where Red was monitoring their progress. I ambled over and watched as Red kept his eye on a three-year-old bay colt who was "running" on a treadmill attached to the bottom of a frothing whirlpool. Periodically Red would also encourage a four-year-old chestnut mare to keep moving on the hot walker that was just to our left.

As he worked, Red, who is of Italian, German, and Danish heritage, told me he grew up in a semirural area outside Jersey City, New Jersey. "We had a farm up by the Delaware Water Gap where I spent a lot of my youth. I came to California when I joined the navy at seventeen. I went back to Jersey for two years afterwards but couldn't take the weather. You think you always want to go home, but when you get there it's not the same."

Red's first connection with horse racing was in New Mexico. "I was rodeoing and got talked into buying a racehorse by a couple of guys. Come to find out, they knew less about racehorses than I did." Red shook his head and laughed. "I had a construction company at the time, quit it, and went about racing horses. I had an early stroke of good luck and, like everybody else, thought I could make a living at it for the rest of my life. I trained for quite a few years, eighteen or nineteen, but I've been fixing up hurt horses all my life. That's my enjoyment in life, patchin' on horses.

I take horses that other people wouldn't feed and try to get them sound. That's why I started Tatiana Farms."

Red was an early supporter of magnetic field therapy. He brought the first "blue boots" to California and started selling them. "I thought they were great. They were a portable battery-operated magnetic unit that you could strap onto a horse's leg. I have one now that comes from England, which you can plug in directly to an electrical outlet. It's much stronger and covers a wider area. You can do sore backs and the whole body. It has a blanket and you can put it anyplace you want."

Red also got into laser-acupuncture before it was fashionable. "I've worked with the veterinary, Dr. Hill, it seems like all my life. When I first got into racing, I went to work for him and we've been friends ever since. I don't think he even gives a shot anymore, he's that kind of a veterinary. He works for the state and does his healing with lasers and screens and that kind of stuff. He used to be called weird. Now he goes all over the world and teaches."

Red became track superintendent as a result of a strike at Golden Gate Fields. "I had some ideas about what made for a kinder racing surface for horses, and the pay was more lucrative than what I was making training horses. I was in the HBPA and one of the biggest complainers about the conditioning of racetracks. When the strike came up I saw an opportunity to put my theory to work. But Scott and I inherited a theory that neither of us liked. The theory was that you had to have so much humus in a racetrack to make the bounce, to keep the horses from hurting themselves. We had a lot of problems fighting that theory the first few years, but when we were given the authority to apply our own ideas, track conditions began to improve dramatically. We went from being considered 'stupes' to setting track records."

Since Red seemed to take pride in setting track records, I asked him if that was the best standard for judging the condition of a racetrack. "Yes, and the kindness to the horse," he replied. "If a horse has a kind surface to run over, he will get ahold of the racetrack and it won't hurt him. He'll carry his speed and not fall apart. He'll keep right on running. Horses that can run, that are real racehorses, dig in and try hard. But if they try hard and the racetrack is a hindrance to them and they can't get ahold of it—it's too hard or too deep—it take its toll and they give up. It's self-preservation. Most people would give up too."

Red elaborated on track conditions. "The track varies every fifteen minutes. The weather at Golden Gate is so variable that you make yourself a wreck trying to maintain a consistent racing surface. Fans want the track to remain the same at twelve-thirty as it is at two-thirty as it is at four-thirty. And that's impossible, unless you make it so bad that it's bad all the time. Generally, what we try to do is get the right mix of the clay and the silt against the humus. The coarse sand has to be to the point where it's binding together with the clay, so that when a horse hits it, he can grab ahold of it and keep on going. The clay and silt content can't be so high that when it rains it turns into a sea of slop. If you have too much clay, when it rains, it gets so slippery you can't walk over it, much less run over it. So you have to hit that perfect medium. Every time we harrow the track, the track changes. On a dry track the small fine stuff keeps coming up to the top of the surface, and the bottom parts keep setting up harder as the coarse stuff goes down. You don't want that separation, which is why we renovate so much at Golden Gate Fields. We get criticized because we try to mix it up daily."

A typical workday for Red begins at six in the morning and extends through the afternoon races. When there are problems he stays over and sleeps in his shed. The first thing he does in the morning is check the weather and then look at the racetrack. "During the rainy season we seal the track every night in case it's gonna rain. How hard we seal it depends on the amount of rain we expect to get. If we expect a light shower we just seal the top of it and come out in the morning at four and harrow it back up and have a great racetrack. If we expect two or three inches of rain during the night, we have other equipment that we set the track up with to make sure water doesn't get into it. We have wood floats and iron floats and rollers, and we set it up so the water cannot penetrate and make a real deep and treacherous track. There's nothing worse for riders or horses than to have a deep, muddy racetrack."

Constant criticism, Red admitted, is one of the debilitating aspects of his job. "Hell," Red snorted, "we even got criticized when Simply Majestic ran that mile and an eighth in 1:45 flat and set a world record against Judge Angelucci. That's an interesting story. Charlie Whittingham is a personal friend of mine. I thought the racetrack was perfect. So I asked him, 'Charlie, bring a good horse up for one of our stakes races.' He said, 'I'll bring Ferdinand up.' I said, 'No, I don't want the best, I just want a good horse.' We were teasing back and forth. Anyhow, a race came up and he shipped up Judge Angelucci. Simply Majestic came up on the same van for the same race. Well, the Judge ran second and Simply Majestic just loved the racetrack. We got condemned because people thought we set the racetrack up. We did work hard on it. We wanted a perfect racetrack to get national recognition that Golden Gate Fields has the finest racetrack in the world. But we didn't set it up for any particular horse. The horse was like two to five. What are you gonna do, bet? That's crazy."

The transformation of Golden Gate Fields into one of the better racing surfaces in the country, in Red's opinion, goes back to when Kjell Qvale was the principal owner and director. "He told me personally, 'I don't care how long it takes you, do what you have to do. Make it the best.' And we have. That's still management's position under Ladbroke, the new owners. We're probably the highest-paid tractor drivers in the world at Golden Gate Fields. We work hard at it and take pride. Because we know, if something goes wrong, someone will say, 'That stupid asshole don't know what he's doing.' And it could have nothing to do with what we did or didn't do. It's supposed to be sunny weather and all of a sudden it rains at three in the morning. And just like that we have the track three-and-half inches deep and no chance of getting it set up to keep the rain from seeping into it. Or the wind can shift in the afternoon. We can put a load of water on and the wind can come up five minutes later and dry it out and we have a cuppy racetrack for the next race and we have no control over it."

Temperature changes can also dramatically affect the track's condition. "When the temperature drops four or five degrees and that north wind comes up"—Red shook his head—"it will suck the water out of the track and set it up so fast, we can't get around fast enough to drop the teeth in the harrows between races and put enough water back in the track. The track will turn hard and dry in a matter of minutes. It's a constant guessing game, what to do next."

Some handicappers believe that the tides from San Francisco Bay affect track conditions. Red has his doubts. "Years ago, they used to say, 'Well, the tide comes in and that's what changes the race-track.' They said Golden Gate Fields is built on a dump. If the tide would come in the dump would float up to the top. Well, that's bullshit. Years ago, at three o'clock in the afternoon the racetrack would change. Everybody said it was the tide. Well it wasn't the tide that was doing it, it was what the people who were working on the track then were doing. They wanted to get away early and would water with abundance on the seventh, eighth, and ninth races, so as soon as the last race was over they could go home."

Red and his men have to try to keep the track in consistent shape not only for the afternoon races but also for the morning workouts when the horses are trained. That means they often have to work at night. "We can't just forget about the track when the races end. We have to do something to compensate for what happens to the track in those twelve hours between the end of the races and when training begins at six the next morning."

To be a top-notch track conditioner, it was becoming apparent, requires talent, hard work, and intuition. Besides having a feel for his equipment, a trackman has to be in tune with the weather and be a bit of an alchemist to mix earth, air, water, and the sun's fire in their proper portions. The process, as Red explained with one of the elements, water, is not without paradox. "Moisture, for instance, does two things. It will set a racetrack up hard and it will also soften it. To compact the track you have to have moisture, so you can pack it and hold it together. When you have it hard, you have to get it wet again to rip it up and get it soft. So you're constantly looking for that perfection. But it's not a science. You just have to go by your intuition and experience over the years."

Red echoed Scott Dorn's belief that the best racing is always right after the first rains, when the natural water gets into the ground. "That nitrogen, or whatever you want to call it, comes with the rain. The racetrack gets moisture down deep and the top stays a little bit dry. If it could rain a half inch every night I'd be the happiest guy in the world. We'd always have the fastest, kindest racetrack in the world. But the weather is always changing, and that's why our track varies. People complain, 'You had it slow, you had it fast.' But that's bullshit. We aren't gods. We try to maintain a consistent racetrack. Sometimes we come out looking great and other times we look like dummies."

When Red gets accused of changing the racetrack during the day, he gets a little bit irritated. "I grant you, the track changes," he admits. "It changes every ten to fifteen minutes. Between races it changes sometimes. We try to do the best we can. I've been called in front of the union twenty-five times for hollering and screaming and being a wild man with my men. Half the time they're mad at me because I'm telling them do this, do that—especially now that we have CBs and walkie-talkies in the tractors. Now I can tell everyone exactly what I want done every minute during the races. I can come around to the backside and see that it's dried up more and tell my water truck, 'Hey, slow down between the five-eighths pole and the three-eighths pole.' Or 'speed up' or whatever I want to do. Years ago, we just did the same thing over and over again, whether it needed it or not. That's why track surfaces were so uneven. It didn't make any difference, if the water truck was going over a shady area that was already so wet that the truck was sliding sideways, more water was still routinely put on. That doesn't happen anymore because we're in constant communication."

In recent years handicappers have paid a lot more attention to the subject of track bias, especially regarding post positions. I asked Red for his opinion. "That word, *biased*," Red insisted, "shouldn't even be in the dictionary. It's a manmade word, because they don't have any other description. It's an illusion. When we work on the track we start at the rail and rip out to the outside of the racetrack. It's in the state law that we have to have a consistent racetrack.

Why would we want to have a path anywhere that was deeper or faster than the rest of the racetrack? The horsemen would be on us in a minute. Horses have to have equality."

Red agreed that, depending upon a horse's running style and the distance of a race, a certain post might be an advantage or disadvantage. But he insisted that was a different thing than a track generally being biased in favor of certain post positions. For him, when a certain part of the track seems hot or cold, other factors are at work to sustain the illusion. A major reason, in his opinion, is simply the way the pills come out when the post positions are selected. All the favorites can draw inside posts or outside posts for several days running. When they win, Red reasoned, it's not because of a track bias in favor of their post position, but because they are the best horses.

Another factor that contributes to the perception of a track bias, Red feels, involves the jockeys. "The leading rider says, 'Well, this horse didn't handle the inside too good, maybe it was too deep.' So he moves out four feet. Everybody else figures, 'Well, he's the leading rider, he knows what he's doing. I'll move out four feet.' It becomes a self-fulfilling thing."

Red and I discussed the pitch of the track. Since the whole racetrack is pitched at an angle that slopes down toward the rail, I asked him if the track didn't have a tendency to slide and accumulate down toward the inside. If it did, wouldn't that make for heavier, slower going for the horses running there? "Every time you go around with the harrows," Red admitted, "the ground moves down a half inch toward the rail. That's why at the end of the day, or every two days—depending on the weather conditions—you have to take that berm and move it back up to the outside. The whole racetrack just moves down during the day. It goes down around the turn and everywhere else. Sometimes you get caught. There isn't enough time between training in the morning and racing in the afternoon to get that berm back up."

So the inside might be a little thicker then? "Yeah, but that would only be the first two-and-half feet off the rail. It's real soft, and no one should be down there. The only time a horse runs down there is when the jock has no control over him and the horse is bouncing off the fence. The official racetrack is three feet off from the rail. That's where it's measured for a mile racetrack. Everybody wants the racetrack to be harrowed right up to the rail, but if you just throw that dirt underneath the rail, it builds up faster and it's harder to get back up. We try and keep an apron that's a foot clear from the stanchions of the inside rail. When it rains we have to compact that berm by the rail, and that area gets a little harder. If we don't, the water gets trapped and doesn't run off the racetrack."

Red said that over the years the pitch of the track has been changed to promote better drainage. "Our turns are pitched at an angle of seven degrees now, where they used to be five. Our straightaways are pitched at five degrees, where they used to be four. You can't dry the track out in the winter if too much rain seeps directly into a racetrack. Once it gets in the racetrack it goes deep. It has to run off."

I could see that a greater pitch would make for better drainage. But I wondered how that would affect the horses. Wouldn't a greater pitch make it harder for them to run evenly and increase the chance of injury? Red shook his head and replied, "No. It's actually easier on them. There's only about a sixteenth of an inch difference in height between a horse's inside and outside feet, and the inertia of running holds them to the inside. So in fact, the more of a pitch you have, the easier it is on a horse. He really doesn't even have to change leads. If he goes into the turn and he's hurting, he doesn't have to change leads to keep from going farther out. Most people don't even know that's happening. We do it for self-preservation and to make a better racetrack. The pitch going into and out of the turns has also been changed since Scott and I took over, and people don't even realize it. A horse goes into them in a nice smooth fashion and comes out of them in the same way, instead of an abrupt change."

Red and his crew also pay quite a bit of attention to the starting chute. In his opinion it's one of the most critical places in a race, especially in a sprint. "If a horse slips in the chute he loses all chance of winning. That's why we go in there every other race, sometimes every race, because you have to have the horses with good footing. We pull the gate off and go in and water and harrow the chute so you have a consistency coming onto the main track. Water used to collect around the six-furlong chute, but Scott re-engineered the slope of the ground behind it so the water now drains away from it."

Every now and then in a horse's past-performance chart the *Daily Racing Form* will comment that it "jumped tracks" in one of its races. I asked Red if the reference was to tire tracks. "Yeah— but they shouldn't be there. The only time they are there is on a muddy track, when the gate crew has to pull the gate off the track in a mile or longer race and the crew isn't able to obliterate them completely. I can only think about three days where that happened here. That was when we had thirty-one straight days of rain, and the racetrack was up over our ankles. Under those conditions, it was difficult to even make the races go."

In fact, sometimes the weather is so inclement and track conditions so bad that the afternoon races have to be canceled. Usually that decision is prompted by the jockeys when they consider conditions so dangerous that they refuse to ride. But Scott Dorn, or Red in his absence, can also close the track down. Most often, however, it is only the inner portion of the track that is shut down during the mornings in order to protect the running surface for the afternoon races. In those cases the "dogs" are put up, and trainers are forced to work their horses outside the series of orange rubber cones that line the track. Works around the dogs are usually much slower, both because of the off-track conditions and the greater distance the horses have to travel.

An important part of Scott and Red's job is to monitor the weather constantly during the rainy season. One of them is usually on the telephone every thirty minutes trying to get an update from the National Weather Service or the Coast Guard. They also have weather radios in their tractors, so they can listen to updates while they're watering and harrowing in the afternoon. "It's a constant battle with the elements," Red reflected. "People look and see the tractor coming around, harrowing out, and think that's the whole job. Well, it's not. If it was, we could put the tractor on remote control. Mr. Crook, the head of Tanforan years ago, wanted to do the whole job with one tractor. We asked him, 'How we gonna make the turn to get back in the chute?' He didn't have an answer. At the Meadowlands racetrack in New Jersey, they have two tractors that have harrows on them so big that they do half the track at a time. They never stop. In the wintertime they're going twenty-four hours a day. All day and night long they just keep turning it over because they're afraid it's gonna freeze or set up. They never water in wintertime, they just keep harrowing. We had a freeze-up this year at Golden Gate and harrowed all night long, and it still didn't make any difference. That was one morning we decided to close the track."

Since trainers have to live with track conditions on a daily basis, I wondered what kinds of comments Red got from them when he went for his morning coffee at the track cafe. "There are over a hundred trainers on the backside," Red reflected, "and everybody has a horse that has a preference. And everyone is under pressure. Trainers are under more pressure than anyone else. They have to perform. If their horses don't perform, somebody else gets the horses. It's as simple as that. And somebody is always there in the clubhouse to tell the owner that they're smarter than the guy who's got the horse. That's the way the racetrack is. It's a cut-throat business. It probably shouldn't be that way, but that's the way it is."

Red elaborated about the preferences of different kinds of horses. "Horses that are real racehorses, that dig in and try every jump, have to get ahold of that racetrack. They don't like it too soft. They can't be slipping and sliding. If they slip and slide, they just wear themselves out and die. Plodders, cheap old route horses that have one lick in them, maybe an eighth of a mile running at the end, don't care what kind of surface they run over. They can only run so fast and that's it. A trainer with a horse like that wants a soft track, because it's not gonna hurt his horse to run on it as much as it will one of those faster horses."

Older, sore-footed horses sometimes blossom on fast tracks with lots of bounce. Red explained why. "A fast racetrack is the per-fection. When the bounce is right, it's like the horses are running on a sea of titties. Any horse can run on it. That's why sometimes we get these old horses that are running way down at the $6,250 level in eight and change and people say, 'What the hell is going on?' Usually it's a horse that has all the ability in the world, but he's been running on a track that hurts him. When he suddenly hits a racetrack that is to his liking, he runs his eyeballs out. We get horses that have run on a less kind surface and go right up the ladder here. When I was training, I even had one, a sprinter called Bold Nada. I claimed him for $6,500 at Bay Meadows in the fall and took him to Santa Anita. I raced him a couple of times there, when there was a layup between Bay Meadows and Golden Gate Fields, and then brought him back here. The horse ran six times and won five allowance races. He ran down every time in nine and one, that was his race. He ended up making $45,000, when that kind of money meant something. There are still horses today that are the same way. When Simply Majestic came here and set that world record, he was like that."

Every year more horses get injured, and a lot of trainers blame the racing surfaces for breaking them down. I asked Red for his opinion. "The reason horses break down more now is that we used to only race about eight months out of the year and rest the horses in between. Now we're racing 365 days out of the year, and there's a lot more stress on the horses. We had more breakdowns this year on the racetrack than we had in the last three years. And people contended it was our racetrack that was breaking them down. That wasn't it. It was people bringing horses that had already injured themselves and running them at our racetrack. Those horses liked our racetrack so much that they outran themselves and broke down. But they were already injured. Racetracks don't break horses down, owners and trainers break down horses. They run them with prob-lems and look the other way or try and mask them. And it's not necessarily greed that's doing it, it's just the pressure of being in the game. That's ninety percent of it. They have to have a horse running or they get asked, 'Why are you here? If you're here to run, run. If you're not here to run, get him off the ground.' So if you only have a few horses, you run them until there's nothing left, because the pots are so great that you have to take the chance. The only way to deal with the problem is to have the horses be qualified. The majority of the good trainers have learned that you can only run a horse so many times. Then you gotta give him a rest or he'll break down and make you give him a rest. That's why I started Tatiana Farms."

Red is gambling there is a bright future for convalescent ranches like Tatiana where owners and trainers can send their horses to get them freshened up and sound again. "It's less expensive than keeping a sore horse at the racetrack. A sore horse don't do nobody any good, an owner or a trainer. See that mare over there on the walker, when she came here she was just a sack of bones and couldn't walk. They sent her up from Santa Anita. She's ready to go back now, but the owner called and said, 'Give her another three weeks.' The man knows his horse. Bryan Webb is his trainer, and Bryan's been in the racing business long enough to know what's going on. He's happy with what we've been doing here for a whole year. People are realizing that they have to take care of the horses they got, because it costs so much to replace one. You can't just discard a horse like a pair of socks and write it off anymore. There's no one who's got so much money they can just keep claiming horses and giving them away. You have to repair them and get them back to racing."

Red walked over, switched the whirlpool and treadmill off, and led the bay colt over to the hot walker to join the chestnut mare. I asked him how he felt about the racing of two-year-olds. "Well, mine's still out in the paddock." He pointed to a small corral. "People talk about banning two-year-old racing, but I don't think that's even the issue. I think it's an economical burden on the person who owns the horse to run them that young. But if they want to go and run their horse as a two-year-old, before he's developed, and try to get that flash in the pan and hope he holds together, that's their prerogative. Years ago we used to race two-year-olds late in the year for only a quarter of a mile. Now we start them much earlier, and they go 4½ furlongs and up."

Red feels that, besides being bad for the horse, running two-year-olds distorts the whole racing program. "If you're gonna race two-year-olds, you have to have a lot of them at the track to fill the races, because they're constantly falling by the wayside. It's a racing secretary's nightmare. At Golden Gate Fields there's something like thirteen hundred stalls. But because trainers sneak their two-year-olds into their barns before they're supposed to, he's only got nine hundred horses that are actually racing. That's why you see the same cheap horses all the time. There's not a lot to choose from."

On the other hand, Red believes that with a more balanced program, "A racing secretary might have a thousand head of sound running horses that he could pick and choose from. He would have different categories of horses in them stalls. But if you have to give up three hundred stalls for two-year-olds you're in trouble. Because the rule of thumb is you have to have twice as many two-year-olds in the barn as normal because only half of them are ready to run. Pretty soon all the racing secretary has to choose from in making up the daily card is a barnful of two-year-olds. It comes to the point where you have to ask yourself what the program is."

I asked Red if he thought it would be helpful to cut back on the number of racing days, which in California had grown to an astounding 485 days in 1989. "I don't think cutting back the number of racing dates is the answer," he replied. "Self-management is the answer. Keep getting fresh horses. Don't try and run the same horses all the time, and if something happens to a horse, get him off the racetrack. There are plenty of sound horses out there that can't get on the racetrack. The racetrack is not the place to heal up horses."

If Red were the racing secretary, he would shake up the complacency of those trainers who just sit around and collect day rates. "We are the only part of the horse industry," he emphasized, "that doesn't make a trainer prove that his horse is ready to run. In the quarter horse and trotting industries, to be eligible to run, you have to run to the clock. You have to go so fast and so far before you're allowed to run in that category. The thoroughbred industry operates on the assumption that the trainer knows best, that he can do as he sees fit. If a trainer wants to run a horse and give it a race and drop it down and bet on it, he can do that. I've contended for years that we have so many horses here in northern California that we should make them qualify. There are lots of horses that are ready and willing to run that are not able to get stall space on the track because there is an abundance of sore horses in the barns that are not ready to run. You can watch every maiden race that runs, and I watch every race that runs, and six out of the twelve horses should not be in the race. They might be too slow, they might be in the wrong category, they might not be fit. But that's just because of the way things are set up now."

So how would Red have horses qualify—would it be by time? If a horse ran 1:11 flat in a trial race, would he put him in, say, a $20,000 maiden race? "No, because times vary by the time of day and the track conditions. The way to determine where a horse belongs is with training races. I would have them run three-quarters of a mile, and if you run one, two, or three in this training race, at this designated claiming price, then you're eligible to run for the money. You get so many races to try out. If you don't make it, you're not permanently banned. You just have to go someplace else to get your horse in better shape and try again. You'd have to give up that stall at Golden Gate Fields so another horse that's ready to run has a chance. My theory is based on the idea that Golden Gate Fields is a racetrack, not a training center. When you get here, you're supposed to be ready to run. It makes it easier on everyone. Easier on the owner, because his horse is there ready to run. It makes it easier for the racing secretary. He can write races for horses and get a comparable field of horses that the public will bet against, not a four-to-five horse and the rest of them at twenty or fifty to one."

Red believes that qualifying races would also keep more owners in the game. "An owner will accept getting beat by a length," he explained. "But he won't accept getting beat by twenty lengths and having his friends give him the hoorah and say to him, 'What the hell did you run that piece of shit for?' But he will gladly pay the bills, until he bleeds, to prove that his horse can run. Then, if he comes for several weeks and sees in a schooling race that his horse can't run, he'll say to himself, 'Hey, this horse can't beat nobody. Why should I put him in front of the public and get ridiculed? I'll just take him home and give him away.' "

Red is skeptical, however, that his ideas will be embraced. He knows every trainer on the backside is intent on keeping his prerogatives. "It's the appeal of individuality," he reflected. "That's why we have so many trainers. They all have theories and they all have the same outlook, 'There's no son of a bitch gonna tell me what to do.' I was the same way. But for the betterment of racing and in order not to keep turning over owners, things have to change."

One of the best things that's happened to racing in the past few years, in Red's view, is that they've extended the racing career of maidens. It's no longer unusual to see a five-year-old horse trying to win its first race. "If they don't make themselves ineligible," Red approved, "they can keep on running. That's why I got this mare right here. It gives everyone a better chance."

But most handicappers I know, I told Red, would say, "Hey, if this horse hasn't broken its maiden by four, forget it."

"Yeah," Red countered. "But that's not necessarily true. There could have been circumstances that kept a horse from winning. The pressure before was so strong that trainers felt, 'Just do whatever you have to do to get their maiden broken.' Now there's no pressure. If the horse is hurt you take time off, fix it up, and bring it back. We had a race last spring at Golden Gate Fields with four five-year-old maidens in it. They run down there in nine and one. They were coming head and head and finished boom, boom, boom. They carried two of them off again because they broke down. But they ran their eyeballs out. Santa Anita has had older horses running for years. You look it up and there'll be some well-bred horse that's seven years old that had problems when he was young, but had some ability, and they gave him the time. And that's no more than right."

Red and I discussed his philosophy of handicapping. He started off with an apparent paradox. "Why are horses favorites?" he asked. "Because they ran good last time, that's why," he answered. "Why are there so many beaten favorites?" he asked. "Because they ran their eyeballs out last time. My point is their trainers didn't give them enough time to come back to themselves before they ran them again. They ran them again because there was a race in the Condition Book that fit the horse, that was the reason. And that's what makes handicapping. The guy who can balance out all the things and read between the lines, he's the winner."

I wondered what Red thought would happen if his idea of qualifying races was adopted and every horse in a ten-horse field was fit and had a legitimate shot to win. I told him I knew a number of gamblers who would say, "That's a handicapper's nightmare. It's a race to stay out of."

"No, it's not," Red disagreed. "It's a race to bet because you have an opinion and get better odds. That's what you're there for. Your brain against everybody else's. Gambling is a disease, but it's a disease of your mind. The only reason you bet is that you figure you're smarter than every other son of a bitch in the place. I know that's why I bet."

Red didn't have much sympathy for gamblers who play the chalk in a weak field. "Yeah, but what fun is that? They're not gamblers. They could stick their money in the goddamn bank. They're just looking for a cinch that's gonna pay sixty cents. They aren't gamblers, they're cinchers. The definition of gambling is you pay your money and take your choice. Don't give me a silver platter. 'Here, you give me two dollars, I give you two-sixty back.' That's not gambling. If you want to designate a gambler, he's the guy that's got his brain. He's betting that he's smarter than everybody else. He can figure out what's going on."

Red has a jaundiced view of the typical fan reading the *Racing Form*. "He's the guy reading past performances, right? He's not reading what's gonna happen today. He's figuring, 'The one horse did this, and the six horse did that, on this given day, and he went this far and this fast and the racetrack was this, blah, blah.' Listen, I know the best gamblers in the world. I know millions of them. Sometimes they win, ninety-nine percent they're losers. It's a mind game. The racetrack and gambling is a mind game. And there's so many factors to take into account.

"But then again," Red backtracked, "if trainers had to prove their horses before they could run, everyone would have an even shot. The track would also handle more money. Most people wouldn't bet on a four-to-five shot if their life depended upon it. Me, I go have a cup of coffee. Forget it. I don't need that kind of gambling. I don't wanna invest my money to get back a few pennies."

From what he has learned as a trackman, what would Red advise the fan in the grandstand to pay attention to? "Everything," he replied. "You watch the racetrack. You have to watch the weather. You have to watch the equipment, the way it's being worked. If you're gonna be a gambler, you have to take everything into consideration. There are some old guys who come out at twelve o'clock every day and put their stick in the racetrack to see how hard and deep it is. Sometimes they even pick some of the dirt up and feel it. Years ago there was a guard around who kept the fans from doing it. I told the guard, 'Let them come.' We're not here to hide anything. We're not here to do anything but help everybody, because if we help everybody, they're gonna bet. If you try to pull some kind of a scam on them, they're not gonna bet. People are not stupid."

Red talked about the wind from a handicapping perspective. "Most generally, when the wind comes up it means that the track is gonna get faster. Unless the wind gets too high, and it dries out the track so much it cups out. Then the track is gonna be slower. It depends on the velocity of the wind and how much moisture is in the ground. If you're gonna bet, you have to take that into consideration. You can't just say, 'Well, this horse ran 1:08.4 at Golden Gate Fields last time, how come he got beat running 1:09.3 this time.' Any number of circumstances could explain it. It could be the track is not as tight as it was. It could be the pace. It could be that the horse wasn't quite as strong as he was the other day."

Red elaborated about his gambling philosophy. "I gamble very sparingly anymore, but when I do I gamble a lot of money at one time. I pick horses that I know can run and try to match them to the conditions of the racetrack. During the racing meet at Golden Gate Fields I seldom gamble anymore. Driving the tractor all day long, I don't get to the grandstand that much to be able to gamble. I gamble during the fairs and the first part of the Bay Meadows meet."

It seemed a lot of horsemen on the backside had told me they used to be heavy gamblers but had cut way back. Red had an explanation. "Well, it used to be, before year-round racing, that the season was short and going to be over, so you were more of a fanatic. Now, there's racing every day. You can pick your spots. You like a horse, you know a horse, you watch a horse. I've had great success with the horses I send back from this farm. I know how they came to me and how they were running and how I sent them back."

"Yeah, but that's inside information," I told him.

"No it's not," Red responded. "If a fan is an astute gambler, he should never be in the grandstand but down in the saddling paddock. He should have his binoculars, be at the saddling paddock every race watching every horse being saddled up, then go get a vantage point and watch them warm up. And then go make his decision. Nobody is gonna make any money in this business not watching the horses."

What does Red look for as a negative sign in a horse that's warming up? "I look for stiffness. Inability to have a fluid motion," Red answered. "If a horse isn't gliding, if he's hitting the ground with a short, jarring stride, he's not gonna run. Very few horses can just go out and run without warming up. That's why jockeys run horses back and forth and up and down, to get them loose."

What about fans that don't bring binoculars to the races and watch only the post parade? "So all they did," Red chided, "was watch a horse walk by. They missed the most important thing. The warmups just before the race are very important. You have to look at how the horse is acting. Is the horse washed out or too nervous? Did they warm it up a lot or not at all? There are horses that get so nervous that they tie up in the post parade. Their muscles get cramped and they lose their ability to run. So it's a science, and you have to study it. If you want to beat the races, you have to pick your spots, watch the horses consistently, and get to know them. It's just like any other job: If you're gonna be a success, you got to know all the ins and outs. Instead of making a blind gamble, learn something and get the edge. Around the racetrack, you hear guys say, 'I got the edge.' It doesn't matter what it is, you have to go at it intelligently. You got to educate yourself."

Part of educating yourself is being able to distinguish good information from bad. When Red was training, he used to go to the saddling paddock before every race to get his edge. "I knew every horse by sight. And then I'd go up and sit in my box and listen to everybody's racetrack bullshit. Guys would come up and tell me my own horse was gonna win. I'd ask them, 'How do you know my horse is gonna win?' They'd tell me, 'The owner told me.' I'd say, 'I own the mother. How do you know he's gonna win, tell me that? Maybe you're smarter than I am. Maybe I'm missing something. If I knew he was gonna win, I'd go bet five hundred instead of fifty dollars. So tell me, how do you know he's gonna win?' "

Red had a couple of patched-up horses he had to deliver to Bay Meadows, so he concluded our talk with a warning about tipsters. "These guys go from box to box and tell everybody this horse is gonna win, that horse is gonna win. That's how rumors get started on the backside, and then it goes like wildfire in the grandstand. The word gets out that so-and-so said his horse is gonna win, and a horse's odds plunge from ten to one to nine to five. Well, he might have said, 'I think my horse is gonna run good.' By the time the sixth person's got it he thinks it's a lock, bets big, and loses his shirt. You have to remember, nobody is giving away money at the track."

A couple of weeks later I visited Scott Dorn again. While much of what Red had said fascinated me, I wasn't totally convinced by his dismissal of the notion of track bias. Panama had reinforced my doubt when he reflected, "Sure, Red's gonna deny that a track bias can exist. If he admits to a bias, it doesn't reflect well on his job. He's got a vested interest in denying it." When I mentioned Panama's comment to Scott, he was even more adamant than Red.

"I don't believe in it either. I mean I've been on the racetrack for over thirty years, and it only came up five years ago, this whole trip about track bias."

The only thing that can temporarily create a bias, in Scott's opinion, is bad weather. "Sometimes after a rain," he grudgingly admitted, "if we've sealed the racing part of the track and put up the dogs to keep the guys in the morning from running to the inside, there can be a bad spot. Let's say we set those orange cones out at twenty or twenty-five feet from the rail and everybody trains in the morning in the same place, then they can dig a trench by those dogs. If that happens, the part closer to the rail is bound to be better than the area next to those dogs. So, in a twelve-horse field that afternoon, the horses that are in the stalls from the seventh hole out are gonna start on a worse racetrack than the horses on the inside. The same thing is true going around the turns, if the horse has to run wide and can't get to the inside. Those things can happen to you. But they happen everywhere."

What about the track draining toward the inside during a rain? Wouldn't all that water and slop drifting down create a negative inside bias? "It does drain to the inside," Scott agreed. "But the only time the inside might be a little slower is when it starts to dry out, not when it's wet. When it's really pouring down, the inside is probably the best place to be. And the harder it rains, the better it is, because it actually packs it down. But on an off-track, I don't care how proven the horse is, you can have a problem with that horse. People can't talk to these horses. When a horse wakes up in the morning he doesn't tell you, 'I just don't feel like I'm a hundred percent.' The Mike Tyson fight last night with Buster Douglas is the same thing. I mean, that wasn't Mike Tyson we saw. For years we thought he was the best. And then look at last night. It's the same thing with a horse. Any horse can get beat, and it might not have anything to do with its post position. And you have to remember that a horse runs at different distances from the rail during a race. So just because he's the one horse doesn't mean he hugged the rail the whole way."

Scott emphasized the disadvantage a horse has being in the one hole unless he has enough speed to get to a clear early lead. "Being on the inside next to the rail," he elaborated, "is not natural to a horse. I mean, when he trains in the morning he doesn't run with that kind of pressure, even when the trainer sends them out in groups of four to get them used to running side by side. During a race, if you have the steward's view coming down the lane, there's also bumping going on all the time. It's bound to happen. All the jockeys are trying to get to the rail, they're not going in a straight line. So if a horse is trapped and has the rail right next to him, and a horse to his right and one ahead of him, that's an uncomfortable place to be. At Golden Gate Fields some inside horses, as they come out, will even bobble because they want to make a left-hand turn and go back to the barn area. They don't want to run. Those are horses that will lug in at the start, and the jockey has to pull them the other way to get on with it. The horse that's out a little farther has more room, feels a little more relaxed and can go faster. You see the same thing with humans. Some of the greatest sprinters in the world don't win on the inside as much. It's actually easier to run around a bigger turn than a sharper one."

On the other hand, since all the horses are lined up equal in a horse race, the inside horses have the advantage of not having to run as far. "If a horse runs four-wide the whole way during a race," Scott agreed, "he's run an extra sixty or seventy yards. That can be the difference in being beaten by eight or nine lengths. But, generally speaking, horses slant in toward the rail at the start, and horses in the one or two posts will often get pinched off unless they're rockets and can get out."

An outside bias, Scott acknowledged, is sometimes created in wet weather when the track crew inadvertently removes too much material from the inside of the track. "The horses in the first few posts will start slipping because they don't have anything to grab ahold of. When they take off, they need a big push. But if they go down and hit the hardpan and their feet slip out from under them, they're going to stumble. Probably the only time that it makes much difference is when we have a lot of young three-year-olds that have never run in the mud and they get stuck on those inside posts. What happens is they get off slow, and all that mud hits them in the face, and they say, 'Whoa, I don't like this. I don't want to do this anymore.' And they quit."

Reflecting on the challenges of his and Red's job, Scott threw up his hands and said, "If it wasn't hard on horses, we'd pave the track. It would make our job a whole lot easier to say, 'Here you go, run on a blacktop.' "

Scott doesn't think an artificial surface like Equitrack is the answer, either. "There's only one track that has it. That's at Remington Park. Right now, Equitrack has too much personality. All it is is oil-soaked sand. At Remington, in the heat, they've had nothing but trouble. You're not supposed to water this stuff or do anything else. It's been around for five or six years. Bay Meadows almost bought into it, but they couldn't get the guarantees they wanted. We go to that seminar every year in Tucson, and last year we heard about what's been happening at Newcastle in England with synthetic surfaces. They use Equitrack on some of their training tracks there. A British guy was asked what he thought about Equitrack and he said, 'Naw, that stuff's no good.' Of course, that's a matter of his opinion. But myself, I've never touched it, never seen it."

As it is, Scott and Red have their hands full working with a natural track. In order to bolster the fans' understanding and confidence in their work, they plan an informational campaign. "I'm working on something right now"—Scott beamed—"that we will post every day so the fans will know what we've done with the track. We're also going to have photographs of our equipment. It will include a number system that fans can key from and know that if a certain piece of equipment has been used, it will probably affect the track in a certain way.

"You know," Scott mused, "we get accused of playing with the racetrack all the time. But all management would have to do is call me up and ask me to doctor the track for a Pick Six carryover and that would be it. I'd go straight to the press and tell them that they tried to do that. But that isn't going to happen. They'd never do that. I mean, what difference does it make to them, one Pick Six carryover? Sure, if it gets big we're going to have a better day than normal, but in reality people don't understand that we get ours up front. When you go up to that window and bet, we got our 5.5 percent already. We don't care who wins. The horse could pay $70.00 or $2.20. The only time we would care is if the horse only pays $2.10 and there's a minus pool. As long as the horse pays $2.20, it doesn't matter to us. We really don't have an incentive to be crooked and try to change things."

Scott also laughs at the notion that he and Red could fix a race so that a big-priced horse came in. "Red and I have both said this many times. If we knew how to fix the racetrack, we'd only have to do it for one day and you'd never see us again. It can't be done. I'm willing to be shown. How do you make a racetrack that guarantees long shots are gonna win. It's impossible. If it could be done, all track superintendents would only have to work for a day, two at the most, and they'd have a lifetime's worth of money, tax free. Because you wouldn't be playing exactas and shit, you'd just play the horses straight to win and place and make enough to never have to work again."

7

HOW SORE IS YOUR HORSE?
The Track Veterinarian

I had gone out to catch the last three races on a Wednesday afternoon and ran into Frisco. He was scratching his head and trying to handicap the first leg of the daily triple, which was for bottom-level claimers. "Jesus, where did they get this bunch of sore-legged losers?" he moaned about the quality of the field. "Five of them haven't done anything but break their maiden in slow times, four are dropping down from bad races, and the tenth horse, the *Form* says, pulled up lame, for God's sake. How can they be running a lame horse back in a week? If you gave me a shot of Bute, I could probably outrun a couple of these nags. The only way to bet this race is if you went out this morning with the track vet."

Though Frisco wisely decided to skip the triple, his comments about soreness and the track vet were germane not only for cheap claimers but for a majority of the races on the typical daily card.

With the advent of year-round racing, the unhappy truth is that most horses are over-raced and, despite anti-inflammatory medications, suffer from chronic soreness and a variety of infirmities. Even when this isn't the case, horses that try hard often come out of a competitive effort feeling less than a hundred percent. Handicappers are constantly guessing how much a horse's last race has taken out of him and whether he will be too sore to run well today. Track management, for its part, is aware of the problem and employs a track veterinarian to try to ensure a horse's racing soundness. But "racing soundness," as we shall see, is a matter of degree.

I decided to broaden my knowledge and sharpen my handicapping skills by looking up Dr. Dean Goeldner, Track Veterinarian at Bay Meadows and Golden Gate Fields, to see what he could tell me about the body language of an unfit horse. "What," I asked him one morning at Bay Meadows, "is a sound horse?"

Dr. Goeldner, a candid and affable man in his early forties, looked at me and said, "I wish I could answer that more easily. One of the things we need to come up with is a working definition of racing soundness, because we all use the term, but nobody wants to put words to it. The truth is that there's a large gray area between soundness and unsoundness that we constantly have to use our individual judgment with."

Goeldner has an unusual background for a track veterinarian. He grew up in suburban Wichita, Kansas, as part of the first generation of his family to leave the farm. After graduating from high school he attended Northwestern University, where he completed an undergraduate degree in the history and literature of religions. About his undergraduate degree Goeldner wryly noted, "That certainly isn't the typical prevet background, believe me."

Goeldner's interest in a veterinary career was initially stimulated as a result of a year he spent working with a small animal practitioner in Colorado. He found the work engaging enough that he subsequently enrolled in the veterinary program at Colorado State University, where he earned his DVM in 1975. His first exposure to horse racing came as a student urine catcher in the test barn at Centennial Turf Club in Littleton. "The official veterinarian there only used vet students from Colorado State as his urine catchers." Goeldner grinned as he reminisced about his student days. "And, though it might seem like an unappealing job, I discovered I actually enjoyed the testing procedures and found racing an interesting environment to be in."

After getting his vet degree, Dr. Goeldner migrated to northern California so he could work with both small animals and horses—a professional combination that Colorado did not provide for. It wasn't long, however, before he discovered he enjoyed being around horses best of all and began specializing in that direction. Goeldner accepted his current position at Golden Gate Fields and Bay Meadows in 1985 after completing a two-year equine residency at the University of California at Davis and seven years of private practice.

It didn't take me long to understand that Dr. Goeldner's job of weeding out unfit horses is a challenging one. In all but the most obvious cases there are a number of factors he has to weigh before recommending that a horse be scratched from a race. On the one hand, he can't be so draconian in his judgment that the racing secretary, trainers, management, and even the fans start screaming because of the short fields. On the other hand, he doesn't want to see a horse break down on the track, have a jockey hurt, or incur the wrath of the fans because the horse they bet on was distanced or pulled up lame.

Given his liberal-arts background and interest in ethics, I asked Goeldner if one of the attractions of being a track vet, as opposed to having a more lucrative private practice on the backside, might not be greater freedom to do what is in the best interests of the horse. "Oh, I think so," he agreed. "I frankly admit to the private practitioners here, both the ones whom I'm fairly close to and the ones that I'm not, that I couldn't do what they do. Because it would be difficult for me to live with myself, or I would be refusing to do things that would probably lose me clients. When you're a private vet, you're under a lot of pressure to help a trainer get another race out of a horse. You're constantly tempted to over-medicate a horse rather than recommend that he be rested."

Goeldner outlined a typical working day—from the morning inspections on the backside that he and his colleague, Dr. Diane

Isbell, perform, all the way until after the horses have crossed the wire and headed back to their barns in the afternoon. "Typically, I do a dozen or two morning inspections a day and Dr. Isbell, my colleague, does the rest. She starts at six in the morning and inspects until maybe one o'clock. I come in around nine-thirty and look at maybe an hour's worth of horses. But most of my job involves looking at the horses in the afternoon, from the time they come into the paddock until they pull up after the race."

The basic monitoring tool Goeldner and Isbell use is the health card that is kept for every horse on the grounds. Each card includes the horse's name, breed, trainer, tattoo number, color, sex, and medical history among other things. "On the days that the horses are going to race, the relevant cards are pulled and put into order by our secretary and we come in, pick them up, and go out and examine the horses in the trainer's barn. The trainer is expected to have the horse ready for us to inspect. Some trainers use ice on race day to cool a horse's legs out, but we don't allow the horses to be standing in ice when we look at their legs. If a horse has bandages, those have to come off."

Ah yes, bandages. Nary a handicapper exists who hasn't felt an acute rise in anxiety when a horse he likes in the *Racing Form* comes onto the track heavily wrapped. Is the horse a step away from breaking down, he asks himself, wondering if he shouldn't sit out the race, or are the bandages merely a trainer's ploy to keep his horse from being claimed? "Well, bandages, from the point of view of the bettor, can sometimes be very significant," Goeldner agreed. "But a lot of times they're red herrings. Basically, what you see are two kinds of bandages, rundowns and front wraps. Rundowns are usually small and wrapped right around the back ankles, though trainers will occasionally put them on the front legs too. Rundowns are meant primarily to protect a horse's ankles from the bottom of sloppy tracks—where they go through the surface and scrape against the bottom—or to protect them from 'burning' against the sand that is typically mixed into racetracks as winter approaches."

Some horses run down badly, Goeldner explained, because, "as their foot hits the ground, their ankles tend to drop down more and scrape against whatever surface is there and produce a 'straw-berry' kind of wound. But rundown bandages, even when they go up a ways on the back legs, are strictly for protection and probably don't mean much in terms of a horse's soundness."

What about those instances when there is so much tape around a horse's ankle that it bulges? "Normally, all that means is that the trainer has put in some extra padding for a horse that runs down a lot. But if it's really blatant," Goeldner cautioned, "maybe this is a horse that runs down so badly that he doesn't have the spring and resiliency in those legs, nor as much drive as he should have. Those horses you might want to take a closer look at as they're warming up."

Front wraps, on the other hand, are generally more serious. "When you see a tall wrap on the front legs that goes up just below the knee or the carpus," Goeldner warned, "those wraps are more likely to indicate a weakness in a tendon or ligament. Those kinds of front wraps are intended to support the suspensory apparatus, and, if I were a bettor, I would attach more significance to them. Sometimes you'll even see a big bulge on a front wrap, which probably means it's covering and supporting an injury like a par-tially bowed tendon."

Once the bandages have been taken off during the morning inspections, the next thing Goeldner or Isbell do is date the health card and write down "TN," which stands for temperature normal. "We don't actually temp the horse. We expect the trainers to tell us if the temperature is abnormal—because if the horse is sick, they don't want to run it anyway. Normal temperature for a horse ranges between 99 and 101 degrees. But since most of them are racing on anti-inflammatories or Phenylbutazone, their tempera-tures are generally on the low end of that range."

While inspecting the horse in its stall, Dr. Goeldner and Dr. Isbell will note on the health card anything unusual about its ap-pearance. The groom is then asked to lead the horse out of the stall, walk it down the shed row, give it a turn, and bring it back so the vet can see how it moves. "We're looking for any abnormality in how it's walking," Goeldner explained. "A horse generally changes the way it moves to accommodate some sort of pain. We're looking for a horse whose front feet are spread wider apart than normal, because that's a good indication he's starting to hurt somewhere. I'm looking for shortness of stride. If a horse isn't reaching out, he may be hurting or stiff. I'm also looking for head-bobbers, those horses that raise their head and shoulder when their leg comes through because they don't want to put their weight on it."

Goeldner emphasized that most of a thoroughbred's problems involve their front legs. "We don't have too many problems with the back legs like the standardbreds, trotters, and pacers do. Anyhow, I'll watch the horses in the morning as they turn because at the turn, the inside front leg takes a little more torque and weight, and you often see more of a pain response than you would on the straight."

After the groom brings the horse back to the stall, Goeldner palpates its knees, shins, tendons and suspensory ligaments, ankles, and feet, while also looking for swelling and heat. "I'm looking for tenderness. If I'm seeing anything in the gait or feeling anything in the legs that I think is abnormal, then I'm flexing joints and manipulating the legs around to see if I get a pain response. I'm also looking at the bottom of the hoof and the shoes. I'm looking for a foot problem like a quarter crack or, if he's grabbed his heel in the last race, if he's still a little tender to the touch."

When Goeldner senses something unusual, he'll often take the horse out and jog him up and down the road that runs between the barns. "The classic gait for veterinarians to evaluate abnormalities with is the jog or the trot. With a walk you can't see as much, and once they get to galloping or loping you can't see much at all, unless they're just really short and choppy. But at the jog, you'll see most problems, because it's not as free a gait and it takes more concussion. A horse's pain responses show up most in a jog."

Goeldner explained the major criteria for scratching a horse. "If we feel the horse has a problem that makes him unlikely to run competitively, or that's going to make him head-bobbing lame out there on the track, or if he has a problem that may be made significantly worse because of the stress of racing, those are the kinds of reasons we're likely to scratch a horse. Now I would love to be able to tell you that every horse in a $10,000 race is perfectly sound, and the only difference is their difference in abilities. That's not the case. I wish it were. Some of them are horses that used to be allowance horses and bowed a tendon, and now they're coming back and we just hope that tendon doesn't blow again in the middle of a race. We want that tendon to be cold and tight, and as long as it's not painful to flexion, we're going to let him run. But when that tendon gets soft and warm and a little ouchy when we touch it, then we're likely to take that horse out."

Minutes Away was an example of what Goeldner was talking about. He was an ex-stakes horse with a bowed tendon that had come back and won something like five races in a row at Golden Gates Fields in the high claiming ranks before being scratched at the gate one day. "Tendons are probably the hardest thing for us to evaluate," Goeldner emphasized. "We juggle a number of factors when we're evaluating a bowed horse. But probably the one we give the most weight to is how the horse jogs and moves. The problem with a bowed tendon is that the horse with the marginal tendon is going to move fine until it blows. Even though it's a little warm, a little painful, a little soft to the touch, he's going to jog like a million dollars until he completely tears it apart. Then he's going to be dead lame and practically broken down. By then it's too late. So, deciding what to do with those horses is one of our toughest decisions. Because, in my experience, a fair number of bowed horses, like Minutes Away, will go out there and race just fine, while others won't, and you cannot absolutely predict which one of the two will happen."

Golden Gate Fields and Bay Meadows have a pool of about two thousand horses they draw from for their meets. What percentage of them, I wondered, get put on the vet's list and become ineligible to race? "I don't have a total figure. But I can tell you that an average of three or four horses a day are on the vet's list, and we probably take one or two a day off. The reason they go on the list can vary from injury, to sickness, to lameness, to soreness, to exhaustion, to bleeding, to failure to have a Coggins Test. And once a horse is on our list in any of those categories, it has to fulfill certain requirements to get off. Horses that have suffered from exhaustion, are lame, sore, or unsound, all have to do a five-eighths-mile work for one of the regulatory veterinarians. We have to watch the horses work and then, when they come back, examine them. We jog them for soundness and also give them a blood test to make sure they don't have drug levels above what's allowed for race day."

After a horse has passed its preliminary morning inspection, it is looked at again by the state veterinarian in the receiving barn, where all horses are required to be forty-five minutes before they race. Apart from rechecking for racing soundness, horses are also sequestered in the receiving barn to protect the gambling public from any last-minute tampering.

The horses are then moved to the paddock and saddling area, where Goeldner looks them over again just before they race. He watches them circling in the paddock area, paying particular attention to any notes he or Dr. Isbell might have made during the morning exams. "Some of the horses we looked at earlier," Goeldner elaborated, "weren't bad enough to be scratched. But our notes might say something like: 'He's moving a little wide' . . . 'Striding a little short' . . . 'The tendon looked a little thick today' or 'His knee is a little filled. It's not sensitive to flexion, but it's a little warm.' My point is that we're watching these horses in the paddock with these notes in mind. I'm looking to see if they are taking that short stride or beginning to warm up and move more freely. I'm also identifying horses as they go along, so I can pick them up after the races and know what I'm looking at."

Once the horses leave the paddock, Goeldner watches them in the post parade and then follows them in the track car as they warm up and jog out to the backstretch. "This is the last line of evaluation most of the time," Goeldner reflected. "That horse that was a little short in the morning—is he now striding out comfortably and moving freely and evenly on both sides? I want to see that freer movement, and most of the time I do. Racehorses are like human athletes, they're a little stiff to begin with. But they can usually get out there and work the kinks out and get to moving pretty good as soon as they start warming up. And as long as they do that, then that's fine and we go on with them."

It's important for Goeldner to watch the horses warm up on the backstretch, because some problems become evident only when there is weight on their back. "That horse we okayed in the morning," he emphasized, "can be a different horse with 114 pounds on his back in the afternoon. He may suddenly start to show me a head bob and that hunch in the shoulder with a real uneven, rough gait. Or maybe he's still running even but he's getting choppier and choppier, and when the jockey tries to get him into a canter, he's taking tiny little steps. Or maybe the jockey, no matter how much he warms him up, can't get him to extend and want to reach out and be comfortable at a faster gait. Those horses are either lame or sore, and I'll usually converse with the jockey at that point."

Typically, Goeldner will ask the jockey questions like, " 'How does this horse feel to you?' . . . 'Is he even, are you comfortable with him?' The jockey might say, 'He feels pretty rough to me.' . . . 'I'm not comfortable with him,' or 'Yeah, he's getting better' or 'Let me run him a little more and bring him back to you and see if he's getting better or worse.' And I'll give the jockey the benefit of the doubt that way. If he can take the horse out and move him up the backside two or three times and the horse starts to get more comfortable and freer, then we'll go on with him. My decision about whether or not to let a marginally sore horse run is complicated by the irony that just because he's sore doesn't mean he can't win. He may be the kind of horse that tries hard, and that's how he gets sore in the first place. Eventually, though, soreness will adversely affect performance. And if a horse is getting worse, then I'm going to recommend to the stewards that he be scratched out of the race."

I was curious if horses coming off of a layoff are generally stiffer and in greater need of warming up. "You'd think that," Goeldner said, "but often if a horse has had enough time off to get over his problems, he's a little better at that point. He may have been off because he had surgery or to just let the soreness and heat he developed over several months of racing cool out and calm down. He may be coming back off a big problem like a bowed tendon or a slab fracture of the knee, a cracked cannon bone or something like that. But if they've given him enough time off for his problems to resolve, he often comes back sounder than he left. I make notes on horses that are coming back off a layoff to take a look at them. But, by and large, those are not my problem horses. The problem horse is, more often than not, the horse that has run every ten to twelve days for the last six months, and he's just getting sorer and sorer each race, and when do we say enough is enough?"

That brought up the question of how many times a horse can be expected to run competitively before he begins to tail off. "That's hard to tell," Goeldner reflected. "It varies a lot from horse to horse. I don't know that there's a general rule. But if you watch the way most horses are handled around here, in terms of how often they're entered and raced, the ones that raced more often than every two to three weeks for more than a month or two at a time start to tail off."

Personally, Goeldner would like to limit the number of starts a horse can make. However, the politics of doing so would be pretty volatile. "I will readily admit that, if someone ever adopted my thoughts on this, there would be a large outcry from the horsemen, because I'd be eliminating some horses that could easily and comfortably race more often. But there are so many horses that don't race comfortably, that I think it would be more humane to the horses to limit the number of starts. The only other alternative would be to limit the number of racing days. But I don't think we are in the position, at this point, to do that. The associations, the state, and a lot of the people involved in racing are all too avid for the dollar to cut back on the number of days they race. So the only way you can protect the horse is to limit the number of starts he can make."

As a handicapper, and fan, I liked the idea of some sort of limitation that would protect both horses and gamblers from the infirmities of over-racing. I pushed Goeldner for a more specific proposal. "I would say a horse should not make more than fifteen to eighteen starts a year, nine starts in any six-month span, and probably not more than three starts in any thirty-day period. When you start going beyond those numbers, I don't think there are very many horses that are productive and paying their way at that increased level of racing. Besides limiting the number of starts, I think each horse would benefit from a mandatory sixty- to ninety-days "turnout" away from the track each year to rest, heal minor problems, and generally freshen up."

What about Red Lowery's opinion that horses should have to prove their soundness and running ability by being competitive in qualifying races in the morning? How would that impact on Goeldner's job? "It wouldn't change my job or bother me if you did that. Red's right to an extent, in that there are horses on the grounds that are not being productive and paying their way from the racing industry's point of view. But backstretch politics might torpedo Red's proposal. It's difficult, once a trainer's been assigned stalls, to take one away from him. If a trainer has two or three really good horses and four or five marginal ones and you're the racing secretary, you're not going to bug him about his marginal horses because he might take them all away, and then you wouldn't have his good horses either."

What about the racing of two-year-olds? Is it the case, as Red claimed, that nearly half of them wind up not running and taking up stall space because they develop the typical juvenile problems like bucked shins? "I don't know if it's half," Goeldner reflected. "But certainly a lot of two-year-olds develop problems. If it was my decision, we probably wouldn't race two-year-olds. But, the economics of the industry being what they are, it's pretty hard to keep them from racing."

As I listened to Goeldner's response, it struck me that most horsemen lament the racing of two-year-olds, but few of them are willing to resist the big pots that are put before them. Unless some kind of economic incentive is developed to encourage owners and trainers to wait on their horses until they are three, young horses are going to continue to be broken down prematurely.

One possible approach, which would take both the economic needs of horsemen and the welfare of young horses into account, would be for the state to take a stronger position. If the state was willing to take a smaller cut out of the betting handle, say 4.5 percent instead of the current five-plus percent tax bite, they could discourage two-year-old racing by putting more money in a special category for three-year-old races, which would have as one of its conditions that no horse would be eligible if it had been raced as a two-year-old. It would be a creative way for the state to reward those horsemen who waited on their horses. Besides protecting the health of two-year-olds, the whole racing program would also be improved, because by waiting on horses until they are three, they would generally stay sounder and have longer racing lives.

I asked Goeldner whether he thought the idea of a special three-year-old category had any merit. "That would certainly help," he agreed. "But the Breeders' Cup kind of does that now. While they do have two-year-old races, they also put up a lot of money for older horses. Older, more mature horses have a much better shot at winning those races. There's now a reason to have a sound five- or six-year-old where there didn't use to be."

Dr. Goeldner had talked about the body language of a horse in terms of looking for soreness. But what about a horse that is sweating in the paddock and post parade or comes up to the starting gate in a lather? How important, I asked him, is that in assessing the racing soundness of a horse? "It can be real significant. But it can also be deceiving to the bettor," Goeldner cautioned. "The horse that's a little lathered between his hind legs on a medium warm day is not of any concern to me. The horse that's sweating up around the neck and dripping water off his belly on a cool day would concern me. On a hot and muggy day, they're probably all going to be sweating. You're going to have trouble distinguishing those that are washing out from those that are working up a healthy sweat. But if it's a normal or cool day and you see a horse sweating on the neck, dripping from the belly, and up high on the hip— especially if that's associated with a lot of hyper behavior before the race where the horse is rank and difficult to handle—those horses, in my experience, aren't going to run very well."

Once the horses have warmed up and reach the starting gate, Goeldner watches to see how they load up. A horse can be scratched for a variety of reasons, including unruliness, flipping over, bumping his head, or getting off his feet. "It's a judgment call," Goeldner explained. "If a horse just rears up a little bit, he's allowed to go on. Sometimes a horse will hurt an adjoining horse when he's fallen and his legs are thrashing between the stalls, because the stalls aren't separated all the way to the ground. That happened last week, when we had to scratch a horse that had one of its legs inadvertently cut up by a fallen horse."

Goeldner's example illustrated once again that anything can happen in a horse race. In fact, it reminded me of something that had happened to The Stone and me the week before when we had both bet on a filly stretching out of a sprint. She had broken from the gate alertly, opened a clear early lead, and then suddenly bolted. We didn't know what to think. "Maybe she's never been on the lead before and got lonely," The Stone sarcastically cracked as he tore up his ticket. "She probably thought the race was over and it was time to go back to the barn."

Goeldner laughed at The Stone's quip and said that a horse can bolt for a number of reasons. "It can be a physical problem. Especially when he gets to the front turn, has a problem on the left front leg, has to take that left lead and go around the turn, and he doesn't like that and starts to get out and all of a sudden he's on the outside rail. What I'm saying is that horses sometimes lug in or drift out because they're experiencing physical problems and try to compensate for them in the way they move. But a horse may also be reacting to the jockey or be spooked by something he sees."

Red Lowery believes that the pitch of the track helps keep a horse from drifting out, but I wondered if it also didn't put more pressure on its left front leg. "Banking the track probably does help in keeping the horse's weight from wanting to travel out," Goeldner agreed, "but he's also having to take a little more concussion and bear more weight on that inside left leg. Given the fact we race counterclockwise and the way the turns are banked, you would think we would have a lot more problems on the left front leg than we do on the right. While I haven't ever done a study of it, my guess is that it's not as predominant as you might think. We have a lot of problems with the right front leg as well. And I think the reason for that is that injury tends to occur with a combination of speed and fatigue. Especially in the stretch, when the horse is getting tired, and that's when they're beating on them to get everything they've got left out of them. That's when you end up stretching those tendons and ligaments. You get weak steps, you get bad steps, you get missteps, and they're on the right lead at that time because they switched leads at the top of the stretch. So they're more likely to hurt their right front leg than their left one at that point. That's probably why we see almost as many right leg problems as left ones."

Once the horses break from the gate, Goeldner pays close attention to how they're running. "If it's a sprint," he explained, "I'm in the car you see that follows the race around. If it's a route, I sit up at the quarter pole and wait for them to come around. In both cases I watch the race to see if there are any problems developing. I'm looking to see if a horse breaks down, pulls up, or stumbles. When something happens, we try to spot it as quickly as possible."

When there's a spill, the ambulance rushes to help the jockey while Goeldner looks after the welfare of the horse. "Usually it's some kind of leg injury, and I'm assessing what the problem is and doing whatever I can to keep the horse from hurting himself even further. If we get to a horse and find a severe injury like a broken sesmoid or badly pulled suspensory ligament, I've got a splint that I can get on him and get that part immobilized while we wait for the horse ambulance to arrive. Fortunately, we have a very nice ambulance-trailer with a lot of hydraulics on it. We can lower the floor to ground level so the horse doesn't have to step up or hobble up a steep ramp. He just walks right in. Then we have a partition we can move over and kind of pin him in against either wall, so he doesn't bounce around in there as we get him off the track."

Goeldner has a radio in his car that he uses to alert the trainer's vet on the backside so that he can start treating the injured horse as soon as it arrives. In a really bad situation, where a horse is down, unable to rise, and may have to be destroyed, Goeldner can administer a lethal injection right on the racetrack. "We try and avoid that, because it's always an ugly situation when we have to winch a dead horse into a trailer and haul them off in front of the crowd. Nobody wants to see that. That's one of the really down sides of this business. But it does happen and I have to deal with it. Thankfully, most of the time we just get the horse off the track, and the bulk of treatment is done by the private vet on the backside as soon as the horse gets there."

Assuming there are no problems during the race, Goeldner gets back to the finish line and waits for the horses to jog back, unsaddle, and walk off the racetrack. "I'm looking for some very important things at that point," he emphasized. "To me the three or four most important steps I watch all day are probably those that a horse takes just before he unsaddles. Because that tells me, more than anything, how he's coming out of the race. If he pulls up really uneven or lame at that point, then I know I have a serious problem. How he walks off the track is also important to me. But those few steps he takes as he jogs in with the rider still on his back really tell me a lot. He might have run second or third, but if he jogs back in lame, he may make the vet's list anyway. Contrary to what some trainers and owners think, performance does not equal soundness."

The idea that a horse could run well and then pull up lame after the race seemed odd, but I remembered something Red Lowery had told me when he had reminisced on his experiences as a trainer. "Horses are going to break down and come up lame," he said, "because they're fragile animals. Originally they were a beast of burden, but over the years we've bred them for speed. And when you put them in conditions of excessive speed they get tired and hurt themselves. That's also what happens with human athletes. A real racehorse has a desire to win that's so strong that they will run over that safe barrier and hurt themselves. That's why a lot of times you'll see a horse cross the wire sound, finish winning, and then get eight jumps past the jock's room and be dead lame."

Since we were talking about lameness, I broached Frisco's question about how a horse could be designated as lame by the *Racing Form* and then be allowed to run within a week. Goeldner had an explanation. "The *Racing Form* is in a tough spot, because they're operating under a deadline. If a horse gets eased, pulled up, or has a bad performance for some reason, they usually just call it 'eased.' If they really feel that the horse looked lame, that's what they write down. But they never check with me or any of the other vets about it, and we may not agree. We may think the horse pulled up for another reason. Any time a horse doesn't finish a race or finishes thirty lengths behind, he's either going to make the vet's list or the steward's list. In both cases the horse has to have a published five-eighths of a mile work before he can race again. If he's on the steward's list, that's all he has to have. He can go out and work five-eighths and enter a race the next day. But if we have him down as lame and he makes our vet's list, not only does he have to make that work under our observation, he also has to come back and be examined, jogged for soundness, have a blood test and the blood test has to come back clean. It takes longer to clear the vet's list, and usually a horse can't come back in just a week. In fact, if he's got a real problem, he can't get sound that quick anyway."

Besides watching for lameness when a horse pulls up after a race, Goeldner also looks for bleeding from the nostrils. The first time a horse bleeds visibly on the track, he automatically goes on the vet's list for two weeks and then must do a five-eighths-mile workout, without bleeding, before being allowed to race again. The second time a horse bleeds he goes on the vet's list for thirty days, and the third time he visibly bleeds, even with the use of Lasix or Furosemide, he is barred permanently from the track. Fortunately, Goeldner reported, "We don't see bleeding from the nostrils as much since horsemen started to use Lasix. I've only had four or five this meet."

Of all the drugs used in racing, Lasix is probably the most controversial. The two biggest racing jurisdictions have opposite policies. California allows it, New York does not. "Lasix continues to be controversial," Goeldner explained, "for a number of reasons. One reason, medically speaking, is that no one is real sure how or why it decreases bleeding. I say decreases because Lasix doesn't usually totally stop the bleeding. What it does is reduce the amount significantly enough to allow a number of horses to perform back to their best potential.

"Lasix is also controversial because it is an acknowledged di-uretic. It causes a great deal of fluid to be lost through the kidney and urinary system. Some people think that the increased fluid dilutes or masks the urine sample enough so that you might not pick up an illegal drug that you otherwise would catch in a horse that hasn't had Lasix. The lab chemists have done a great deal of study on this issue, however, and they're reasonably convinced that, if Lasix is given three to four hours or more before the race, the diluting effect on the urine is over by that time. In fact, the medications committee on the racing board here in California just extended the time horizon from three hours to four, just to be on the safe side. There are also specific-gravity tests you can make on urine to see if it is diluted. One suggestion that has been made, but not yet implemented, is that we check the specific gravities right here in the test barn and if the urine is too diluted, we would just keep the horse around until we get a more concentrated sample."

Critics of Lasix worry about the genetic consequences of allowing horses with a propensity to bleed to win big races and then go to the breeding shed. They also point out that twenty years ago, eighty percent of the horses in California weren't running on Lasix the way they are now. The traditional approach trainers took toward dealing with bleeders was to withhold water before a race and use only dry feed. I asked Goeldner if he thought there really was more bleeding going on today or if some trainers are just taking advantage of Lasix for other reasons. "I think the answer to both of those questions is probably yes," Goeldner answered. "What was discovered by Dr. John Pascoe, who started doing research on this problem at U.C. Davis a number of years ago, was that when he went out and started scoping horses after they ran, a number of them had bled, even though you couldn't see anything from the nostrils. Pascoe used an endoscope, which is a flexible tube with a light on the end of it, and stuck it up a horse's nose and into the trachea. He discovered that while only two to four percent of the horses actually bled visibly from the nostrils during a race, as many as seventy-five percent of the horses had some blood in their trachea after a race. What that meant was that lots of horses were bleeding, but not so badly that the blood came out of their noses. So then the industry realized, 'Hey, we have more of a bleeding problem than we realized we had.' "

The basic dilemma about Lasix, in Goeldner's view, is whether or not it has any inherent performance-enhancing properties of its own. "Recent research indicates that it might," he stated, "and you see some trainers trying to take advantage of that possibility. One barn will have only a few horses on Lasix and there will be others where practically every horse is running on it. Or you'll see a horse that hasn't been running on Lasix gets claimed and suddenly he's on Lasix. Trainers are always looking for an edge. If Lasix is shown to be performance enhancing, it may have to be discontinued or replaced with another drug. The bleeding problem, however, is too serious and too pervasive to be ignored completely."

The ultimate fate of Lasix will probably hinge on the results of further testing. Meanwhile, other ongoing research offers the hope that there may be another solution to the bleeding problem. Preliminary studies in the plateaus of Utah and Colorado seem to indicate that when young horses are raised for their first year in higher, cooler climates—similar to the environment they first evolved in as a species—their lungs develop faster and more fully and are more resistant to bleeding. One implication from these studies is that the greater incidence of pulmonary bleeding in recent years may partly be a product of low coastal breeding and urban pollution during the early stages of a horse's life.

A number of other horsemen think that increased pulmonary bleeding in horses is a product of having fed them a diet too high in hybrid grains rather than the more traditional grass, alfalfa, and oats. Experiments with diet changes may bear this out.

Besides Lasix, the other medications widely used in racing are the nonsteroidal anti-inflamatory drugs, or NSAIDs. In California these include Banamine, Naproxen, Arquel, and Butazolidin. Trainers are allowed to use only one of them at a time, and by far the most popular is Butazolidin, or "Bute" as it is affectionately known on the backside. Critics of drugs like "Bute" believe that their nearly ubiquitous use in modern times is a product of too much racing. One horseman told me, "Most of the horses we run are chemically maintained. The horses get so sore from over-racing that you need an army of vets to keep them running. With year-round racing, horses don't get rested enough. The financial pressures and temptations on owners and trainers are so great that they'll do almost anything to get another race out of their horses."

On the other hand, most trainers believe that drugs like "Bute" and Lasix are necessary. "Lasix is a hard drug to get rid of," Bill Morey told me. "Many of our horses bleed, and Lasix makes their performance more consistent for the gambling public. We also need medications like 'Bute' because most northern California horses are a notch below southern California horses and have more physical problems and soreness. We need these medications here to help the horses train and run more consistently. I'm not talking about running lame horses. The amount of 'Bute' they let us use isn't going to make a lame horse run sound. If racing medications like 'Bute' are banned, then local injections of things like cortisone into horses' joints will be used three or more days before a race. The result will be that more horses will break down as their joints degenerate."

Chuck Jenda echoed Morey's argument and took issue as well with critics of year-round racing. "I think Lasix definitely helps," he told me. "There would be a lot of horses that couldn't compete without Lasix. The small amount of 'Bute' we use isn't a cure-all. What it basically does is help out the horse that has a little arthritic problem. Without 'Bute' he wouldn't want to train as hard or eat as well because this thing is just kind of gnawing at him. If the horse has a serious problem like a bowed tendon, a couple of tabs of 'Bute' isn't going to help him. With regard to blaming year-round racing for increased use of drugs, I think that's a stupid argument, because it's my decision and the owner's decision when to race and when not to race a horse. They could race 365 days a year, a hundred races a day, it doesn't make any difference. It's the responsibility of the people who own the horses and train the horses to make that call. If the horse isn't fit and ready to run, he shouldn't be on the racetrack. I think year-round racing is great because that means I can bring a horse in and out at any time and not worry about missing a race. Before, when there was less opportunity to race, there was more pressure to run a horse that maybe wasn't quite ready."

Jenda acknowledged there are some horsemen who have neither the courage nor the intelligence to rest their horses when they need it. "Unfortunately, the horse is the one that suffers in that situation. But that's why we have a track vet. It's his job to make sure that unfit horses aren't running."

Steve Boyer, a private veterinarian working on the backside at Golden Gate Fields and Bay Meadows, had another view of the medications controversy. "There are non-performance-enhancing medications that human athletes use all the time like aspirin, antihistamines and cortisone creams that alleviate minor aches and pains and allow them to compete. Why shouldn't horses, as equine athletes, be able to race in comfort, too, with the benefit of both ancient and modern technologies? Why deny them the benefit of medications like 'Bute' and Lasix just because they are racehorses? It's not illegal for major league pitchers and football players to get cortisone shots periodically to allow them to compete. What we need is a medications policy that will allow a horse to run to its optimum potential without enhancing his ability beyond that. There is obviously a fine line between effective use of a medication and abuse. It's a bit of a gray area that has to be defined. Some people feel a no-medication policy would be better for the horse and the gambling public, but I don't think it's best for either the horse or the gambling public. I think that medication can be used humanely and wisely to maintain the competing life of a horse and keep him running comfortably and consistently so the handicapper can feel more confident in his assessment of a horse's chances to win."

Goeldner took exception to part of Boyer's argument, pointing out that horses, unlike humans, aren't given a choice about the drugs that are injected into them. He agreed, however, that popular assumptions about the use of NSAIDs like "Bute" are in error. "It's important to remember these drugs are anti-inflammatories," he emphasized. "They're not pain-killers as some people mistakenly believe. They're more like relatives of aspirin. They're anti-inflammatory in that they'll decrease some of the effects of inflammation, but they don't block pain. By decreasing certain inflammatory processes in the body, a medication like 'Bute' may allow a horse to run back to his normal potential. 'Bute' has to be given at least twenty-four hours before the race and, when it is tested for after the race, it can't exceed certain microgram levels. If it tests out a little high the trainer gets a warning. If it tests quite a bit higher he will get fined."

If "Bute" is not a performance-enhancing drug, I asked the good doctor, what difference would it make if the amounts injected were higher? "That's a difficult question to answer," Goeldner acknowledged. "I'm not sure I've thought it through enough to give you a good answer. But the current level of 'Bute' allowed is five micrograms per milliliter of blood. The thought is that if 'Bute' is administered at that level or below, it will not markedly affect a horse's performance. Whereas, if he was at ten, fifteen, or twenty micrograms, maybe at that point he has so much anti-inflammatory activity going on in his system, it might allow him to perform through some pain that he otherwise shouldn't be performing through—which could be dangerous both to him and the jockey."

Even though anti-inflammatory drugs like "Bute" are permitted, I'd heard rumors that some trainers continue to inject cortisone into the joints of their sore-legged horses. I asked Goeldner if this practice was legal. "Injecting cortisone into the joints of horses is not illegal," Goeldner said. "I think it's ethically questionable at times, in fact, probably most of the time. But you also have to realize that cortisone and cortisone derivatives are perfectly good anti-inflammatory agents and perfectly reasonable therapeutic modalities to use. But when it's done for a joint that's inflamed, rational veterinary procedure says that that horse should be rested for a period of time, after that injection, to allow that joint to cool out and calm down. And if that's done, then I think that using cortisone is a great procedure. Unfortunately, what's more likely to happen is that the horse gets injected and feels and looks great, so a trainer is tempted to run him. And they run him much sooner than they should and ultimately you pay a price for that because you start to wear down cartilage and you end up with an arthritic joint."

What about autopsies? Are they ever performed on horses that break down? If so, and it becomes apparent that a horse has been running with a degenerated joint, is its trainer ever reprimanded for injecting too much cortisone? "That's a multipart question," Goeldner answered. "The answer is yes, we do autopsies. They used to be performed by the trainer's practitioner with a report submitted to the state veterinarian. Now there's tougher monitoring, and all horses destroyed on the track are autopsied at the state diagnostic laboratory at U.C. Davis. But in terms of actually proving that a joint has been injected, that's very difficult to do in an autopsy situation. Especially if the joint's been broken open in the process of the injury and exposed to the environment, there's practically no way to pick up that drug. And even if it's not, there's usually so much tearing and bleeding in that area that it's very hard to go in there and tap it so that you could demonstrate a presence of the drug. Having enough evidence to bring someone to task for injecting a joint is almost impossible. But, yes, if you go in there and see a joint that has practically no cartilage left in it and see all kinds of arthritic spurs, or a joint capsule that's all thick and red, you know that horse has been racing on very inflamed joints, and probably the only way he would have been comfortable enough to race was if he had been injected. In those cases, you can certainly say something to that trainer. And I've been known to do that. But I'm just trying to prick their consciences, because I have no legal grounds to bring them in on anything. But our testing methods are getting better all the time, and the day may come when we can pick up things we can't pick up now. Once that happens, maybe we'll have some leverage we don't have now."

In human sports, as witnessed by the case of Olympic runner Ben Johnson losing his gold medal, there's been a huge controversy around the use of anabolic steroids. I asked Goeldner if they are used in equine medicine as well. "They're legal, but they have some side effects down the road—probably not for the racing animal as much as the one that's going to the breeding shed after his racing career is over. One side effect is that they can affect fertility. They can also affect behavior in some fillies and geldings by making them overly aggressive. At present there is no limitation on the use of steroids in horse racing. One reason is that equine drug testing has not been set up in such a way as to easily detect them over time, as it has been in humans.

"But steroids," Goeldner cautioned, "can be a plus or a minus depending upon the nature of the horse and the way he moves.

You have to remember we have two categories of steroids, the anabolic and the corticosteroids. The corticosteroids are the ones that go into joints to decrease inflammation. The anabolic steroids are the ones that go systemically to build up muscle mass. These come from the adrenal gland. Your body produces these things normally. You have them in your system, it's just a matter of how much. What modern technology does is take them and produce them synthetically and put much larger quantities into the animal depending on what you want to achieve. In terms of anabolic steroids, my guess is that they're not that heavily used in racing because there's no known correlation between building muscle mass and greater speed. When I was in private practice I used them, not for racing, but in show horses. Even then, I didn't do it routinely. With a racehorse that's coming off an illness or severe disability, steroids might build him up faster. But a normal horse that's on a good training program with good nutrition probably doesn't get that much of an edge off anabolic steroids."

Surrounding the entire controversy about drugs and horse racing is not only the question of which ones are legitimately therapeutic, but also what kinds of penalties should be meted out for violations. As a private vet on the backside, Steve Boyer thinks the current controlled medication program is in need of improvement. "The penalties lately seem to be increasing heavily for offenses that in the past were considered minor. I think the penalties are inconsistent. For example, one trainer was suspended for six months and fined $2,000 for a cocaine positive. He appealed that to the CHRB and was denied and then went to civil court and got an injunction. Another trainer can give a horse that is having trouble breathing an antihistamine that you can buy over the counter and it's considered a more serious offense than if you load a horse up with cortisone or use more than one of the approved nonsteroidal anti-inflammatory drugs and it traces positive in a test on race day. A trainer can be fined $1,000, lose a purse, and be put on probation for there being trace elements of an antihistamine in his horse. Vets get fined, too. It's ridiculous to be so punitive about antihistamines unless they are found in more than trace amounts. Most of the time the antihistamines were given ten or more days before a race and just haven't cleared a horse's system by race day. The small amounts present couldn't possibly affect the outcome of a race."

Goeldner had some sympathy for the inequity that Boyer had raised. "As we get more and more sensitive methods of testing that can pick up a drug in the system further and further out past the point of administration, we have to start dealing with that situation. Because we might be able to pick up a drug that has procaine in it two weeks after it was injected. Well, that procaine is not going to affect a horse's performance at that point, but trace molecules may still be in his system and we'll find them. What the answer to that part of the problem appears to be is that we are going to have to establish, over time, cutoff levels for legitimate therapeutic drugs, just like we have for 'Bute' and Lasix. So if you have a low trace element of an antihistamine that's a legitimate therapeutic drug, we'll consider that insignificant and not a problem. The question is still not answered, however, as to whether or not you establish those kinds of levels for prohibited substances. Three molecules of cocaine may not be performance enhancing, but is there any way to justify them being there at all? So that's the controversy."

One of the truths of technological society is that new drugs are being discovered at a faster rate than tests can be developed to detect them. Almost everyone connected to racing is understandably troubled by the prospect that who wins a race might be reduced to the question of not who has the best horse but rather who has the best vet. About the ethical dilemma involved Goeldner said, "I did have a private veterinarian tell me, 'If I had a substance that I could tell a trainer was gonna move his horse up and guarantee him that it wouldn't be detected, there's hardly anybody in this racetrack that wouldn't be sorely tempted to use it.' His point was that it's just so competitive a business that everyone is looking for an edge. That's why we constantly have to improve our testing abilities."

I was curious if Goeldner thought that most horses were well meant when they were entered into a race. "By and large," he responded, "a trainer doesn't send his horse out there to give it some exercise. Because a horse has only so many races in it. And each time it is sent out there is a real risk of injury and there is always some wear and tear. So, you better take advantage of every opportunity and not just go out there for the hell of it. You better give it your best effort."

Goeldner reflected on the predicament of handicappers. "The bettor in the grandstands usually feels that he is not privy to inside information that could affect a horse's performance, and that's probably true. But, it's not like all of us on the backside know about it either. I'm as flabbergasted as they are when I see a twenty-to-one shot bet down to two to one. I don't know how that happens, but obviously the scuttlebutt has gotten around that this horse is ready to run."

While Goeldner is prohibited by CHRB rules from gambling, his job requires that he be a kind of reverse handicapper. "I'm watching the other end of the race." He smiled. "I'm watching horses that are starting to drop back, having difficulty on the turn, that are taking those short, choppy, wide, flailing strides in the stretch. I'm trying to pick who's going to run last, if you want to look at it that way. And that's almost as hard as picking who's gonna run first."

Goeldner's comment reminded me of the story about two handicappers who were mired in such slumps that they decided to wager on who would come in last. Unfortunately, they didn't have any better luck with that, because some horse would always be eased unexpectedly. Goeldner nodded in acknowledgment and said, "About two weeks ago there was a horse that, to my mind, was of marginal soundness. Like I said before, there is a gray continuum of soundness to unsoundness. It's no black-and-white situation, and I'm the one that has to draw the line and say, enough is enough. Anyway, there is this horse that is kind of on that line, that I'm not sure I want to see running anymore, that was probably twenty to thirty lengths behind the field—running his little heart out in the stretch—and he caught two eased horses to finish third. So, what do I do? Do I put him on the vet's list or let him run another race?"

8

INQUIRY
The Steward

*R*onnie Beau and I were in the grandstand for the ninth race and a couple of cheap routers were fighting it out, nose to nose, down the length of the stretch. At the last jump it was too close to call, and the photo sign went up as they crossed the wire. It was the third photo finish of the day, and our nerves were beginning to get a little frazzled.

Ronnie had bet against Wilmot, the eight-to-five favorite who was dropping in class from Santa Anita, in favor of a six-to-one shot named Drouilly Fuisse, and those were the two horses involved in the finish. Unfortunately, I had supported Last Attack, the second favorite, who had run out of the money. Ronnie, who had already lost two photo finishes to favorites, moaned pessimistically, "The way my luck has been running today, the chalk is gonna kill me again."

As we waited for the results of the photo, a couple of other gamblers in our section, who were hardly paragons of objectivity, offered their opinions about who had won. "The one horse caught the four at the wire," insisted one ticket holder who had bet on Drouilly Fuisse. "Whatsa matter, don't ya have eyes?" the cab driver behind him, who had backed Wilmot, countered derisively. "The inside horse, the four horse, held on by a head."

One thing was certain, though. The horses had already run their race, and now the decision was up to the stewards, who were perched, like distant gods, in their booth high above the grand-stand. As the moments dragged on with still no result posted on the tote board, a third handicapper who was sitting beside us volunteered, "If it's taken the stewards this long to decide, there's a good chance it will wind up a dead heat." To which Ronnie responded, "I hope not. If we have to split the pot with the favorite, it won't pay anything. I've got ten to win on the one horse and put him on top in the exacta, too."

Just then the photo light went out and the crowd held its breath as it waited for the numbers to be put on the board. When 4–1–8 went up, Ronnie Beau shook his head in disbelief. It had been that kind of day. Wilmot, the favorite, had hung on by a nose. In disgust Ronnie tossed his losing tickets in the air and, as they fluttered back toward the ground, whimsically chanted, "Inquiry. Inquiry."

The racing gods or the stewards must have heard him, because the Inquiry light came on and the 4–1 numbers began flashing on the board. Simultaneously, track announcer Larry Collmus clicked on his microphone and advised everyone to "Please hold all tickets. The rider of the one horse, Ron Warren, has filed a protest against the rider of the four horse for interference at the top of the stretch."

Ronnie Beau was suddenly stooped over and rummaging through the tickets on the ground. "This is undignified," he quipped. "I mean, if it was a steward's inquiry, I might stand a chance to have my number put up. But, ah . . . here the little buggers are . . . how many times does a jockey-prompted inquiry result in a disqualification? The stewards don't like to get shown up. If the riding infraction was that flagrant, they would have caught it themselves. My only chance is if they don't make a quick decision.

The longer the inquiry, the better the chance that they've seen something to justify taking the four horse's number down."

Ronnie Beau's reasoning proved prophetic. Forty-five seconds later the numbers stopped flashing and Collmus came back on to advise the crowd that, "After reviewing the tapes of the race, the stewards have ruled there will be no change in the order of finish. Coming up on your video monitors will be three shots of the incident: a head-on shot, a quarter-pole shot, and a pan shot. While the tapes will show there was some slight brushing at the top of the stretch, the stewards have ruled the contact was not severe enough to warrant a disqualification."

As we headed out toward the parking lot, a couple of handicappers were still debating the photo finish. "How come," one of them said, "they showed the rerun of the brushing at the top of the stretch but never put the photo finish on the video monitor the way they usually do?" To which his pal cynically responded, "One of the stewards probably had his money on the four horse and his cronies gave him the benefit of the doubt." While I was not inclined to share this darker view of how stewards make their decisions, I was interested in who these powerful, but largely anonymous, men are and how effective they are in ensuring the integrity of racing. Upon their competence rests not only the outcome of a particular race, but ultimately the health of a nearly $10 billion-a-year industry.

So it was that a couple of weeks later on St. Patrick's Day I found myself in the steward's booth high above the grandstand at Golden Gate Fields. After years of sweating out photo finishes and inquiries with my friends in the grandstand, I was getting to see, firsthand, what really goes on. I had prevailed upon Chief Steward Leon Lewis, and he had graciously allowed me to sit in and observe how he and his fellow stewards, Charles Dougherty and Dennis Nevin, monitor the afternoon races.

Since we had twenty minutes before the first race, Lewis filled me in about his background. Adjusting his bifocals, he told me his first contact with racing was in Napa, California, in 1945. "I was a young lad and horse crazy. I had grown up around horses and wanted to be a jockey. I worked at a training track where a lot of horses wintered and some young horses were broken and gotten ready for the races. I worked for a man who had a couple of thoroughbreds and began galloping for him. I started race-riding in 1946, and Frank Prior, who won the Kentucky Derby on Elwood, had my contract."

Lewis's jockey career, however, was short-lived because of a combination of injury in a spill at Pomona and the fact that he was still growing. "I could see I was getting too big," he philosophically reminisced, "and the weight problem was coming."

Not one to dawdle, Lewis tried his hand at a variety of jobs around the racetrack, sandwiched around a hitch in the service. He was a jockey agent, worked in the parking lot, punched tickets as a pari-mutuel clerk, groomed horses, trained them, and rode as an exercise rider before he went to work as a racing official.

In California all stewards are employees of the California Horse Racing Board (CHRB), a state-appointed agency, and the normal career progression is for them to variously put in time as a patrol judge, placing judge, paddock judge, and clerk of scales before being elevated to the top spot.

Lewis described the first of these jobs. "Patrol judges are the officials stationed out on the track in those little stands. There's usually three or four of them, and it's their job to watch for any interference during the running of the race and report back to the stewards. There's a patrol judge at the quarter pole, one at the finish line, one at the three-eighths pole, and some tracks even have one at the half-mile pole. There is no need for a patrol judge at the gate, because the starter there reports to the stewards about any problems at the break."

Of all racing officials, Lewis explained, the placing judges have the simplest but most controversial job. It's their responsibility to determine visually the top three horses as they cross the finish line, mark their numbers down on their programs, then show them to Lewis, who is the man who declares all results official. "We have a photo-finish camera," Lewis said, "but that's merely an aid for us to verify what the placing judges see. If the photo-finish camera happened to break down, we would take the numbers of the placing judges, how they saw the horses finish."

At smaller tracks stewards sometimes double up as placing judges. Lewis related a humorous incident that had happened at Stockton a few years back when he was on duty and they didn't have any placing judges. "The stewards' stand was in the center of the field, and they had to send the photo finish in a little bag from the top of the grandstand on a wire across the track to us. Anyhow, here come four horses thundering down the stretch, all together at the finish line. Well, normal procedure is, you mark down on your program the way you think you see them. And then you verify it with the other two stewards. And if one fellow has it one way and the other two another way, well, the first guy is ruled out: majority rules. We tentatively decided the finish was 7–10–9–8 and phoned that over to the mutuel department. But we decided to wait for the photo before making it official. And we waited and waited until we finally called over there and said, 'Send the damn photo down.' Meanwhile these four horses are walking around waiting for our decision for what seems like hours. Finally, here comes the bag, we reach in and pull out this piece of film. There's nothing on it. So we call back and ask what happened. The photo man started to make all kinds of excuses. To make a long story short, he wasn't even in the booth when the horses crossed the finish line to start the photo machine. So we called it as we saw it and put the numbers up on the board. Well, the crowd went wild. They were screaming and hollering, jumping over the fence, doing everything but throwing bottles. Jack Meyers, one of the stewards, was so nervous he called the police. In fact, they came and got us after the last race and escorted us out. My point in mentioning this story is that being a placing judge can be a very touchy thing in the absence of a photo. But things happen and you can never get totally away from the need for human judgment."

Even when photo finishes are available for the stewards to review, they aren't always shown on the video monitors after a race. I asked Lewis how that could be justified. "Sometimes the finishes are so close," he explained, "that to put them on the screen the image would be blurred. If you can't show a clear-cut picture, sometimes you're better off not to show them anything. We could needlessly start a riot. But we do save all the original photo finishes. The ones that are hung up for the public to see are copies."

The first race on the card was set to go off in fifteen minutes. It was a maiden allowance race for three-year-old fillies going a mile and one-sixteenth. From the steward's booth I could see the horses that were about to run circling in the paddock below. Lewis pointed to Paddock Judge Floyd Prospero and said his main job is to check the equipment on each horse. "We try to be consistent and make the horse wear the same equipment each time. If there's going to be any equipment change, say like blinkers, it has to be approved by the stewards in advance and is so noted on the bottom of the program for each race. The horses that are wearing blinkers for the first time have to be schooled out of the starting gate and be approved to wear them. Or, if they're coming off, it's the same thing."

Lewis elaborated about blinkers. "Let's say that a horse is a three-year-old and he's run two or three times and shown erratic behavior during a race. He might be the kind of horse that gets in front and then stops and waits for the other horses, or maybe he gets to looking up at the crowd or shying from other horses. So the trainer thinks, 'Gee, this horse might perform better if he can't see so much. Maybe we should try blinkers.' The trainer has to work his horse out of the gate with the blinkers on and get approval from the starter. The starter tells us and then, if the trainer still wants to put blinkers on his horse, we let him. But we very seldom let a horse change equipment off of a winning race, unless the trainer can show us that the horse did something in the race that would merit putting blinkers on. Some racing officials think that there should never be an equipment change allowed off of a winning race. I've found that by saying never, you get yourself in trouble sometimes. You're better off judging each case on how it comes to you. So I never say never."

As the horses were galloping off from the post parade, Lewis described the four video cameras that monitor the running of each race at Golden Gate Fields and Bay Meadows. "There's a pan camera on top of the grandstand that follows the horses all the way around the track. We have a second camera at the bottom of the stretch that gives us a head-on view of the horses coming toward the finish. Then there's a third one at the quarter pole that gets the horses from the three-eighths pole, around the turn, and the rear view of them going down the stretch. And finally, we have a camera at the three-eighths pole that gets a head-on shot of the horses coming out of the far turn and down the backside. So it's pretty well covered."

During the actual running of the race there is a division of labor among the three stewards. Lewis and Dougherty watch the race through their binoculars, while Nevin scans the four video monitors that are mounted in his corner of the booth and looks for any infractions. The starter and the three patrol judges are also directly plugged into the steward's box so they can phone up if they see anything that might warrant a disqualification. When an inquiry is conducted, it's one of Nevin's jobs to have the technical people replay the relevant part of the race from the perspective of at least two of the cameras. Given all the people involved in watching each race, as well as the video and photographic documentation available for review, I could see it would be almost impossible for the stewards to declare a winner a horse that hadn't actually won a race and get away with it.

The first race was about to go off. The horses had completed their twelve-minute warmups and were entering the starting gate. Lewis excused himself and waited, while peering through his binoculars, for the last filly to load into her post position. As the horses broke from the gate Lewis pushed a button that was mounted to the wall next to him. When I asked him about it, he told me the button automatically shut off all the pari-mutuel machines. It's important that he synchronize his move with the horses breaking from the gate, because any delay in closing the machines might give last-second gamblers a big edge. They could, for instance, make sure a speed horse that figured broke cleanly from the gate and still have time to place a big bet.

While Lewis and Dougherty used their binoculars to watch the horses run down the backstretch, I joined Dennis Nevin in his corner as he scanned the four video monitors. I didn't see anything unusual but, once it was over, Nevin picked up his phone and asked for a replay of the horses breaking from the gate. Regarding Azusa, the eight-to-five favorite, he commented, "The one horse damn near dwelt in the gate."

On second look I could see that Nevin was right. I also noticed some bumping at the start and asked Nevin about it. "With young horses," he explained, "there's going to be some erratic running out of the gate. Unless it's really flagrant, we won't take a horse's number down for bumping out of the gate. In quarter-horse racing it's more important to watch, because they don't have time to recover like the thoroughbreds do."

One of the two placing judges came into the booth and showed Lewis how they had rated the finish on their programs. Lewis picked up the phone and told the pari-mutuel department to put up the official sign. If it had been a photo finish he would have compared the photograph with the placing judges' numbers and made the final decision.

The telephone rang, and Lewis was informed by the horse identifier in the receiving barn that the eight horse in the third race, Teddy's Grey, was now a gelding. Lewis in turn called the track announcer so he could inform the public. I was curious how come they had just found out about the horse being gelded and asked somewhat facetiously if it had been cut on the way to the receiving barn. Lewis smiled and said that someone had probably screwed up on the paperwork, and that was one of the reasons why everything is always double-checked.

Another change that often vexes handicappers is a late scratch in a race. I had promised The Stone, who is always on the lookout for trainer ploys, that I would find out how much freedom trainers have to scratch a horse. He was particularly interested because in the past week he had bet a couple of triples where a horse he had singled in the seventh and eighth races was a late scratch and he was forced to take the post-time favorite, a horse he did not like. Lewis understood The Stone's predicament but said the only time trainers aren't allowed a late scratch is if doing so will reduce the field to less than eight. Even then trainers may sometimes be allowed to do so. "The most obvious reason is because of weather conditions. If a horse hates the mud, for example, we'll normally let the horse be scratched regardless of the size of the field."

The horses were now coming out of the paddock for the second race, and a big cheer came up from the crowd. Jockey Ron Hansen, who is one of northern California's leading riders, was on a seven-year-old mare named Naski, and it was his first day back after a six-week ban that Golden Gate Fields management had imposed upon him as a result of an alleged bribery attempt and complaints from Las Vegas casinos. After several hearings, the racing board had ordered Golden Gate Fields to reinstate Hansen, and the reaction of the fans below indicated they generally supported that decision. Lewis told me that the stewards had looked into the alleged bribery charges over a year earlier and had not found sufficient grounds to warrant an action. His feelings toward the Las Vegas casinos, who had been complaining about northern California "steam" cashing in some long-shot bets, was unsympathetic. "You don't hear those guys complaining to the media and the FBI and asking for an inquiry when they make a killing and nobody cashes a bet. They just think they should never have to pay anything out."

Since Lewis had mentioned the word *inquiry*, it seemed an appropriate time to ask him how the stewards decide to call one during a race. "Well, I can't answer for anyone else," Lewis qualified, "but I look at the race and, if I see some interference that I think costs a horse a better placing, then I think the number should come down. You also have to remember that just because two horses bump, that doesn't mean you're going to bring one of their numbers down. There's no place in the rules that says this is a noncontact sport. There's almost always some contact leaving the gate. Horses don't run in a totally straight line. If you wanted to watch every little detail, you could have an inquiry on almost every race. I don't know if you'd have any changes or not, but you could definitely have an inquiry."

I was curious how the stewards dealt with chain-reaction situations, where one horse lugs in or drifts out and bumps a second horse who then bumps a third one. "We don't take a horse down for inadvertent bumping. If a horse on the inside drifts out and bumps a horse in the middle and it bumps a third horse on the outside, we'll take the inside horse's number down, but not the one in the middle. Even though the one in the middle may have cost the horse on the outside a better placing, there is no way of knowing how well he would have run if he hadn't been bumped. In situations where there is inadvertent bumping, you can only disqualify the horse that started it all and chalk up the rest to racing luck."

When the stewards take a horse's number down, they will sometimes also suspend its jockey for negligent riding. "Most of the time when I look at a race," Lewis reflected, "I look for some way not to disqualify a horse or suspend a rider. If, when we're reviewing the video with the jockey the next day, he shows an attempt to keep his horse straight or if the horse is lugging in and he straightens him out, or if the horse is trying to run out and he takes ahold of him, then you can exonerate the rider from any rule violation. But if the jockey just lets the horse go helter skelter and it slams into another horse and makes another rider pull up and shorten stride or alter course, then that's grounds for disqualification. In that case you can believe the next day, after the film review, there will be a ruling suspending that rider for five days and maybe more."

What would be an example of an infraction justifying more than five days? "If you thought it was a deliberate act. Say a rider is in front and looks back and sees a horse closing on the rail, and the front rider just guides his horse in deliberately to stop the other rider, then that's a deliberate act and we'll probably give the rider fifteen days. And if the horse fell and there was an injury or something, it could be thirty days or anything we wanted to give. When that jockey hit Julie Krone with a whip back in New York, I think they gave him six months."

A common complaint heard in the grandstands revolves around handicappers who think that jockeys stiff their mounts. Almost any afternoon you'll hear more than one gambler moan while tearing up a losing ticket, "Did you see that jockey strangled my horse in the gate?" or "The bum deliberately pulled up behind a wall of horses and got himself trapped," or "The crook deliberately burned my horse out on the front end," or "The jock raced wide all the way when he could have saved ground by going to the inside." I asked Lewis if the stewards had ever put a rider down for not trying. "Yes. We gave a rider thirty days once in Fresno for failure to persevere with his mount because we thought he had a chance to be in the money. It's pretty hard to put a jock down for moving too quick on the front end, because a lot of horses don't rate all that well. That same fan who thinks the jockey is burning his horse out on the front end would be screaming that the jockey was strangling his horse if he tried to rate him."

It's not unusual for jockeys to ease up on their mounts when they know they aren't going to be in the money. Jack Kaenel had told me he didn't see any point in beating a dead horse and would rather save something for its next race. "Well, you know, I'm not one who insists on jockeys using their whips too much," Lewis reflected. "I'm a little bit the other way. In fact, we call riders in for overuse of the stick. All you have to do is just watch a horse and you can tell, as soon as he starts shortening his stride, that horse is tiring. So if a jockey is still hand riding him, making some kind of effort, that's enough, because there's no use whipping on a tired horse. He's already putting out all he can. Those bettors in the grandstand who say, 'Well, that jockey didn't hit the horse, didn't whip on the horse,' those same people, if a jockey came out of the saddling paddock onto the post parade and started whipping on his horse, they would want to lynch him. But when they're coming down the stretch, you can hear these same people screaming, 'Hit him, kill him.' My point is, people are really fickle. They're not thinking about the welfare of the horse, all they care about is the two dollars they bet on the horse."

I asked Lewis what a justifiable reason for whipping on a horse in the post parade might be. "If a horse is trying to fall over backward or won't go forward, sometimes a jock has to hit him. But we kind of frown on that too."

Some horses are particularly recalcitrant at the gate, and Lewis had an interesting explanation for their behavior. "Usually, when a horse doesn't want to load, that's a pretty good indication he doesn't want to race. I found that to be true in my experience when I was riding. The horse that is hurting somewhere knows when he gets in that gate he is going to have to run. So he'd rather not go in the gate."

Horses wind up on the steward's list for two primary reasons: for bad performance or because they were eased in their last race. "When we put a horse on the steward's list, we also confer with the track vet and have him take a look at the horse. If the vet sees some infirmity or lameness, then he'll put him on his list and we'll take him off our list. But if the horse is not physically infirm, he'll stay on our list until he can work a decent five-eighths of a mile. He has to be able to work at the average workout time of the morning he works before we consider taking him off."

Fans often wonder why, if a horse is inspected and passed by the track vet in the morning, it runs so badly in the afternoon. "Well, in the morning," Lewis replied, "he's not on the track putting out an all-out effort with weight on his back. The track vet in the morning just lets him out of his stall and feels his legs. If the legs are reasonably cool and the horse jogs okay, the vet is going to say that, at that point, the horse is raceably sound. Now, a lot of times you'll see a horse scratched during the post parade for showing lameness. That's because once they get weight on their back and start to move, if there's something wrong with them it will usually show up. But sometimes it will only show up during the stress of the race. It's impossible to predict before a race how some horses are going to run. There's a whole bunch of soundnesses on the racetrack. There's the real sound horses. There's raceably sound horses that can be sore but will still put out. And there are unsound horses that can't really run at all. And there's a big gray line in between."

Lewis had some tips about what to look for in assessing a horse's soundness. "If you see in the *Racing Form* that a horse has lugged out, or has been hard to control, that may mean he's sore and hurting. Especially with lugging out, because a horse is trained to run and work out on the rail. And when they gallop horses, they do it out in the middle of the racetrack. So a horse, if he's hurting a little bit, he wants to get out, get away from the racing, get to the outside fence and stop. He knows that's where he doesn't have to run. So, if you see a horse lugging out in his past performances, you can pretty well believe he's hurting somewhere. You can also watch horses on the backside, if they're excessively warming up, going back and forth, back and forth, there's some reason they're doing it. And it could be because they're trying to warm him up out of being sore."

The second race, a bottom-level claiming affair, was about to go off, and the three stewards took their posts. Coming for home it was a three-horse finish, and Ron Hansen closed with Naski to get up by half a length. As he crossed the finish line, Hansen pumped his right fist in acknowledgment to the cheers of the crowd. Lewis, who sees horse racing as something of a theatrical event, was enjoying the crowd's response. He was smiling and said, "That's great!"

But Dennis Nevin had a more dour view of Hansen's gesture. He asked for a replay to see if Hansen had started to pump his arm before he crossed the finish line. He also wanted a second look to see if Hansen had given the bird to Peter Tunney, the executive who had suspended him, when he rode past the clubhouse window. After looking at three different angles of the arm pump, Nevin satisfied himself that Hansen was only being exuberant.

Our discussion shifted back to jockeys and riding suspensions. I was interested in Lewis's view of the Big Conviction–Rob An Plunder race where Jack Kaenel's horse had drifted out from the rail and been disqualified. Kaenel had hit Big Conviction two or three times on his left side without the horse's drifting into Rob An Plunder. But with the next hit it did. In that kind of situation, I asked Lewis, how do the stewards determine whether or not to give the jockey days? "You can hit a horse two or three times and a horse might not do anything, but that next one he might. I don't remember the race, but I would think we probably gave Jack days. As an ex-jockey I know you can hit a horse three or four times and he might not show any sign of drifting out, but when you raise the whip one more time the horse knows it's gonna come and he has a tendency to want to get away from it. Horses aren't stupid. A rider will normally have a pretty good hold of the inside rein when he's whipping left-handed to keep the horse in and still be able to hit him. But the reins could have slipped a little bit in his hands just before he went to hit him that last time, and the horse knew he was gonna get hit and he just got out on him. That might have been what happened to Jack in that race."

I sat back and watched as Lewis worked the third race. During the stretch run he commented that it looked as if Joe Judice hadn't ridden his mount out on the two horse, The Visalian. When the video for that portion of the race was replayed, Lewis's initial judgment was confirmed. Lewis got on the phone and left a message in the jockey room that Judice was to report to the steward's office the next morning. A few minutes later a nervous Judice called back up inquiring about the problem. Both teasing and informing him, Lewis asked Judice. "When is the race over, Joe? At the quarter pole? At the sixteenth pole? Or at the wire? The wire, excellent, Joe. How come you quit riding at the quarter pole. Let's talk about it in the morning."

Once off the phone, Lewis explained they would go over the video of the race with Judice in the morning to get his side of the story. "We probably won't give him days. The horse wasn't going to be in the money, but he should have at least given some effort to hand ride the horse. When jockeys don't do that, the fans think they're stiffing their horses. In this case we'll probably only issue Joe a warning."

Speaking of fan perceptions, another controversial area is the starting gate. Fans often wonder why their horses break slowly. A common complaint revolves around the handlers who hold on to some of the horses' tails. "Those are horses," Lewis explained, "that have a tendency to rear up and fall over backward in the starting gate. If the handlers get their tail and hold it to the back of the gate, the horse won't rear up. But that doesn't keep the horse from breaking quickly from the gate. If the handler doesn't let go of that tail at the bell, he'll find himself going down the racetrack with that horse. Because there's no man strong enough that he can hold a horse by the tail and keep him from breaking with the others. It's just an impossibility. I don't care how big a man or how strong he is, when that gate opens, that horse is gone."

Another part of the steward's job is to designate what the track condition is. Lewis explained how they decide. "We generally just look at the track. Sometimes we'll confer with the track clocker and ask him how fast the morning workouts were. We get a workout sheet from the clocker around noon each day. We refer to it a lot when the track is muddy and the dogs are up. If the times are slow, we'll label it Slow. If the track looks muddy we'll label it Muddy. If there's a lot of water on the track we'll label it Sloppy."

Since track conditions can change dramatically as the afternoon progresses, I asked Lewis about the criteria for upgrading or downgrading the track's condition on the tote board. Do the stewards rely primarily on speed, on how fast the horses are running? "If the horses are running sprints in ten and change, it could be labeled Fast or it could be a Good track, too. There's quite a variation within the Fast and Good categories. It could be a Fast track with the horses running slower times, or the track might look a little off and be labeled Good and the horses could be running real fast. So it isn't just speed. I can't give you a simple answer."

The last race I stayed for was the Florida Derby, which was being simulcast from Gulfstream Park. Of the three stewards, Lewis was the only one who had a job to do. Since there was betting on the race at Golden Gate Fields, he still had to shut off the pari-mutuel machines as soon as the horses broke from the gate. The only difference in his routine was that the horses were three thousand miles away, and he was timing his move based on what he saw on the television screen. Lewis also had a direct line hookup to the steward's booth at Gulfstream, so he could get the official results and relay them to the tote board officials at Golden Gate Fields. The actual race, run in a slow time, was uneventful. Unbridled, the five-to-two co-favorite with Pat Day aboard came from just off the pace to win by four lengths, with Slavic and Run Turn getting the place and show.

It was only after the race that things suddenly got interesting. Somehow the direct-line connection to Gulfstream was broken, and Lewis was forced to delay making the results official. Meanwhile, he asked the placing officials at Golden Gate for their order of finish, and fortunately their results corresponded to the unofficial numbers the television showed on the Gulfstream board. Still, it was possible an inquiry might change the results, and Lewis had to be cautious before declaring the results official and paying out any money. Despite repeated attempts, the Golden Gate Fields switchboard couldn't reconnect with Gulfstream, and Lewis had to nervously hope that the simulcast would give the official results at Gulfstream. After what seemed like an interminable time but was actually only about ten minutes, the simulcast camera finally panned to the Gulfstream tote board again, and Lewis could see that the race had now been declared official. Wiping his brow, he called the pari-mutuel department to confirm the results were now official and told them to put the same numbers up on the GGF board. The Florida Derby simulcast left me thinking one important thing: no matter how much technology you have, the human element, fallible as it is, remains indispensable.

While monitoring the afternoon races is the more visible side of a steward's job, their morning work, where they hear disputes and mete out penalties, is just as important and controversial. Horsemen on the backside, just like fans in the grandstand, tend to look askance toward the stewards because of the power they wield. While a fan may lose a bet because of a steward's decision, a trainer, jockey, groom, and anyone else connected to the backside can be ruled off the grounds and even have his license permanently revoked if the offense is considered serious enough. As one backsider who's been reprimanded a time or two said to me, "The stewards are part umpire, but they're even more cop, and it's hard to like a cop."

Stewards, for their part, are in a tough position. They want the cooperation and trust of the horsemen, but they aren't paid to assume the best about human nature. Their primary mandate is to ensure the integrity of racing by keeping the game free of horsemen who try to affect the outcome of a race illegally, whether by bribery and collusion or the illegal drugging of a horse.

Leon Lewis and I talked about these and other matters on a weekday morning in his office. Lewis started off by saying that—given California's Controlled Medication program of allowing race-day medications like Lasix and "Bute"—one of the most difficult things for a steward to deal with is the Trainer Insurer Rule, the rule that holds a trainer absolutely responsible for the chemical condition of his horse when it is entered into a race. If any foreign substances, besides the approved medications in the specified dosages, are found in a horse's postrace urine or blood, a trainer is supposed to be penalized—regardless of the acts of any third parties like his vet, hot walker, or groom.

Trainers understandably fear and loathe the insurer rule. They argue, with considerable justification, that it deprives them of the basic constitutional protection of being presumed innocent until proven guilty. Most courts, however, have upheld the right of state racing commissions like the CHRB, and their stewards by extension, to regulate racing and suspend or permanently revoke any trainer's license for a medications violation or any other act contrary to the best interests of the sport. Their reasoning has been that protecting the public and maintaining the integrity of racing have a priority, and that horsemen knowingly accept the limitation of their constitutional rights when they apply for a license. Even further, the courts, lacking technical expertise and fearing a deluge of civil suits, have been reluctant to undermine the authority of racing's regulatory agencies by contravening their decisions. They have supported the view that racing, like most other sports, should essentially regulate itself.

Chuck Jenda had described the potentially unjust invocation of the Trainer Insurer Rule as "every trainer's worst nightmare." Leon Lewis, not surprisingly, had a different opinion. "I think we have to have the Trainer Insurer Rule," he emphasized. "Without it, I don't think racing would be as good as it is. When we find a drug violation, we have to invoke the rule. But suspending a trainer is usually our last resort. We know there are a lot of gray areas in applying the insurer rule, and understand that a trainer can't be at his barn twenty-four hours a day. Things can happen, say where his foreman gets Butazolidin in the wrong feed tub for one of his horses and the horse winds up with a high 'Bute' level in one of his tests. Well, you can see how a violation might have inadvertently happened in that case. So you don't rule that trainer off. You just fine him or take away the purse.

"But if a trainer is taking advantage and trying to affect the outcome of a race by giving a horse a stimulant or depressant and it can be proven, then there's no place in this business for him. We have to protect the integrity of racing. We have billions of dollars invested in the horse-racing industry that ultimately depend upon the wagering public's confidence in the honesty of the game. The general public doesn't think about the ancillary areas that are economically linked to the racetrack. There are breeding and training facilities, auctions for yearlings, stud fees, and also the farms that grow hay and alfalfa, oats, barley, and so forth. These are all huge investments tied to the health of the racing industry."

I was curious if the stewards had ever ruled any trainers off permanently. "Oh, yes. Larry Kleve is an example. When I used to be with the quarter horses, we suspended Kleve twice and then finally recommended his license be revoked because he was just an outlaw. He didn't do anything honest. The son of a bitch would do anything he could to win a race. Guys like Kleve feed their egos by winning races and don't think they're gonna get caught. They really don't. In fact, Kleve had other people take the rap for him twice. One time when I was a steward at Los Alamitos he had a groom come in and the groom said, 'Yeah, I gave the horse some medicine, the vet didn't know anything about it.' So we gave him the benefit of the doubt there. Next time, another groom tried to say the same thing. We didn't go for it. I think in quarter horses you get more people looking for an edge than with the thoroughbreds. You get a lot of them that come out of Texas, Oklahoma, Louisiana, where they have to live by their wits, and using stimulants is part of the game. They come from the match-racing era, and their attitude is 'Catch me if you can.'"

The phone rang and Lewis answered some questions from an anxious trainer about an upcoming hearing concerning a medications violation. Hanging up the receiver, Lewis sighed and said, "We may have to suspend his license for 120 days. And that bothers me. Because I still have to do it, even when I'm convinced deep down inside that this person didn't have any knowledge of how the horse got the medication. But then, we have to go to the Trainer Insurer Rule. We have to say, 'Well, if you don't know how he got it, then you're not protecting your stable the way you should.' "

Since we were talking about medications violations, I asked Lewis to comment on the highly controversial HBPA drug study that had leaked out in early 1989.

"One of the interesting things about the HBPA study," Lewis observed, "was that it was prompted by the horsemen themselves because they were concerned that some trainers were doing much better with the same horses than other trainers. There were cases where one trainer would claim a horse from another, raise him twenty-five percent or more in class within ten days, and the horse would just gallop. The horse would suddenly look like a stakes horse, whereas ten days earlier, for the previous trainer, he couldn't win for $10,000. So there was quite a concern and a lot of talk, mostly in southern California. Anyhow, the concerned trainers went to the HBPA and said, 'What about us getting a sample and testing winners, just for our own satisfaction, to see if there's any truth to these rumors we're hearing.' Well, the HBPA sent these samples to an independent lab and got quite a few positive tests. So then Truesdail, the CHRB's appointed test facility, went back and started testing their frozen samples and they got quite a few, too. The CHRB took the matter out of the hands of the local stewards and filed cocaine charges against Lukas, Barrera, Stein, Webb, and the others. As you know, all the charges were subsequently dropped because one of the metabolites to prove that cocaine was present was missing when the samples were retested. As far as I know, nothing was ever done about all those other positives the HBPA came up with. Why no one was ever prosecuted, I don't know. But the CHRB took the investigation out of the hands of the stewards at the local tracks, which I think was a big mistake. I also think Truesdail, which is now being sued by Stein and Barrera, was unfairly criticized because the state was not giving them enough money to do rigorous testing. From what I've subsequently learned, they weren't even originally testing for cocaine. They were being told what to test for by the CHRB. Someone at the CHRB was telling them, 'Test for this.' "

I asked Lewis where things stood now. "We have a new Equine Medical Director, Dr. Dennis Meagher, who's the chief surgeon at U.C. Davis. I'm surprised the CHRB even got him to do this, because it's a thankless job. He's making some progress. He's trying to get all the various facets of racing together and say, 'Hey, there's a cloud over our industry. Let's see if we can't get this thing blown away.' But everyone is going to have to work to protect the integrity of racing."

Perhaps the most important thing Dr. Meagher has done, according to Lewis, is to set up a new system for testing. The testing lab is now being given enough money to upgrade its tests on all winners, beaten favorites, exacta partners, and any other horse the stewards want checked. Under the new system, samples that test positive will also be sent to an independent, approved laboratory for corroboration, and referee samples will also be made available to accused horsemen so they can privately verify the results. "So from here on out," Lewis emphasized, "if we get a positive confirmed twice, then there's going to be a hearing and someone is going to be penalized for violation of the rules."

Lewis also hopes that the CHRB will allow local stewards to do their job. "We have the advantage of regularly dealing with trainers and have the perspective to evaluate what is going on better than some more remote racing board comprised of mainly political appointees. Even though the great majority of trainers are honest, we have to protect against the bad apples. It's a cat-and-mouse game when it comes to drugs and drug testing. The chemists come up with something new and pretty soon some trainer will try it. We have to keep up by constantly updating our drug-testing procedures. There's no question that we need a drug research center for horse racing that will allow us to anticipate and keep ahead of any performance-enhancing or -detracting drugs. Dr. Meagher is working on that. The way it is now, an unscrupulous trainer could take small, undetectable amounts of, say, four different prohibited drugs and mix them together—like a cocktail—and have a stimulating or tranquilizing effect on a horse that can affect the outcome of a race."

Lewis candidly admits that detecting performance-enhancing drugs is going to be an ongoing problem. "The bottom line will continue to be that stewards will have to keep looking at those trainers that show dramatic improvement in their horses. I mean, what can a fellow who's claimed a horse do in ten days to move a horse up, that was losing for $10,000, and now he's running for $16,000 and beating horses that are dropping down from $20,000? I mean, the horse just runs off and leaves them. You'll see some of them be on the lead all the way and down at the sixteenth pole, where horses normally tire, and they suddenly change gears. A horse will run up to them and they'll just run off and leave them. You better believe we will look into that."

Another thing Lewis would like to see is a no-medications policy on race day. "There's no question that race-day use of Lasix makes our job more difficult. It also makes it more expensive to test for prohibited drugs. Right now, the industry puts the dollar sign in front of the health of the horse. Because of the economics of the industry, horses aren't given enough time off to heal properly. Instead, we'll do almost anything to get another race out of a horse. Maybe we should cut down on the number of dates. It would be better if we had less racing, with sounder horses. Before the introduction of year-round racing, if a trainer had ten horses, he would have five of them laid off and five racing. Now he can't afford to do that, so we wind up giving NSAIDs and Lasix to horses to keep them running."

Lewis also has strong reservations about the racing of two-year-olds. "They're still babies and their bones haven't fully developed. This makes them more injury prone. If you wait another year you get healthier, sounder horses that don't have to be on all these drugs. They will have longer racing lives. I think we should quit writing two-year-old races. But that won't happen without a strong agreement on the part of owners not to race their horses at two. Then the HBPA could go to management and say, 'Don't write any two-year-old races.'"

Lewis acknowledges that breeders and owners are under strong economic pressure to race their two-year-olds. "You have to look on the other side of the coin. Too bad the coin has two sides. You take a fellow that's got a brood mare that's worth $50,000, he takes and ships her to Kentucky and breeds her to a horse and the stud fee is $25,000. Then he brings her back to California. So you've got a vanning bill. She's got the foal inside her for eleven months. Then you wait two years. Now you've got three years into this foal, before you break them and if you're lucky get them to the races. So the economics do get to you. It costs a lot of money. As a breeder, you want to sell your two-year-old at a nice price. As an owner who's paid a lot of money for it, you want to race it and see a return on your investment as soon as you can. In the long run, however, being patient with a horse is the best policy. Brown Bess is a good example of that. But a lot of people don't have that kind of money or they don't want to wait that long. A horse doesn't come fully mature until it's five or six years old. But you hardly see any six-year-olds racing, because they started as two-year-olds and they're lucky to make it as three-year-olds. And if you saw the list of horses on Butazolidin and other permitted medications, you'd wonder how or why we're racing. What's happened is we've put the dollar sign before the welfare of the horse. And that's just what the business has come to."

Lewis is also concerned about the fan in the grandstand. "I don't think management does enough for the public. For years racing hasn't done a thing for the fan. There's so much competition for the entertainment dollar that racing has kind of fallen behind. I think management should reduce the parking, admission, and program fees. They should roll out the red carpet, whether it's for a two-dollar bettor or a hundred-dollar bettor. Treat the people so they want to come back again. I look at racing sometimes like a giant play. Management is the producer. They have the racetrack, the big stage. Management then hires the racing secretary, who's the director of the play. It's his job to get all of these characters— the trainers, horses, and jockeys—and they're the performers. Together their job is to put on a good show for the public. And that's the way it should be."

Part of Lewis's definition of a good show is that the track conditions should be kept as consistent as possible. "That was a real problem at Bay Meadows. The track shouldn't be deep on Wednesday and Thursday, harder on Friday, and on the weekends they're breaking track records. It shouldn't be that way because it's bad for the horseplayer and the horsemen. The track variants shouldn't be changing. If they're going to keep it deep, keep it deep all the time. If they're going to make it hard, keep it hard all the time."

Lewis also felt that more should be done to see that sound horses are running for the public to bet on. Toward that end, he thought Red Lowery's idea of qualifying races had some merit. "In fact," he added, "they're already an integral part of the racing program in Australia, where they are called barrier races. Here in northern California, some trainers use training races to get their young thoroughbreds ready to run, and we sometimes require older horses to be competitive in one of them before we allow them to come off the steward's list."

Lewis sees some potential problems, however, in requiring all thoroughbreds to run in qualifying races. "In quarter-horse racing, at one time you had to have two training races out of the gate with a certain time to qualify for a race. Until you could do that, you couldn't start. But quarter horses run a short distance, 350 to 440 yards, and they're running almost full blast from the time the gate opens. Thoroughbreds aren't the same. For one thing, some of them just won't work in the mornings. I mean, they just will not put out. But in the afternoons they'll run like gangbusters. Whether it's the excitement of the crowd, the noise and all that stuff, who knows, but their adrenaline gets going and they run better in the afternoon. Another difference is that quarter-horse trials run in a straight course. Thoroughbreds, on the other hand, have to run longer distances, which means they normally have to go around at least one turn. Young horses tend to get into all kinds of trouble going around a turn and it wouldn't show up in the results. A handicapper wouldn't know what happened by just reading the workout tabs in the *Form*."

Another potential problem involves maintaining the integrity of the qualifying races. Lowering his voice in a mock conspiratorial tone, Lewis gave an example. "Let's say I'm Slippery Sam and I've got a nice two- or three-year-old and I put him in three training races and each time I tell my rider, 'Be third.' Now, in each of those races I could have won the race by ten lengths, but I instructed my rider to be third, to cheat. Now I'm gonna go for the money and try to cash a big bet. So here's nine horses in a race and six of these horses, the public can see from the training charts, have already outrun my horse. So now I tell my jockey, 'Today we're gonna bet on my horse, so let's win.' That wouldn't be fair to the public. So we'd have to monitor those races."

The phone rang again and it was an owner defending his right to a claim he had recently made. After hanging up, Lewis explained the situation to me. "This guy claimed a horse, and we don't think he used his money to claim the horse. We got information that a second guy, who isn't eligible to claim a horse, put up some of the money for the claim. Apparently, the second guy told the first guy, 'Well, in thirty days you can put it in my name.' These guys are trying to bend around the rules. We could void the claim if we want to. Or if the previous owner doesn't want him back, just say to the first guy, 'Okay, it's your horse now, but you can't run him for thirty days. You can just feed him, and then if you want to sell part of him, that's your business.' "

I asked Lewis how he felt about trainers in the fast claiming lane who take a horse for $10,000, drop it down to $8,000, and it wins easy. Did he feel the ploy was legitimate or part of a betting scam? "Most of the times, and I know this for a fact," he responded, "they'll claim a horse and get it back to the barn and as soon as the 'Bute' or Banamine or whatever the horse is on wears off, the horse is so sore it can't get out of the stall. Usually it takes them thirty days to get that horse healed back up to where they can run him. So they say, 'Let's get rid of this horse, he's got an ailment, a physical disability and we don't want him.' So, they'll take a $2,000 loss, maybe try to win the purse and get their money back and hope someone will claim the horse. Most people claim a horse figuring that if they can do as well with the horse as the previous trainer, then they are gonna make out on him. If they can improve on him a little bit, then so much the better. Also, don't forget, when you claim a horse you have to raise them twenty-five percent if you want to race them back under thirty days. You can't even run them back at the same level for thirty days. One of the reasons for putting horses 'in jail,' or the thirty-day rule, is to discourage owners and trainers from dropping sound horses and gambling on them."

. . .

It was getting late, and Lewis wanted to get some lunch before the afternoon races began. We concluded with a brief discussion of the other facets of a steward's job on the backside. "We deal with everything from fights to rapes to people not paying their bills to a groom caught smoking underneath the shed row. We don't allow the grooms to smoke underneath the barns or cook in a tack room because of the danger of fire. But they all do it. So if it's brought to our attention, we have to rule on it."

Lewis described the backside as "A city in itself surrounded by a fence. And the people on the backstretch all have one thing in common. They're all addicted with horseshit in their veins. I'll give you an example. There was a woman who trained horses, and she got down and had one horse left. I was talking to her one day and asked her, 'How do you keep going?' She said, 'I got another job.' I said, 'Well, what do you do?' She said, 'I get up at three o'clock in the morning and go clean out laundromats.' She swept them up and mopped them out so she could make enough money to keep her horse and herself eating. So, horse people are really addicted. It's almost as bad as being on drugs. But it's a fascinating business. It has its ups and downs and its heartaches. You can see a fellow that one day has a big stable of horses and is driving a big Cadillac, and the next year you might see him with two or three horses and living in the tack room."

I asked Lewis what happens to people like that. "It's just the cycle," he explained. "A trainer might have one big owner that gets mad at him and takes all the horses away. Or their good horses get claimed from them or just start getting physical disabilities and going bad. Pretty soon they're down to where they don't have much of anything. And then a lot of people get to fighting the mutuel machines over there. Every dime they get they put into the machines, and pretty soon they owe all these bills and can't pay them. But, you know, most people are here because there's something about the animals. I've been that way all my life. I was disappointed one day when I woke up and found out I wasn't a horse. I don't know what there is about them. But I think they're the most beautiful animals in the world."

9

IN THE
WINNER'S CIRCLE
The Owners

Sooner or later every horseplayer is gripped by the fever and fantasizes about owning a racehorse. I can still remember that afternoon when Panama, Frisco, and I were sitting in the grandstand and Pegasus struck. It was the normally hard-boiled Frisco who was smitten. "Hey!" Frisco's eyes lit up as he proclaimed, "Why don't we all chip in and buy a horse. We could form a syndicate! Think of it. Our own colors. Free passes to the clubhouse! Access to inside information."

Frisco's idea was to invest a portion of a modest inheritance into buying a share of a bottom-level claimer as a way of getting his foot in the door. With luck, he enthused, we might even parlay our modest beginnings into buying a two-year-old that became a stakes horse! One thing was certain though: short of hitting the Pick Six, Frisco's syndicate proposal was probably our only shot at ownership.

Our enthusiasm was dampened, however, when The Stone showed up in his postal uniform. "You realize, of course," he intoned, "that it costs as much to feed and train a cheap claimer as a million-dollar stakes horse? You don't have enough money to play this game. You'll go broke paying the bills. Even with the three of you going in, it'll cost you at least five hundred a month apiece, and you won't be able to afford to come out here and play the horses anymore. I'll miss you guys."

The Stone, we had to admit, had a point. We weren't moguls. Why get stuck with backing only one horse? As handicappers, on our worst day we might drop a hundred bucks, but at least we had a shot at picking a winner in every race. As owners there was a good chance we'd be supporting a chronic loser to the tune of a hundred and a quarter a week. If our luck was really bad, we might even claim a horse we couldn't give away.

Fortunately, we concluded, there are people of means who, undaunted, continue to hear Pegasus sing. In northern California Bart Heller has been one of his most enthusiastic disciples for the past twenty-two years. Not only does he breed, claim, and race over a hundred thoroughbreds, but he has promoted the sport as past president of the HBPA and won the thanks of handicappers everywhere through his sponsorship of Sam Spear's daily racing show.

Having tracked down the fifty-one-year-old Heller at his corporate headquarters for Baron's Jewelers, I asked him what sparked his initial interest in racing. He told me he got into horse racing the old-fashioned way. "My dad was a bookie. I was blessed with a photographic memory and a gift for numbers and was reading the *Racing Form* by the time I was seven. My dad never had any horses, but I used to go to the track with him all the time. After my dad and mom split up, I went to live with my sister and began riding horses. Between the time I was eight and twelve I rode in horse shows all over California. I rode in Grand Nationals, Blue Ribbon shows, and everything else. So I've loved horses all my life."

Given the demands of his business, I was curious if Heller still rode. "No." He shook his head. "I don't get on their backs anymore.

But on any given day we've got between sixty and a hundred head at home that I can see right out my back door. And every one of them knows me, though I don't have as much time to spend with them as I'd like to."

Heller described his first encounter with owning a horse. "Twenty-two years ago there were five of us that claimed a horse named Bounce Away for $3,200. We each put up $700 to cover all the costs. That's how I got into owning horses."

Aha, I thought, a syndicate! Just like what Frisco had tried to talk us into before we realized that the cheapest part of owning a horse is buying him. "That's right," Heller agreed, "the cheapest part is buying them. But syndicates have a lot of other problems, because everyone has their own idea of how often and where the horse should run, who the jockey should be, and so on. Something is always wrong, even when you win, with syndicate members."

Bill Morey had related a funny story from a trainer's side about syndicates, which I shared with Heller. Early in his career Morey had agreed to train a cheap claimer that a dozen friends had decided to go in on. "Pretty soon"—Morey had shaken his head—"the phone was ringing every day with one or another of the owners wanting to know why the horse didn't win its last race, when it was going to run again, or why the vet bill was so high." Realizing he'd gotten himself into a thankless situation, Morey soon called a meeting at a local restaurant to simplify matters. Each owner put his name into a hat, and the first names picked were given the opportunity of buying out the others.

Heller grinned at Morey's predicament and explained that after two horses he had abandoned the syndicate idea himself in favor of going in with his partner at the jewelry store. "We started to buy and sell horses for a period of about three years. Then my partner decided he didn't want to own horses anymore, so I went on my own."

The first horse Heller claimed totally on his own was the last day of the meet at Bay Meadows in 1971. "I claimed a horse called His World. And it's really been my world ever since. His World ran for me two times, and I lost him and claimed another horse. I ran him two times and lost him. Then I claimed a horse for $8,500, named after my son—My Boy Scotty—and I ran him back for twelve-five and he won. I took him to Santa Anita and he ran second and then I lost him for sixteen, but I made a big profit."

From there, Heller was on his way. He claimed Brown Giant, who won fifteen races for him. "I claimed him for ten and lost him for twelve-five the first time. Claimed him back for twelve-five and lost him for nine on his last race. But in between he won nearly $100,000. Bill Mastrangelo was my trainer at the time, and we usually had two or three horses. We would claim them, run them, and lose them. We didn't necessarily run them to lose them, but we always tried to run them where they belonged."

Heller's initial luck was good enough that he actually paid income tax for three years in a row. Then he claimed his first filly. "A guy told me, 'Don't ever get rid of her. She'll be a great brood mare,'" Heller recounted with a rueful look of satisfaction. "This was a filly by the name of Pueblo Spirit. She was by Viking Spirit, and Old Pueblo on the brood mare side. She was second some fifteen times before she broke her maiden. People around the track got to calling her the bridesmaid of brides until she finally broke her maiden and then won another race at Stockton."

After that Heller took Pueblo Spirit out to his ranch with the intent of breeding her. Within a month tragedy almost struck. The mare was out galloping in the pasture one morning and broke her knee. "They called me from the store, and I ran out there and they were going to put Pueblo down," Heller recalled with visible emotion, "and I said, 'No, you're not.' We put her in a sling for six months and saved that mare's life. She became my foundation mare, because she produced my first foal, Tiny Heller, which I named after my dad. He was stakes placed and won $77,000."

After Tiny Heller, Pueblo Spirit next threw an extremely quick filly, Roz H, that Heller had named after his mother. "Roz H was a stakes winner and finished second, beaten a nose, at Hollywood Park in world record time for five-eighths of a mile. She made $124,000 in twenty-four starts. That was big money back in those days. Roz H is now following in Pueblo's footsteps. She just had a great-granddaughter of hers."

Brood mares, I learned, can be productive for a long time.

"Pueblo's almost twenty-one years old and still cycling," Heller marveled. "She's down at Cardiff Stud Farm right now being bred to Al Mamoon. I claimed her when she was three and started breeding her at five. So all together she's been cycling for about fifteen years."

Bart and his wife, Ronelle, have stepped up their breeding operation in recent years. "My wife and I went partners with the five horses I already had when we got married. We've been claiming and breeding ever since, building up whatever we can. We have a ranch with thirty-eight acres in Castro Valley, where we live and raise our horses. It's gotten to be a large enough endeavor that we have five full-time people working there."

To pay the bills, Heller gets up every morning, jogs a little, looks at his horses, and then heads off to his jewelry store. He has also successfully reached into the claiming pot with Bill Morey for some pretty expensive horses, like Quick Twist and Big Chill, in the last few years. I asked him if he and Morey had claimed them to race them or with breeding in mind. "Well, they're both stallions. So they certainly could go to the breeding shed. But Bill and I claimed them to race them. I wanted to claim Quick Twist because I had a horse that was worth fifty grand run against him down south and Quick Twist just annihilated him. So when they stuck him in a race up here for fifty, I had the feeling that this was the time to go and I went. Quick Twist was a great claim. He's earned over $150,000 in purse money for us. Unfortunately he's laid up right now with a bad ankle. I don't know if he'll ever run again. We've tried to sell him as a stallion, but couldn't find any takers. You'd think a horse that's won ten of twenty-nine races and earned over $200,000 would be attractive to someone for $10,000, but it's hard to sell an unproven stallion."

Heller credits Bill Morey for claiming Big Chill. "We had run Quick Twist in a race," he explained, "and he ran second and Big Chill third. After the race Bill told me he thought that Big Chill was by far the best horse in the race. So when I saw them drop him in for forty grand, I called Bill up and said, 'I got to go. You want a piece?' And he took a piece of him, too."

Based on his experience, what advice would Heller give to

someone just getting into the game as an owner? "Well, the biggest thing," Heller emphasized, "is that nine out of ten times you're gonna be a loser in this business. You're not going to make money. So you better have fun. If I was just claiming horses, and kept being lucky, I could probably make money in this business. But it's all luck. There are no geniuses in this world, believe me. The key is to have a trainer you're comfortable with. You want a trainer who knows how to handle a horse whether it's sound or unsound. You want someone who can move on a horse. Up or down the claiming ladder, but especially up. It's important that you have confidence in your trainer. Otherwise you won't be comfortable, and it doesn't pay to go into the claiming game."

Heller elaborated, "I've been doing this a long time and I watch trainers. You watch guys like Bill Morey, Lonnie Arterburn, or Jerry Hollendorfer and you can see they move horses up all the time. Terry Knight moves horses up sometimes too. You don't see all their horses moving up. But then no trainer, no matter how good he is, can move every horse up. There are going to be some horses that go by the wayside. Bill Morey moves a majority of his horses up. How many horses have you ever seen claimed off Bill Morey that went on and became stars? There's only a few that have won on a jump raise from Bill. If you really watch the statistics, you'll find that out. And I watch the statistics. I've had two trainers, over the years, that I felt comfortable claiming and running horses with. One was Bill Mastrangelo and the other, in recent years, is Bill Morey. I also have Richard Lewis and Keith Murray, who are very good with getting babies ready to run."

If claiming horses is a risky game, breeding them is even tougher. Bill Morey had described his breeding experience as so disheartening that he was afraid to look at the ledger. "The ledger in breeding is terrible," Heller agreed. "Bill and I have never bred horses together. But you cannot make it as a breeder. If you stop and add up the bills, you'll see why. Your brood mare costs you $500 a month to board at a decent ranch like Cardiff Stud Farm, and she produces no income. So that's $6,000 a year. Then let's say you've paid a $3,000 stud fee. So that's $9,000 right there. Then the foal is born and that costs you $500 a month once it's been weaned. Now you breed the mare back and you have another $3,000 stud fee plus the cost of her board for another year. So just with the mare, the stud fees, and your first foal you've got nearly $22,000 in the package after two years. Now you have your second foal and you breed your mare back again for another $9,000. During all of this time, you haven't yet broke the first baby. But you do have another $6,000 in boarding expenses for that yearling that's just coming up for breaking, plus another $3,500 coming up for the new weanling. So if you take and add up all the expenses with your first mare, you could have as much as $40,000 to $50,000 invested with all the babies before you have your first racehorse ready to run. And then what usually happens with that first foal— after you've bred for her, broke her, sent her to the track, and now she's ready to breeze—is the trainer says she can't run. I mean, this is a business that is the killer of killers. That's why you can't make it in breeding."

Heller is thankful that, at least in California, something is being done for the breeders. "They're giving fifteen percent bonuses for wins, and ten percent of the purse for seconds and thirds. And they're giving California Division Awards and Stallion Awards. The hardest thing in breeding today is standing a stallion. First, you have to get mares to him. If you have a hot stallion, that's easy. But if you've got a stallion you're trying for the first time, you've got to beg, borrow, and steal to get people to breed their mares to him. It's the toughest business going. I have one stallion, Baron O'Dublin, that I'm standing and I'm not going to stand any others, except for maybe Big Chill one day. I basically want to get out of standing stallions."

Instead of developing his own stallions, Heller has decided it's smarter to buy shares in proven ones. In recent years he's bought shares in such blue-chip studs as Flying Paster, Desert Wine, Skywalker, Crystal Waters, Habitony, Endow, and Interco. "I own 2.5 percent of each of those stallions. When you own shares in a good stallion, one of the things you can do is trade part of their earnings toward the cost of their stud fee. I like to breed to the best stallions, so I buy a lot of shares in them. I just bought a share in Somethingfabulous, Unpredictable, and Faliraki. Altogether

I've got fourteen stallion shares, so my mares are going to be busy."

Meanwhile, with a couple dozen mares and their babies to support, Heller has to sell a lot of jewelry to keep his head above water. "Can I tell you something?" he confided. "I haven't had a vacation in ten years. Every dime I make in jewelry goes into feeding these horses. But someday it'll pay me back. God willing, if I'm still alive, I'll hit with a really big horse. It's just been a dream all my life. Some people buy a lot of real estate or fancy automobiles, but this is where I'd rather put my money. If you get attached to these horses, they can break you. That's why I work sixty to seventy hours a week. But you know, you can get highs from alcohol, whatever drugs these guys use on the outside, but you'll never get a high like being successful with a racehorse. It's the ultimate high."

Heller's dream of hitting with a big horse rests with his young stock. Toward that end he has eighteen yearlings and a new crop of babies. "We've had nine foals this year already, but we lost one of them. We think it got kicked by its mother and broke its hind leg above the hock. The vet said there was no way to save it. We had to put it down. So we have eight babies now that are out at different ranches with their moms, who are being bred again. We're expecting another foal tonight and should get another dozen or so babies in about three weeks. We had a big run three weeks ago when we had nine of them, and pretty soon we'll have another run. I love this time of year when the foals are born. They're so adorable to watch as they run and play with their mothers those first few days."

I asked Heller what percentage of those babies would actually make it to the track and then win a race. "That's a good question." He sighed. "Probably between sixty and seventy percent will get to the track. But only half of those will ever win a race. So you're looking at a thirty-percent chance of ever earning any money back. That's your chance. I've had years where a hundred percent made it, but I've had years where nothing made it. So it's a big number."

Apart from losing money, what's the worst thing a breeder can hear? "The worst thing, the absolute worst thing, that I hate to hear from a trainer," Heller emphasized, "is that I've bred a bum, a horse that can't run. But he's got to tell me the truth even though I don't want to hear it. It's tough to accept—when you've spent so much time and money and you know the bloodlines are good— that every animal can't be a winner. There's so many losers, and it's terrible when they tell you your horse can't run. It's like someone telling you they want a divorce or your kid is ugly."

Heller acknowledged that trying to offset the cost of his breeding operation is one of the reasons he's jumped into the claiming pot for horses like Quick Twist and Big Chill. "Another reason is that if I think it's a decent buy, I hate to see a bargain go by. It doesn't matter if it's a $50,000 horse or one going for $5,000. If I see something I like, and they're okay, I'll go. A lot of times I'll borrow the money to claim these horses. I don't always have the cash. But if I think it's the right business move, then I take the shot."

Unlike some owners, Heller doesn't look for a scapegoat when he makes a bad claim. "Win, lose, or draw," he emphasized, "I don't cry about a claim. I don't cry to nobody. If it goes bad, it goes bad. I'm the first one to say, 'Let's take another one' the same day. Because if it's a bad claim, then I want to turn around and see if I can change it. That's my philosophy. You can't second-guess yourself in horses. They're meat and flesh, that's all they are, and anything can happen."

Heller gave a harrowing example. "I had a horse by the name of Basita that was one of the best mud horses going, and Bill Morey worked him in the mud one morning because we knew he liked it, and he took a misstep and broke his leg off. Bill, to this day, doesn't like to work horses in the mud because he had his best horse out there and he broke his leg. We talked about it the other day and it wasn't Bill's fault. It wasn't anybody's fault. The wind was blowing the wrong way and the horse hit a hole or something. Maybe it was the track's fault. Maybe the horse had a weak spot and we didn't know about it. This is an unpredictable business and things happen. You can make yourself sick if you're looking to blame somebody."

Another hat that Heller has worn was as president of the HBPA. He talked about his agenda for promoting the interests of horsemen during his tenure. "When I was the president of the HBPA," he recounted, "I was basically the founder of simulcasting. The board and I were also the founders of Sunday racing and Friday night racing at Bay Meadows. We did a lot of things to improve racing handles to where they are today. My objective when I went into the HBPA was to raise purses for owners. Owners are the only consistent losers in this business, and unless they get some kind of a shot they can't make it. The trainer, the jockey, everybody that works at the track gets paid, while the owners take all the financial risk. The owner puts up that money and hopes that his horse can make it. But if his horse runs off the board, he pays all the expenses, plus the jock mount, plus everything else. The owner is the only one taking it in the shorts. That's why I say this is a losing business and an ego setup for owners. They've got to have some winners once in a while to stay in the game."

Given both his affection for horses and the financial pressures he feels as a breeder, I wondered how Heller felt about the racing of two-year-olds. Did he agree that racing them that young isn't generally in their best interests? "Well, basically, that's a true argument. But financially, most people have to run their horses at two. They can't keep them for another year. If you really look at the system, most two-year-olds don't start racing until May, when they're almost two and a half. That's when you start developing them and find out whether or not you've got a good horse. Whether or not you run them at two depends on the horse. I've got a great mare that was out of Roz H by Desert Wine. I tried her at two and she pulled a suspensory ligament, separating the attached bone. She could work in forty-five and change without asking her. We gave her a year off and brought her back at three. After five months of training she pulled the same suspensory bone on her last gallop on entry day. I just took her home and bred her. So injury can happen at two, it can happen at three—it doesn't make any difference. When they're two, their bones are softer. But what an owner, if he's knowledgeable, and trainer have to do is look at those bones and see if they're too immature and not likely to stand up to the pressure. A good trainer can look at a horse and see if he's immature. You give a horse a little time, you'll make a nice animal out of him. You rush him, which is what a lot of people will do, you ruin that horse for life."

Based on his political experience lobbying for the HBPA, I asked Heller if he thought the state would ever agree to cut its percentage of the handle, and earmark that money for special three-year-old races that would have as one of their conditions that the horse couldn't have been raced at two. "That proposal has no shot," Heller predicted. "On every bill that's been done for changing races, one of the stipulations has been that the state continue to receive the same six percent of the betting handle. The state of California takes out the highest percentage of the handle in the country. We are the most successful, but we way overpay the state compared to everywhere else. They will not give an inch. Every bill that goes through will not allow any change in the distribution of money between the state, the horsemen, and the track operators. I don't think you're going to change that."

I wondered if the state, by taking so much out of the betting handle, is forcing owners to run horses younger. Heller disagreed. "No, I don't know if you realize it but, since I've been in the HBPA, the board has been successful in almost doubling the amount of purse money going to owners in the last ten years. The purses are basically allocated without regard to age. The purses are the same, whether it's for two-, three-, four-, or five-year-olds racing. Horses going a distance do get a little better purse than sprinters, and sometimes babies do too, but not more than five percent either way. You take an old broken-down horse for sixty-two fifty and he's still going to run for that six thousand pot. And you take a two-year-old maiden for twelve-five and he's gonna run for the same amount. Now, the maiden could be a nice young horse that may have a long life on the track. So the broken-down horse is getting a big edge, because it's on its last legs and people are holding it together. The younger horses should probably be running for the higher pots, because they have more potential. But they're all running equal."

Heller supports the egalitarian manner in which purse money is distributed. "You can't, just because you're a breeder, say you should have a higher share of the purse money. That's not fair to that little guy out there who just claimed a horse with his last seven thousand bucks and doesn't have enough to pay the feed bill. There has to be enough there for him, so that when he gets that horse home, he can make some money out of the deal. You've got to take care of everybody at the track. The track is a melange of every walk of life. It's hard to describe some of the people out there. It's a Damon Runyon book. Everybody has their own way. Everybody knows they're the best trainer out there."

I asked Heller what he thought about Red Lowery's proposal for requiring horses to prove their ability in qualifying races. Wouldn't that promote racing by giving the small trainer, who now can't get a stall, a better chance, as well as giving handicappers more confidence that the horses they bet on are sound enough to have a real shot at winning? "Well, that's true," Heller acknowledged. "But then you'd run into the problem of filling races. You might knock out too many horses. Also, every time you run a horse you risk an injury. Good horses don't usually run in training races. Their trainers already know they can run. Why risk an injury running against a lot of green horses, or take a chance that the track conditions are maybe a little bit off in the morning and might hurt your horse? You're better off just running them into shape. Handicappers don't necessarily benefit from qualifying races either, because they don't know who else was in that race, and the running times can be deceiving."

Heller believes that qualifying races work well for quarter horses, because "They have horses standing in the woodwork and need some way to eliminate horses. Quarter horses are also generally sounder than thoroughbreds and can take the extra racing more easily. In the thoroughbred business we're trying to get more horses to the track to fill all these races. We've gone from seasonal racing to year-round racing. We even overlap in our racing meets. We're running horses night and day and using all the horses we've got. And now, with Texas, Indiana, and other states starting up racing, we're going to need even more horses. Thoroughbreds are going to be a big thing."

With people bailing out of the breeding business left and right, where does Heller think more thoroughbreds are going to come from? "Well, a lot of breeders have backed out," he acknowledged. "But I'm staying with it. I might lose for a year or two, but I'll get it all back. I have a feeling it's going to come back. I think people are going to be looking for thoroughbreds and buying anything and everything. Look at the two-year-old-in-training sale Barrett's just had down south. Sure, they had some great horses, but they still had an $84,000 average. We've never seen a sale like that in California before. Of course, I don't know how many games were played, how many horses were bought back. I don't know the whole program behind it. They might have had ringers out there to buy these horses and then they syndicate them later and say, 'We bought this horse for $200,000 and now we're syndicating him for fifteen percent above that.' A lot of scams go into this business. Of course, that potential exists in any kind of business. Racing has its problems, but nothing compared to, say, the stock market. Those guys are geniuses the way they put things together. Racing is a lot more regulated."

In terms of the general public's perception of corruption in racing, Heller countered, "It's important to emphasize that racing people are hardworking people. They really work for that buck. They're out there at five in the morning, and they often don't leave until late at night. If they've run a horse in the last race and they have to cool their horse out, they could be out there until eight or nine in the evening. Then all they have time to do is get something to eat and get to bed, because they have to be up at four-thirty the next morning. Racetrackers are a breed in their own, and you've got to be made for the life. It's a seven-day-a-week vocation, if you're really a racetracker. There's no days off with your horses. They've got to eat, they've got to be trained, they've got to be done every day. You've got to love what you're doing or you wouldn't be doing it."

Heller also has some strong feelings about making racing more attractive for its fans. "I would love to see the racetrack operators cater more to the fans. Racetracks shouldn't be so stingy. They should be more like a Las Vegas to their fans. They should get the high rollers to the track. So what if they comp a few people, give a few extra passes out. People are still going to eat, drink, and gamble. They're going to pay for themselves five times over if you get them there."

What about the little guy? I mentioned The Stone's lament when he said to me one day, "I've been playing the horses thirty-five years. As far as I'm concerned, they ought to give me a free pass. I can go to Reno and play the racing book for free. They even give you a *Racing Form*. The way it is at most tracks, you've already spent ten dollars with parking, admission, your program, and a *Form* before you've made your first bet."

Heller was sympathetic. "Racetracks are short-sighted in their thinking, because they don't understand that the little guy today could be the big guy tomorrow. They've got to get the little guys involved in it, because they don't know who's going to hit it in their business tomorrow and become the big spenders. Once somebody gets racing in their blood, they will be there night and day. Horseplayers are addicted. It's just like narcotics, just like alcohol. Gamblers Anonymous. It's an addictive vice, so it doesn't make any difference if he's little or big. If he's little, he may be big someday. And even if he's not, you need the people. You need the action, the turmoil. Even the little guy who only plays a few dollars, he's talking to everyone about how this one horse got beat or how he made the big score. And you know something, the guys he's talking to get a good taste for racing because he's so enthusiastic about it. What happens is they get curious and wind up coming with him one afternoon to find out about it. It's a subconscious deal, but that's the way it works."

As a promotion policy, what would Heller advise racetrack management to do? "Very simple. I would have free admission to the grandstand one day a week. Have fifty percent off on another day. They packed in the people at Golden Gate Fields a couple of years ago when John Crook was in charge and I screamed at him to do that. They had their big days during a Wednesday, a nothing day. So what if they lose two dollars a head when they come in there? If they buy a hot dog, buy a Coke, buy anything, the track will get that back, plus five percent of whatever goes through the mutuel."

Heller is also disappointed with the direction off-track betting is going. When he originally pushed for simulcasting, part of his philosophy was that off-track facilities would have bands on Friday nights where a husband and wife could come out and dance. "That didn't happen. Except at Pleasanton, where they put on a big feed on a Friday night now and they're packing them in. I went there one night just to see what was going on. They had almost nine hundred people in that little room. That's big action. This is what it was supposed to be all about. They only charge three dollars for these people to go in, and they watch it on TV. The simulcasts have helped double the purses. They bring people in when they give them free tote bags. How many people do you think would come if you told them admission was free? Management thinks that if a fan gets in free one day, he won't come another day. But that's dumb. All fans need is to find one horse they want to follow and they'll come back the next time he runs. I believe in promotion. I run a very successful jewelry business, with what's probably the highest-volume store in California, and I give a lot to the little guys. I bring them back. Once they get a taste. Once the wife gets an item that everyone says is beautiful, the guy can't go anyplace else because he knows if he comes to me she's gonna love it. The key to business is first getting them in and then selling them and trying to keep them happy. Sure, you can't please everybody, but if you make ninety-five percent of them happy, you'll do fine."

Heller concluded with what he considers a classic example of racing's ineptitude when it comes to promoting itself. "I'll show you how bad it is up here in northern California. We had, for the first time in history, an Eclipse Award winner in Brown Bess. How much front-page coverage did you see in the *The San Francisco Chronicle, The Oakland Tribune*, or the *Examiner*? I mean, considering the fact that northern California has never had an Eclipse Award winner before, and each year only seven or eight Eclipse Awards are given out for the whole world, why weren't people out there beating the drum? Sam Spear, with his television program, works his tail off to get publicity, and I'm one of his big backers. But where was the rest of it? They should have had front-page pictures of Brown Bess galloping as her trainer watched her work.

There should have been a headline saying BROWN BESS: AN ECLIPSE AWARD WINNER! And then the public should have been told that one of our homebred mares had gotten recognition as the best female turf horse in the world. Here was a great news story that should have been really played up, and it wasn't."

Ah yes, the story of Brown Bess! What were the odds of an owner with only one horse in training, and a nearly eight-year-old mare at that, winning an Eclipse Award? A million to one? Maybe more. But ever since I had hung out at the rail with Chuck Jenda and learned more about Brown Bess's background, it was clear to me that more than luck was involved and that Suzanne Pashayan, her owner, was an important part of the story.

On my way down to Fresno to talk with Pashayan, I recalled something Red Lowery had said about Brown Bess's success that stuck in my mind. I had commented to Red that at 850 pounds she was such a little mare and yet seemed to run, almost glide, with top weight so easily. "Yeah, and when she was a young horse," Red had countered in his inimitable way, "she couldn't do nothin' easy. Brown Bess had her problems early on, but Jenda and the owner took their time and now it's paid off. It's a great story, a Cinderella story. That's the way racing has been for years. You have to play the cards that are dealt to you. Success in racing is how you play the cards that are dealt to you. It's what you do with what you got." Well, Suzanne Pashayan had played her cards right, and the horse gods had allowed her to draw to an inside, royal straight flush.

When I arrived, Pashayan was in the training arena at Sunnyside Ranch working Petronian, Brown Bess's three-quarter-brother, around some dressage techniques. Petronian, she told me, hadn't shown enough to be a racehorse, so she was in the process of converting him into a show horse. I leaned against the arena fence and watched as she gave verbal commands and tapped the ground to direct the horse. Between gasps of breath, Suzanne called out and explained that mastering dressage, one of the most difficult forms of horsemanship, is her ongoing passion. When she isn't helping run the family tire and horse businesses or campaigning for her brother, Congressman Charles Pashayan, Jr., she spends her time training her show horses.

Twenty minutes later, with Petronian back in his stall, Suzanne eased herself into a redwood chair and told me she started up with horses as a girl of eleven. A friend of the family gave her a thoroughbred show horse in 1955, and it wasn't long before Suzanne became fascinated with pedigrees and persuaded her family to get into racing. She prodded her father, who, with one of his friends, purchased two fillies at a Del Mar yearling sale in 1957. The family breeding and racing operation, Calbourne Farm, got its first big boost with the purchase of its foundation brood mare Duchess Doreen for $4,500 at a CTBA breeders sale in 1962.

It was Suzanne who came up with the name Calbourne Farms. "It's a combination of Calumet and Claiborne Farms. I threw a *U* in just to make it different. Calumet and Claiborne were the two most successful breeding farms in racing history when I started. So I just threw them together and thought maybe it would bring me good luck. And to a certain extent it has."

I was curious how many horses Suzanne, who has never had more than a few brood mares at one time, had to breed before she got Brown Bess. "You know, I have no idea. I never thought I'd be asked a question like that, so I never kept track of every horse we've bred. I had been breeding mares for a number of years before I got Duchess Doreen. I had bred and raced some good horses, including the mare Never More. Duchess Doreen was in foal to Noor when we bought her out of the Ridgewood dispersal. She had Moog and I took it from there. We raced Moog, who was stakes-placed, and then retired her and bred foals out of her. Moog's best racehorse was Fingal. He was by Gaelic Dancer and raced until he was nine. Fingal won twenty-four of sixty-six starts and earned almost $400,000. I also had some breeding success with several other stakes horses, including Rigatoni King and American Grit. I bred Moog to Windy Sands and got Chickadee, who won five races and was also stakes-placed. Then I bred Chickadee to Petrone to get Brown Bess."

I couldn't help but think of W. C. Fields's *My Little Chickadee*.

I asked Suzanne if there was any connection. "Of course!" She laughed and mimicked Fields's droll style. "I get a kick out of watching old W. C. Fields movies. But I also think chickadees are cute little birds. So it was him and the bird that led me to the name Chickadee."

Since Suzanne has developed a definite philosophy of horsemanship, I asked her to talk about it, using Brown Bess as an example. "Well, I like to give my young horses plenty of time. I don't like to race them before they're three. Brown Bess was raised locally at my old thoroughbred farm in Sanger and then taken to nearby Silver D-Bar, which is a training ranch, in the fall of her yearling year. Her groundwork, things like long-lining and lunging, was done there. We also got her used to the bit and saddled her up with all the equipment. But no weight was put on her back until after she was two. She then was broken at Silver D-Bar and ridden for two months. After that I turned Brown Bess out until she was three, at which time we started her back in training at Silver D-Bar, and then sent her to Danny Morgan in Pleasanton for a while before going on to Chuck Jenda. I do that with all my horses, send them to Pleasanton first, in order to psychologically acclimate them to being around other horses and the activity of racing. That way they won't be in shock when they get to Bay Meadows or Golden Gate Fields. You can take a horse out to the gate in the afternoon at Pleasanton and get them used to it. You can't do that at the racetrack during a meet. After training hours are over in the morning, that's it. They have to prepare the track for the afternoon races. So if you have a horse that is a bit of a problem, a place like Pleasanton gives you a little more time to work with them. Generally, I think it's a good idea to kind of ease them in like that, because it keeps things more pleasant for them."

Suzanne is following the same pattern with Wolf Whistle, a two-year-old cousin to Brown Bess that she is high on. "Wolf Whistle is with Danny Morgan now. If she stays sound and everything goes all right, she'll make the move to Chuck Jenda's barn in the spring."

Since anything can happen with a racehorse, especially a two-year-old, I asked Suzanne what she would do if Wolf Whistle doesn't stay sound. "If it's an injury that with time will heal," she replied, "I'll give her the time. If time won't help, then we'll just make a brood mare out of her. That's where the difference is. You have to be able to judge the difference. There are some injuries that no matter how much time you give them, they aren't going to come back and be worth anything. In those cases you have to use your head, because it's really hard on a horse if you keep turning them out and bringing them back and trying again and it's not doing any good."

Brown Bess had had some physical problems as a young horse, but Suzanne had stuck with her. I wondered if there was anything distinctive about "Bessie" that had justified her patience. "Well, physically she was rather smallish, but she was always a very willing horse, even as a two-year-old, and liked to train on the track. That probably influenced me some. When she developed her check ligament problem at three and then again at five, I just felt I wanted to give her time to see what would happen with her. You really never know how good a horse is going to get. It's nice, of course, when they develop. People say Brown Bess was a late bloomer, but as far as late bloomers go, you have to ask yourself this question: If horses were allowed to develop, how long would they really last on the racetrack? The answer would be, I think, that people are in too big a hurry. Too much emphasis is placed on racing two-year-olds. Some of the purses on two-year-old stakes are so big that most people can't resist them. Too many horses are not allowed to mature, and a lot of the attitudes toward racing older horses are based on obsolete notions. The old school said that you shouldn't race horses after they're four. They thought fillies shouldn't be raced after four because it would hurt them on the reproductive end. I think that when you retire a horse from racing, either they're going to produce or not produce. The only thing, in my opinion, that messes a mare up, as far as reproducing goes, is when you pump them full of certain drugs. Like if they have an injury and you treat them with steroids and cortisone and similar medications to keep them running. I think that might have an effect on a mare's fertility. With humans, I think there have been a lot of famous women runners who have had perfectly healthy children. So I think the idea that keeping a filly or mare on the track for a length of time hurts it reproductively is a questionable one. There are a lot of mares that, if you only ran them one season, still would have reproductive problems. I think it's just a matter of luck and nature."

The idea that good horses shouldn't be raced beyond their fourth year was championed by the famous Italian breeder and trainer Federico Tesio. He believed that horses only have so much vital energy and that if you race them too hard, they will lose it on the reproductive side. About Tesio's influence Suzanne reflected, "He had a lot of interesting theories. I mean, the man was obviously brilliant, because he bred twenty-one Italian Derby winners. He also had other theories about color and white markings. He felt if a horse had white on his legs, it meant he's weaker there and would have more leg problems. For him gray was not a color, but a disease of the skin. He also had two thoroughbred farms and moved his horses seasonally like they would naturally roam if they were out in the wild. In the wintertime he'd move them to the south, and in the summertime to the north. He had his own ideas about training his horses. Europeans train their horses differently than we do. They don't put so much emphasis on early speed."

It was interesting to me that Pashayan had chosen Petrone as Brown Bess's sire. Looking at his record I could see a strong European influence. He had won four races in France before coming to the United States. Prominent in his pedigree were French horses like Prince Bio, Wild Risk, and Salome, but he was also backed up with British and Italian genes tracing to Mumtaz Begum and Nearco. I asked Suzanne why she had bred to the stallion. "I always liked Petrone," she enthused. "From the day I first saw him over at Flags Up Farm, I liked the horse. I just thought he was a tremendous individual, a very good racehorse. After all, he won two very good distance races here in California and, I believe, set American records in both those races. The San Juan was a mile and three-quarters and the Sunset is a mile and a half. He was also a very well bred horse. I think Petrone has been a very overlooked horse in the breeding program here in California. He offers the stamina that we need in this state."

Pashayan was alluding to the tendency among California breeders to overemphasize early speed in the horses they breed. About Petrone's fate she lamented, "He's an old horse now. He's twenty-five years old. I've been breeding to him off and on for years. In fact, Chickadee is back in foal to him right now. It's unfortunate that more attention wasn't paid to Petrone when he was younger, because he wasn't bred to the best mares, and he doesn't have very many sons at stud that will carry on his line. He's still capable of a few more crops, though, and he's got Silveyville. That's his best racehorse, at stud, and I hope he does well. Kjell Qvale, Silveyville's owner, is breeding a lot of mares to him, but we'll have to wait until his foals hit the grass to see what happens. It might turn out that Petrone's most lasting influence will be as a brood mare sire."

Every owner-breeder has to decide at some point between continuing to race a horse and breeding it. I asked Suzanne to talk about the factors that go into making that decision. "Of course, it varies according to each case," she emphasized. "But generally, the physical condition of a horse has something to do with it. Obviously, if a horse hurts himself and can't run anymore, that ends it right there. I think if you just feel the horse has had enough or the horse has told you it's had enough, you're not going to run it anymore. With a filly or mare, if a particular stallion is retired to stud and you'd like to breed her, that might dictate stopping on her. Or you might be an owner who doesn't want to get into breeding but feels now is the most opportune time to sell her and get the best price you can. That would also dictate a horse not running anymore. And, of course, with a good colt you have to look at soundness and pedigree and compare how much he can earn on the track as opposed to the breeding shed."

Though Brown Bess will clearly attract some of the top stallions when the decision to breed her is made, for now Pashayan is playing her cards close to her vest. "I don't know when I'll breed her," she told me. "It's a question I can't answer, because it wouldn't be fair to answer it one way or the other right now. The horse will tell us, let us know what to do. Basically Chuck and I will just watch her condition, mentally and physically, and see how she goes along and make our decisions from that."

I was interested in how Chuck Jenda had become Suzanne's trainer. "Very simple. I wanted to change trainers. So I called Willie Williamson, the manager of Los Cerritos, because I knew that Chuck Jenda had been training for his boss, Bill Pascoe, for a while. I asked Willie, 'How long has Chuck been training for Los Cerritos?' He said, 'Ten years. He's been doing a pretty good job.' I said, 'Well, that's good enough for me. If he can last with W. T. Pascoe for ten years, that's all I need to know.' "

It seemed more than accidental that, in picking Jenda, Suzanne had chosen someone with a reputation for patience and resisting the temptation to run a horse when it's not right. She agreed but added, "In the relationship between owners and trainers, if an owner can give that extra time, I think a lot of trainers would take it. But it works both ways. What you need is good communication between an owner and trainer, so they both realize they don't have to rush a horse."

Pashayan also had some advice for owners thinking about getting into the business. "I think people should learn as much as they can before they spend their money. They should never forget good business principles. Like in any business, you shouldn't spend more than you can afford. You have to keep your eyes and ears open and remember you're always learning something. Don't think you know everything, because that's when you get into trouble. If you have a flexible mind and are willing to give yourself that advantage, you're going to do better."

Pashayan cautioned it's dangerous for people to come into the game and assume that, because they've been successful and made money in other businesses, horse racing will be the same. "There are a lot of people who think all they have to do is spend money and they'll make money. While there have been some people who have come into racing like that and done very well, that's not usually the case. That's why you shouldn't spend beyond your means."

When it comes time for a fledgling owner to select a trainer, Pashayan feels it is important to go to the barns and talk to several of them. "After all, the trainer is going to be your employee. If you are going to hire someone to work at your company, you talk to several people before you make your selection, right? I think selecting a trainer is no different than how you would hire someone for your business. You should go on their background, how they present themselves, and their principles and philosophy of training horses. You should use common sense, trust your gut feelings, and don't be afraid that if you select a trainer and it doesn't work out that you can't change trainers. Because that happens all the time. Part of being a trainer is accepting the fact that an owner may want to change trainers. No trainer has the right to tell an owner he can't change trainers. That's an owner's prerogative, because the bottom line is that the trainer is an employee."

Of course, a lot of trainers resist being reduced to the status of employees. From their perspective, most owners are ignorant and should gladly pay the bills without asking any meddlesome questions. "I know that," Pashayan reflected, "but that's the way it is. A condescending attitude really isn't fair to an owner, because after all he is paying that person to train their horses for them and that's where it stands."

Deciding to switch trainers is always difficult. "It's tough," Pashayan admits, "because a lot of times if you take a horse from one trainer, give it to another, and that horse just jumps up and starts winning races, you start saying to yourself, 'Gosh, if I had just had my horses with this new trainer look what he could have done before.' But maybe the other trainer had the horse ready to win. If you switch, you can't second-guess yourself. You picked a trainer and he didn't do well, and now with your new one everything is okay. That's part of horse racing. You have your ups and downs."

Then there is the matter of how far a neophyte owner should defer to a trainer's judgment in where to run a horse, especially if the trainer wants to run it for a tag. "Well, there should be good communication between an owner and a trainer, no matter what level the owner is at as far as knowledge is concerned. There are a lot of owners who come into racing that don't know anything. It would be very difficult for them to judge where to place a horse, because they just don't know. But a trainer should try and educate them as much as possible and present his position on where to run a horse based on his experience. Trainers should also recognize that there are owners who have been around long enough, have

256

enough knowledge, so they should have good communication in deciding where to run a particular horse."

I was curious if Suzanne had ever run a horse for a tag at a trainer's suggestion and lost it to the claiming box. If so, how did she feel about it? "Yes, I have lost horses," she said. "But that's a tough question for me to answer, because I don't want to make any trainer look bad. Because, you see, at the time the decision was made, it was made at that time. And, of course, down the road—if you lose the horse, and they turn around and do really well—the first thing you're going to say is, 'Gosh, we shouldn't have done it.' And the next thing you're gonna say is, 'The doggone trainer talked me into it.' And that may not have been the case. Hindsight is always twenty-twenty."

Pashayan believes that most often, when an owner and trainer drop a horse down in a claiming race, there's usually a good reason. "Either the horse can't run, or he's got a problem and they don't want to deal with it. Then too, a lot of owners want their horses to be claimed because that's basically their business. They may be breeders, pinhookers, and trainers who like to develop young horses but don't want to be at the track all the time. They bring a horse so far, they run them and hope they get claimed and then go out and breed or buy another horse. People who enter their horses into claiming races for the purpose of selling them want them to do well, because then more people will claim from them in the future. So you see, there are several different answers to your question of losing a horse. You can't bring it down to just one situation or person."

Our discussion about losing a horse to the claiming box wasn't just academic. As a breeder and owner, Pashayan had risked losing Brown Bess in her fifth race for a $50,000 tag at Bay Meadows. At the time, the four-year-old filly had only broken her maiden and was coming off a bad race at odds of fifty-three to one. So the risk of her getting claimed wasn't high. But if she had been claimed, a $50,000 return, by the lights of most breeders, wouldn't have been too shabby. The downside of the gamble, of course, was, "If someone had claimed Brown Bess and she went on to do for them what she's done for us, how would we have felt then? On the other hand, suppose they claimed her and we never heard of or saw her again? We would have said, 'Wow, I'm glad we got rid of that one.' "

Owners, like fans, have opinions about the jockeys who ride their horses. I asked Suzanne, as a horse person and owner of Brown Bess, what Jack Kaenel does that is particularly good. "I think Jack's very patient as far as Brown Bess is concerned. He uses very good judgment in evaluating a race instantly to see where he should be in that race. If you watch all the different tapes of Brown Bess's races, you'll see that Jack doesn't always ride her the way he did in the Yellow Ribbon. He puts her in different places depending upon how the race comes up. You can have a plan, but a lot of times a race doesn't come up that way and you have to adjust. I think a horse with the class, tactical speed, and smartness that Brown Bess has is probably easier for Jack to ride like that."

Smartness in a horse, however, can cut two ways. "A horse can be smart and like what they're doing or they can be smart and know that they don't want to get involved. When they're contrary, it's like they're saying. 'Nana-nana-na-na, I'm smart enough to know that I'm not gonna do this. Boy, I'll show you.' A really good racehorse is probably a very intelligent horse and, of course, has the competitiveness to hang in there. By intelligence I mean the horse is aware of what he has to do and that makes it easier to train him. I'm not saying that all good horses make it easier. Some of them have nasty temperaments, like Gate Dancer and John Henry. Others won't work in the morning, like Buckpasser. He hated to work in the morning. He had to have four horses go out with him. But I think he knew what was expected of him in the afternoons, and he went out there and did his job. Real racehorses are professionals."

Pashayan is, of course, well aware that a horse like Brown Bess doesn't come along very often. Most owners consistently lose money in their quest to visit the Winner's Circle. In 1989, fewer than half of the 91,000 horses in training around the country won a race, and only twelve percent of them earned enough to pay for the cost of their training. "You always want to visit the Winner's Circle," Suzanne agreed. "That's what keeps you going. Winning is the fruit of your labors. You've been patient and worked your way through all the problems and now you've seen some success. It's like raising a child. You take care of them when they're little, then hopefully when they grow up they will be a success. When your horse wins, then you really feel like the whole thing is worth it."

Our conversation had essentially circled back to the importance of patience. Yet a lot of horsemen, on the claiming side or with small stables and shoestring operations, consider it a luxury when I bring up a horse like Brown Bess as an example. "Well, when you have the bucks," they'll almost universally respond, "it's a lot easier to have the patience."

In conclusion I asked Suzanne how she would respond to that argument. "Well, racing horses is very expensive," she acknowledged. "It's quite an investment at any level. For most people, spending a few thousand dollars for a horse is a lot of money. For others, spending a million dollars is a lot. It all depends upon what you have and can afford. But some things you can't get away from. If the welfare of the horse is connected to the economics—where you have to run a horse that is not truly able to run, to survive economically—then I think you're in real trouble."

10

MATCHMAKER
The Racing Secretary

*I*t was a sunny Wednesday morning, about forty minutes before the first race, and Panama was in his usual spot in the grandstand sipping coffee and noting late scratches, first-time Lasix horses, and equipment changes on his *Daily Racing Form.* When I sat down next to him, he was still shaking his head about the race that Stalwart Charger, a rapidly developing three-year-old, had run the previous Saturday afternoon. "Man," he marveled, "he just crushed that field in the California Derby. Did you see those fractions, :21.4, :44.4, 1:08.3, and 1:34 for the mile? Gonzales just geared him down the final eighth and he finished up with an easy 1:46 and change. Too bad he's not nominated for any of the Triple Crown races. He might give Summer Squall and Mr. Frisky a run for their money."

Panama was less enthused, however, with the card in front of him. "Boy, they're really scraping the bottom of the barrel today," he remarked. "Seven of the races on the card are for cheap maidens and claimers. Umphrey must have blown his wad on that great card Saturday."

Panama was referring, of course, to Robert Umphrey, Racing Secretary at Golden Gate Fields, whose responsibility it is to write the conditions, bring in the horses, and dole out the purse money for every race of the 110-day meet. In the process he not only exerts considerable influence on the texture of the daily cards, but sometimes even on the outcome of particular races. As Chief Steward Leon Lewis had observed, Umphrey's function is a lot like being the powerful director of a theatrical event.

Bob Umphrey, for his part, doesn't quite see his job that way. "Basically," he countered in his office one morning, "I'm a placator. My job is to placate Ladbroke, Peter Tunney, the horsemen, the owners, and the fans. You walk a tenuous line, to say the least, as a racing secretary."

The thirty-seven-year-old Umphrey, whose personality combines equal parts of cynicism and charm, comes from a family with deep roots in racing. He grew up in Hallandale, Florida, about ten minutes from Gulfstream Park, where his father trained for a while and then was an assistant trainer to some big outfits like Bud Lepman's, Joe Bollero's, and T. W. Kelley's.

"I'm a racetrack brat," Umphrey explained with an amused smile. "I worked rubbing horses every summer and during school vacations from the time I was ten years old. That's where I got my money to go to school. It's the only business I ever worked in. I mean, I've had a paper route and worked at the track. That's it. I've never been in the real world. There's that old saying, 'You think those fences are to keep people out? Well, buddy, they're to keep us in.'"

Umphrey confided that he originally wanted to be a veterinarian. "I enrolled in the prevet program at the University of Florida, but then realized I wasn't diligent or intelligent enough to become a vet. Man, you really had to pound those books. Then I thought about becoming a trainer—but that's a tough racket, what with the help situation and a lot of heartbreak with the horses. So, I wound up with a degree in marketing. I think I made the right move getting into this end of the business. It's a little more secure, with the opportunity to take some time off. I only like to work about nine months a year. That's all you can work in this business without getting burned out."

After graduating from Florida, Umphrey started off as a clerk doing past-performance charts in the racing office at Gulfstream. "That's the way everybody starts," he explained. "Then, if you're ambitious, you become a patrol judge or placing judge, move up to assistant racing secretary and finally, if you're crazy enough to take the job, you become the racing secretary. Things went real fast for me because I was raised in the business, had a real good grasp of the job, and knew a lot of people."

By the time he was thirty, Bob Umphrey was racing secretary at Hollywood Park and helped organize the first Breeders' Cup. "That was really nice," he reminisced. "I could hardly believe it. Dealing with the quality of the horses at Hollywood Park during the regular meet was also really interesting. But then things got to the point where I just wasn't happy."

The source of Umphrey's unhappiness was Marjorie Everett, the notorious majority stockholder at Hollywood Park, who among other things liked to terrorize trainers by mailing out copies of each new Condition Book to all the owners. "I said to myself, 'What am I doing working here for this crazy lady? I've got to be nuts. I'm not going to last very long.' So the opportunity showed up here and I availed myself of it. I loved the big horses down there and everything about it. I just couldn't work for Marje Everett anymore. I would never have left if it weren't for her. She made my life too miserable. I couldn't print anything out on schedule. Everything I did she started to second-guess. She wouldn't let me do my job."

Umphrey elaborated about the kind of racetrack politics at Hollywood Park that led to his moving north. "The first two and a half years were fine. But things started to unravel with a horse called Greinton, who was trying to win the California Golden Triple, a series of crazy races that Marje dreamed up. The three races involved were the Californian, The Hollywood Gold Cup, and the Sunset. For the Californian, a horse had to win going a mile around one turn on the main track at Hollywood Park. The Gold Cup was at 1¼ miles on the dirt and the Sunset was 1½ miles on the grass. I didn't think you could breed a horse capable of doing all that. I said to Marje, 'What kind of horse is going to do this? Why even bother to get the insurance policy?' But we did, for a million, and Charlie Whittingham had a little horse called Greinton that ran like :32.2 and won the mile race over Precisionist. Then he won the Gold Cup. And now we're to the 1½-mile Sunset on the grass, which is a handicap race. So I put 121 pounds on the horse. I thought that was tough. Greinton wasn't really a 1½-mile horse and had only been winning on the dirt. Well, Marje flipped out. I said, 'Listen, lady, you do everything else around here, you can weight the horse, too.' "

From then on it got uglier. "Greinton almost won the Sunset. He got beat by a Jerry Fanning horse, King's Isle, by about a nose. King's Isle broke down after the race. But it was unbelievable. The insurance company, before the race, said that Whittingham had got to me. Oh, it was beautiful. They didn't want to pay off. They said I should have handicapped for scale weights. I said to them, 'Do you know what scale weights are?' They said 'No.' I said, 'Why then they'd all be equal, you idiots. Get outta here. I have Greinton at 121 and he's giving six pounds to the next best horse and you want them even? Well, be my guest. Go Charlie!' It was nuts."

After that it was just a question of when Umphrey could get out of town. He moved up to northern California in 1986 and has been Racing Secretary at Golden Gate Fields ever since, while also helping out in the racing office and working as a placing judge at Bay Meadows during their meets.

Umphrey elaborated on the description of a placing judge's job that Leon Lewis had given me. "You start off by posting the numbers as the horses are running. You call over and tell the people running the tote board what numbers to put up. And then when they hit the wire you write on your program how you see the finish. For instance, it might be 3-2-Photo 4-1. In that case, we'll tell them to hang up the 3-2 and then look at the photo for the show. Even though we know the order of finish a lot of times, we always put up the photo for anything less than a half-length as a safety factor. If you don't do that, pretty soon you keep getting finer and finer until you get like Larry Collmus, that wacko announcer of ours, and start calling whisker finishes. Larry likes to take his shots calling those close finishes.

"The actual photo for judging the finish," Umphrey explained, "comes from a narrow strip that is part of a running film." You can't get several angles on the finish, but the photo finish does show the horses crossing an imaginary line as each nose crosses the wire. If it appears that two or more noses are on the line, Humphrey continues, "you don't want to be separating the horses. You want to make a decision that you can live with and show. My attitude is, 'Hey, I'm not splitting these horses.' I mean, we're talking about maybe a hundredth of a second or something. In those cases I just dead-heat them. I think you're better off making two winners, even though they pay half as much."

Umphrey's job as racing secretary, however, is another kettle of fish. Just looking at his desk tells you a lot about the nature of his job. The first thing you notice lying across its breadth—like a flowchart of the entire meet—is a large cardboard calendar upon which he has listed, in pencil, the races that are scheduled to run in the future. The pencil is important, because Umphrey often can't find enough horses to fill a particular race and has to write in a last-minute substitute. Usually it's one of those ubiquitous bottom-level maiden or claiming races that make fans groan. Besides his calendar, Umphrey's desk is also covered with bound copies of every serious handicapper's best friend, the recap charts from the *Racing Form*. "Recap charts are a constant in this job," he explained. "We'll have a race with five horses in it and I have to go searching back through the charts and find some other horses that have run against them and then convince their trainers it's a good spot to run in. An incredible number of the horses we ask to run in a race do win. We call them the 'hustle' horses. We hustle a lot of winners, because the spot may not look that good in the Condition Book, but we know who's in it. A lot of times a non-winners-other-than-allowance race may be easier than a $25,000 claimer, and we'll mention that to a trainer. So we use the charts quite a bit as a reference point to hustle horses for upcoming stakes, things like that. Charts are one of my most valuable tools, for sure."

I was interested in the broad context within which Umphrey's job is defined. At the beginning of each meet, he told me, he guesstimates the amount of purse money he will have to distribute to the horsemen and then figures out how many races, in each category, he should write into the Condition Book to take care of everyone's needs. Usually Umphrey projects the amount of purse money he will have based on the horsemen's 5.5 percent share of the previous meet's betting handle and builds from there. "Like this year we have a situation where we're going to have Santa Clara simulcasting from the beginning of the meet. We have Vallejo on line, so that will give us an increase. But we're also going to take a hit here, because we'll lose some on-site attendance."

I was curious how Umphrey felt about simulcasting and off-track betting. Many horsemen and fans fear that, with the escalating costs of urban real estate and the growth of off-track betting, racing may well become primarily a studio sport, with only a few tracks running live races and the rest of the country receiving their satellite signal. Is it the case that off-track sites really generate more revenue? "They do," Umphrey replied, "but we don't realize as much as people think. You have partners when you have off-track betting. Everyone wants their piece. So you take a hit on track, when you have another site. Especially when you have something like Vallejo, which is only twenty miles away."

Does the same relationship hold with simulcasting? "For sure. Let's say we simulcast from Santa Anita. We have to cut up the income with them and then the off-track sites as well. So those races really get cut up. We realize a lot more money on our own races. We're of the opinion here at Golden Gate Fields that simulcasts are good to the extent that it's a race worth watching. We're not going to simulcast a race to increase the handle, but because it's a race fans want to see. Like last week we took a race from Santa Anita because Brown Bess was going in it. If she wasn't in the race, I couldn't have cared less about that race. I loved the horses that were in it, but as far as bringing that race and making our card longer, there wouldn't have been any reason to do it without Brown Bess."

Umphrey put his corporate hat on and gave me a breakdown of the numbers he works with. "This year, we predicted that we would have a total handle of $317 million in 110 days. That included off-track betting, simulcasts, the whole works. From that we originally figured we would have an average of $117,000 a day in overnight purse money to distribute. Then there's another $30,000 a day that we set aside for the stakes program. So we're generating about $150,000 a day for purses, and I take that and try to get the most for my money when I write the races for the Condition Book."

Umphrey distributes the purse money by writing so many maiden and claiming races, allowance races, overnight handicaps, and then stakes races. He has to distribute the purse money in such a way that he gets at least nine races for every card. The more money he puts on the high end for stakes races, the less money is available for midrange races and the more cheap races he has to card. Almost always, the average purse money distributed on the weekends is higher than during the week, because that's when attendance and the betting handle are greatest and the big stakes races are run.

Umphrey elaborated. "Yesterday was kind of low for a Saturday—we only wrote races for $108,000. But we had a stakes race for $50,000 too, so actually our total purse distribution was $158,000. Through the first thirty-eight racing days, I've given out $4,361,000. I'm currently averaging $114,776 a day in overnight money. We projected $117,000 a day, but management is a little leery because some of the satellite facilities aren't doing as well as we thought they might. We budgeted Santa Clara at $200,000 a day, which would be a heck of a nice satellite. But they haven't really made that place into what they should. I haven't been down there, I should go take a look at it. I've heard the location isn't good, the amenities aren't good, they give the fans nothing. If we could cultivate the Santa Clara–San Jose market, that would really help us get more purse money for the horsemen here in northern California."

Since San Jose is much closer to Bay Meadows, I wondered how that affected the on-site handle there. "They get hurt at Bay Meadows. There's always a struggle between host tracks and satellites for 'impact' fees because of that problem. For every person who comes to San Jose, the satellite there has to give Bay Meadows three dollars for the right to the signal. But it doesn't matter to San Jose, because otherwise they'd have nothing. It's just a matter of how much they're going to make. If San Jose would improve their amenities, everyone would benefit. It's just a shame that it's not run better and that we don't get to run the satellite sites. They're all run by local Fair people. You have to be a Fair site in California to get the signal. So it's not like the people in San Jose or Pleasanton are a bunch of guys who got together and said, 'Let's open a parlor.' Pleasanton is a very good site. They're really going for it. And it's stupid not to, because all you're going to do is make money, if you do it right with a good restaurant and a nice atmosphere. The more conveniences and things you do for your fans, the more money you're going to make. But some of these places are just backwards, and San Jose is a prime example. Managed right, that site could easily generate $300,000 to $400,000 a day. Instead they have some dumpy building down there that nobody wants to go to."

If one side of Umphrey's job is to write races and distribute purse money, just as important is assigning stall space and finding the horses to run in them. I asked him how many horses were on the backside. "We probably have 1,300 at Golden Gate and another 800 at Bay Meadows, of which maybe 350 are utilizable. Then we get horses from Pleasanton, Sacramento, and Santa Rosa. The total pool of horses that could run within the next thirty days is about 2,200 horses."

Surprisingly, no statistics are kept on the age distribution of those horses. "That's a good question," Umphrey noted. "I never thought about that. I've been pretty disappointed with the three-year-olds so far. A lot of the races have been weak, especially the stakes. Just looking at my calendar here, I'd guess maybe twenty to twenty-five percent of the horses are three-year-olds. Two-year-olds are a little more difficult to say. Like right now, on March fifteenth, they're not even supposed to be on the grounds. But I know they're here. I'm not blind. We have some trainers here that ship out their sore and tired horses and sneak in their two-year-olds into those stalls as early as January, even though they're supposed to wait until April first. They're just trying to get the jump on everybody. The ideal situation is to have all of them training at Bay Meadows during our meet. But unfortunately, with the evening quarter-horse meet on over there, there's a range war going on for stalls. It's ugly. We kind of resist the quarter horse meet because we know it has to hurt the handle for thoroughbred racing. Peter Tunney, our general manager, doesn't think so, but I tell him he's crazy. Anytime there's $400,000 being wagered at night, it has to have an effect on us. If a handicapper got banged last night, how is he gonna come back today? You could hit the ninth-race exacta here for $400 and go lose it at the quarters and come out empty. So it's got to be a drag, especially with the hard-core players."

Umphrey thought the best gauge for how many two-year-olds are running is to look at the Bay Meadows fall meet. "Over there," he guessed, "they probably have twenty-five percent two-year-olds, thirty percent three-year-olds, and the rest would be older horses. What really bothers me is not so much the age distribution as the number of maidens we have here. Out of that pool of 2,200 horses I mentioned, probably at least 1,100, or fifty percent, of them are maidens. And of the maidens, probably 750 or 800 of them want to run at the bottom for twelve-five. So that's part of the problem, there's too many bad horses."

I told Umphrey that from a fan's point of view, I'd rather have maidens than those cheap sixty-two-five claimers running all the time. At least there's some potential mystery there. Once in a while a good horse will jump out of one of those races and go up the ladder. "Oh yeah, they're ugly," Umphrey agreed. "Those sixty-two-five claiming races get pretty tiring. But talk about mysteries: how did twenty-two tickets get five out of six yesterday? It was one of the worst cards I've ever written. I said to myself, 'Well, there's only one good thing about this card, it will get me a Pick Six carryover.' After the first two races, which were pretty good prices, they started coming pretty much to form and I thought to myself, 'I may not even have a carryover with this lousy card.' In the last race the long-shot winner, Hronec's horse, just held on for the last jump. I think she was the only horse that would have given me a carryover. I love carryovers for the simple fact that it gives me more purse money. From my standpoint, it's one way to get more people here. I like to see it get really big and then for thirty people to hit it. I don't like to see one guy hit it for $98,000, because I know that money's gone out of the system. If twenty people hit it for $5,000, you know they're gonna put some of that back in the ninth and tenth races. I know there are arguments against the Pick Six, but I like it. And you know something, these are good handicappers in the Bay Area. These people are tough. It's amazing how many days I think it's impossible to hit the Pick Six and someone pops for it."

Panama and I have often wondered how many big tickets are played when there's a large Pick Six carryover. Rumors abound in the grandstand about big syndicate action. "I'd have to say that there are some big tickets played," Umphrey agreed. "But they don't necessarily hit it. People think that you need a $90 horse to get a carryover. But that's bullshit. That's the horse the big ticket players will have. It's the contentious race where there's five or six horses that they get burned, because even big ticket players have to single a few races. I mean, unless you go totally crazy, you have to single about three races. You have to beat a Terry Knight or Jerry Hollendorfer horse. If one of their horses gets beat, then that's where you help your chances with the carryover. The $90 horse doesn't help you because it's usually a maiden twelve-five and the big players just go all. The small player is only going to beat the big player by hitting on a singleton that they miss."

Our discussion moved to the kinds of races Umphrey writes. Bill Morey had complained there isn't as much purse money for mid-range horses as he would like to see. The result is that owners pull their good claiming horses from local trainers and send them to Hollywood Park and Santa Anita, where the purses are better. Morey feels that less money should go to the big stakes and more to the midrange races. Umphrey had a counter-proposal. "I've got a question for Bill. Why do we give these cheap beetles $6,500 for breaking their maidens? They should be getting $3,000. If there's less money made available at the bottom, maybe we'll get rid of some of these bad horses and improve the quality of racing. There are too many people who keep bad horses in training and, even though you and I aren't horse trainers, we know that these horses are never going to win. They just keep soaking these owners for forty dollars a day. I'm not talking about Bill Morey here, he runs a very good outfit. He wins. But there's so many people that try to make it on day money and on some horse that can't ever win. Instead of telling an owner after his horse works five-eighths in 1:04 in a drive that his horse can't run, they just string him along. Wouldn't it be better to tell that owner to save the training expenses and try with another horse? There's just too many people taking up stalls and hurting their owners because they have no chance. There are some trainers here who if they beat another horse it's almost a miracle. We have a trainer here who's got a horse that's ineligible. So she'll ship it to Portland and get it eligible again. This horse will come back, but it will never win. It's a dog. A lot of these horses are jokes."

I was curious how Umphrey felt about qualifying races as a means of upgrading the racing program on the bottom level. Would it be unrealistic to implement something like Red Lowery's proposal? "No, it's not unrealistic at all. They do it at the Kennel Club," he teased. "The quarter horses do it. Here all they have to do is get an okay from the gate and have three works at five-eighths of a mile. I mean some of these owners are really duped into believing their horses have a chance to win. We already have some eligibility rules, and I'm all for tightening them even further."

In that regard, Umphrey has done some things that haven't made him very popular with a number of trainers. "These cheap maiden races for four-year-olds and up. If they've had three or four starts and not finished in the top four, they go to the back of the bus. It's true that some horses fall in the cracks. They may have been running down south for $50,000, but you've got to do something. What's the use of letting these proven losers in again when Bill Morey has a horse that got hurt as a three-year-old and is now coming back cheap, but he can run. Bill's horse might be a useful horse, but he can't get his horse in because these other horses that go off at a hundred to one keep getting in. The horsemen didn't like my tightening of conditions for older maidens at first, but now they're seeing the merits of it. It helps make those maiden twelve-five races a bit more palatable. Now, I'm just talking about older maidens. With the three-year-olds, I think you have to give them more chances to develop."

Since there are some 7,600 thoroughbreds in training in California, with another 20,000 out on the farm, it would appear that there are plenty of horses around from which to upgrade the caliber of racing. But Umphrey thinks those statistics are misleading. "Those numbers include brood mares, yearlings, and weanlings," he pointed out. "Tommy Robbins, the racing secretary at Santa Anita, probably draws from a pool of 5,000 horses, and now with the two-year-olds, it's probably higher than that. I've got around 2,500 horses to draw from up here."

Nevertheless, Umphrey explained, he still has to write a lot of cheap maiden and claiming races, because "There just aren't enough good horses to go around. It used to be during the fairs you could lay up. But now with someone like Greg Brent over at Pleasanton writing an allowance race with a $23,000 purse during the summer, how the hell are you going to lay up? The money's too good. The truth is that there are only so many starts in a horse, and year-round racing has exacted a heavy toll. Right now, we're dancing to keep even. There's just too much racing. Horses used to come here and then go to L.A. Well, now they never stop. You look at Pomona right now, with Santa Anita going, and they're writing $50,000 allowance races. At one point of the year you've got Santa Rosa, the Orange County Fair, and Del Mar all running at the same time. There are so many opportunities for horses that nobody wants to stop. And with horses it's definitely a pyramid shape. I mean, you've got a Brown Bess on the one hand, and then 4,000 horses at the bottom, and the grind just wears out a lot of those cheaper horses."

The situation is even worse with New York racing, in Umphrey's opinion. "Right now, it's pretty ugly. Horses that previously couldn't get stalls are now mainstays. The trickle down is evident.

Neighboring tracks used to get good horses from New York, but they no longer have the horses to spare.

"Even at Santa Anita, you see cards now you'd never have dreamed of before. I mean, you'll see two bottom-level maiden $32,000 races on a Saturday card. We're just running out of horses. There's just too many spots and not enough good horses. That's why I run these five- and six-horse fields. The bettors don't like them, but I have to. If I don't let the five -and six-horse fields go then the owners are going to do what Morey says they will and send all their horses to L.A. If I cut back on the number of races for those smaller but classier fields, then the next time there won't be five horses but only three horses to run in the race and it won't fill. Then pretty soon the whole card will consist of those races you hate to see—nothing but maiden $12,500 and $6,250 claimers. All these cheap, recycled horses coming back at you every two weeks with everyone wondering, 'Who's gonna win today?' It becomes a handicapping joke and isn't good for racing. I mean, I constantly get stung. I wrote a race for Wednesday for seven horses, but already it's down to four. Morey's horse bucked shins, Hollendorfer's horse got sick today, and Greenman's horse had a penicillin shot and the vet didn't tell him."

While most fans like bigger fields because they usually jack up the odds on the horse they like, Umphrey, perhaps influenced by the demands of his job, wasn't so sure about the betting logic. "I think you have a better chance to win with smaller fields," he countered. "I'm not a believer in twelve-horse fields. People see the big odds and get excited. But you kill people with those big fields. I mean they just make for a lot more losers. I think it's better to bet a seven-horse field where you can tee off on a horse and have a decent chance. But beyond that, twelve horses in every race gets a little tough. I mean, I get tired of handicapping them, if nothing else. When I used to work at Gulfstream Park, there would be twelve horses in every race and people got exhausted trying to handicap them. I think you drain people with that many horses. If it's a contentious race people will bet with even a four-horse field. You also have to remember that people only have so much money to bet. Everybody thinks if you run twelve races with twelve horses in every one of them, that people will still be pumping at the end. But I think you're more likely to be tapped out. If you don't hit anything early you're gonna be dead. You only have a certain amount to bet. Especially if you go to your credit card here. I mean that's a slick deal. They've got worse interest rates than the mob. The fee is exorbitant. I mean it's ten dollars to get a hundred? Give me a break. I don't mind losing the money, but goddamn I don't want to give it to them. Don't tell me it's gonna cost ten dollars to get a hundred, pu-leeze."

Besides writing and filling races, Umphrey also has the controversial job of assigning the weights for handicap races. He gave as an example the Miss America Handicap, which is an ungraded stakes race for fillies going 1¹⁄₁₆ miles on the dirt. "This guy, Willard Proctor, just went nuts on me because he thought I had assigned his horse too much weight. He's a good friend of my dad's. I was at Santa Anita on Wednesday, and he's looking for me growling because his horse has only won two races. But I'm looking at who she raced against. She's six lengths to Gorgeous and Akinimod. She's been running with Imaginary Lady. It's not like she's been running against bad horses. Anyway, she wound up carrying 116 pounds. Gary Jones and I then got into a row about the weight on Fantastic Look. She had won the Fantasy when it was still a Grade I and beat Imaginary Lady. She carried 121 pounds going off against Akinimod at two to one. Well, I have 121 pounds on Fantastic Look for the Miss America and Jones is beefing. I say 'Are you crazy. I don't see Akinimod in this race, Gary. You're two to one with Akinimod carrying that much weight.' "

Two local horses, Amy Louise and Dawnelo, were also in the race. "Dawnelo is really getting good," Umphrey observed. "She's an improving filly. If she gets mud, watch out. All these Grey Dawn horses, if you ever see any of them running in the mud, pound on them. I mean, they're like alligators in the mud. Grey Dawn horses have a definite mud pedigree, just like Northern Dancer's run well on the grass and the Mr. Prospector line gives a horse a lot of early speed."

With handicap races Umphrey tries to vary the weights in such a way as to bring the horses together at the finish line. "You try to do that," he explained. "But to me weight is one of the most overrated factors in the history of racing. The trainers like to cry and tell me they can't run with the weights I assign, but I just say, 'Pu-leeze, spare me.' The more important handicapping factors to me are the track—is it favoring speed horses or is it a closer's day? The pace. A clean trip. There's so many other factors that are more important than weight. I mean you can't put enough weight on a horse like Simply Majestic when he's running at Golden Gate Fields. My only role with him in the Kensington Handicap and the Golden Gate Fields Budweiser Breeders' Cup Handicap was to put enough weight on him so I could get somebody to run against him and not have him ship out on me. So I'm walking a fine line. I got 128 pounds on him and Parisella knows he's gonna win but says, 'Oh, shit. What do I do after I carry 128.' I mean I could put 140 pounds on Simply Majestic on the dirt here and he'd still win. The turf is another matter. That was a great controversy here. People were saying that I 'gave' Simply Majestic his last race when I put 121 pounds on him on the grass. But he wasn't that great a turf horse. I mean he only beat a plodder like Ongoing Mister by a nose on the grass. I had to listen to Chuck Jenda and all these geniuses tell me what to do. They should read the *Form* and they'd see that he's not the same horse on the grass. Everyone was complaining about the weights for the Bay Meadows Handicap, too, but the weights were very fair. Chuck Jenda had no intention of running Brown Bess in the Bay Meadows Handicap. He had too much to lose. The weight was just a convenient excuse. I mean, running on a soggy turf course, Simply Majestic was hardly a lock and the results of the race proved it. Ten Keys won it and Simply Majestic finished fifth. But don't get me wrong about Jenda. We discuss things a lot. We go at it, but we understand each other. He's a super trainer, he really is."

I wondered how Umphrey felt about the racing of two-year-olds. Does running them that young create problems down the line for a racing secretary in terms of the injuries they take and the shortening of their racing careers? "Well, I guess Wayne Lukas would be the one to finalize your theory," Umphrey speculated. "Wayne doesn't have a lot of four-year-olds, but he has a lot of champions. But before you come down on him, you have to understand that Wayne has so much money invested, he has to go for it. And if you can get a horse that's athletic early and win a couple of graded races, you're out on him. You give $800,000 for him and he wins a Grade II or a Grade I with a pedigree like Lukas buys and man you're out on him. Wayne's had some good three-year-olds, very few four-year-olds, and a lot of great two-years-olds. Lukas has the best horses you can put your hands on with money, whereas a guy like Shug McGaughey has the best horses you can breed. I think, in the right hands, and raced properly, two-year-olds can run early."

The pressure on Umphrey, from owners and breeders, to write spring races for two-year-olds is considerable. "I've had so many people call me that I'm putting them in the next Condition Book for April eighteenth. Theoretically, they're not supposed to be on the grounds until April first, but like I said before, I know they're already here. It'll be interesting when the *Form* comes out and they already have three works listed on them in March. It'll be interesting to see if anybody gets fined. That would be fun. But I think 4½ furlongs for the ones that come around early is okay. I mean, the breeders and pinhookers are already cranking them up for these two-year-olds-in-training sales like they just had at Barretts and Del Mar. I don't think that's very good. You're going in there and buying a horse and you don't know what they've done. They've probably injected him and he's on 'Bute' and everything else to make sure he can work a quarter mile in :21 and bring more money. That part, I don't like to see. But a two-year-old in the right hands, I can live with. We all have things we have to do, and thoroughbreds are bred to race."

If D. Wayne Lukas is an example of one kind of approach to racing, what about the other side of the coin, someone like Charlie Whittingham? "Well, with Charlie, his babies don't run until September. And the first two times they run, they usually get the shit kicked out of them. Then the third time, boom, you're in November and Charlie's got them going 1¹⁄₁₆ mile and here they come. If you look at Charlie's barn, he's got six- and seven-year-olds. So there's the two different styles. Lukas and Whittingham are one-two in money won. Charlie does it with older horses and Lukas does it with two-year-olds. Who's to say who's right? Maybe if Lukas waited longer his young athletic horses wouldn't stretch out and win the distance races. Look at what happened after the hype on Saratoga Six and Houston. What was it Wayne said about Houston? 'The greatest horse I've ever laid my hands on.' Pu-leeze, Wayne. Yeah, you only paid $2.9 million for him, you better hype it up and get some partners, buddy."

Getting back to the more practical dimensions of his job, I asked Umphrey how he felt about trainers scratching their horses. Would he prefer they not enter at all or take his chances that a questionable horse will run? "I'd rather they didn't enter, because it affects my set. Like today I'm trying to get a ninth race for Friday. It's a good day, Friday, so you want a nice race in the last. I had ten horses in and then three guys take out, and now I'm running seven in the last race. That's no good. We'll get killed by a lower handle."

Umphrey's last comment raised an interesting question. Is his competence as a racing secretary ultimately measured by how big a betting handle he generates during a meet? Or more specifically, if he writes a certain kind of race and notices that people aren't betting it, does that affect what he writes in the future? "I don't think you really see that. There are good races and bad races, from a handle point of view, but you have to have them. But I'll tell you, from a handle perspective, fillies suck. Handicappers just don't bet on them. It's amazing. Fillies do about seventy percent of what the colts do. I don't know why, but the public doesn't bet them as much. I never even thought about it until I started looking at the figures. I'd call Red Grant over in mutuels for the figures after a race and he'd say. 'Another goddamn filly race.' We'll have colts running the race before and be up forty or fifty grand and then I'll come up with what I think is a good filly race and we'll be down fifty. It's incredible, but the handle really takes a hit on fillies. I don't have a prejudice against fillies, but maybe they are more fickle and the bettors know something."

What handicappers *do* like to bet are distance and grass races.

"Probably our ideal, best-bet race," Umphrey reflected, "is a $50,000 race on the turf with twelve horses going 1⅛ miles. People just love to bet those races. One of the biggest joys we have every year is a two-mile turf race on California Derby day. It's for $20,000 claimers, and last year I even put a $25,000 purse on it. I got to feel like Tom Robbins at Santa Anita for once and write a race with a bigger purse than the claiming price. More people talk about that two-mile race. They just love it. I've got to the point where this year I even scheduled two preps for it. Some people don't like to bet it, but what are you going to do—bet every race? It's a fun race to just watch. People get a charge out of seeing the horses go around the track twice."

Another interesting dimension to Umphrey's job is the politics of assigning stall space. If there is a universal truth on the backside, it is that no trainer ever feels he is given enough stalls. How does a racing secretary decide who gets what? "Well, you have to do some research. But basically you learn by experience that certain trainers run their horses and others don't. What you want are trainers with live stables who run their horses and don't just take up stall spaces with tired and sore horses. But you can't always tell. For example, Lloyd Mason I thought was going to be a good outfit for me, but he went backwards this meet. He was trying to make it big in southern California. But they picked his bones and sent him back. He lost most of his good horses, like No Commitment and Sanger Chief, to the claiming box down there. He's just now getting his outfit back together.

"Bill Morey is real steady. He asked for thirty-six spaces and I know he's going to use them. His number is set. Gil Matos is another of my favorites. He's a good trainer, a good guy, and comes to run. We keep an index card for every horse a trainer has that he wants a stall for. What I do is look at the P.P.s [past performance charts] for each horse and the workout tabs to see whether it's likely to be a runner or just take up stall space. So what we do is circle what look like the live runners and tell a trainer that he has that many stalls. Now, I've tentatively excluded one of Gil's horses, Sensitive Copy, and he'll probably come in and say, 'Shoot, he's a $40,000 grass horse.' And I'll come back and say. 'But Gil, he doesn't have any works, when is he gonna be ready?' I'll probably bend and give him the stall space anyway because I know Gil wouldn't have him here if he wasn't going to run him. So what happens is I'll send Gil a letter that says he's been approved for twenty stalls, so he can plan. Most of the trainers are geared up to have twenty stalls. They have four grooms rubbing five horses apiece or five grooms rubbing four apiece."

Once a trainer has been assigned his stalls, the matter doesn't end there. Umphrey elaborated: "Now, Gil will get his letter saying he has twenty stalls and come in and say he just claimed Southport Express and needs an extra stall. Meanwhile, maybe he'll ship one of his horses that needs a rest out for a month or six weeks, and by the time he's ready to come back a space will open up because one of his other horses will have been claimed or needs a rest. It's a constant flow. Horses are moving in and out, getting claimed and being turned out all the time.

"Chuck Jenda has about thirty stalls this year. He runs a different operation than say Jerry Hollendorfer. The 'Dorf' has fifty-five stalls here. How can we not give him fifty-five? He runs to those stalls. He also has forty more stalls at Bay Meadows. His percentage of starts to stalls is outstanding. For a 110-day meet like we have at Golden Gate Fields, you like to see a ratio of about five starts per stall. So for Hollendorfer that would be about 275 starts. Well, shoot, he'll run 350 or 400 times with his horses. He'll also go down to Santa Anita, play with the heavyweights, bring me back the kinds of horses I need. He's very good at claiming horses like Chancy Leigh and moving them up here. So, I've got to love the guy. If a horse can't run, he's not going to keep it in training so he can bilk some owner and make fifty cents a day. He'll say, 'Hey, later with this one. Let's get one that can run.' He's aggressive and progressive. The only problem I have is that he's friends with too many people. He gets away with murder. He'll take a horse like Lot's Curiosity, run him cheap for twelve-five, he whistles, and then he runs him back for thirty or fifty grand. He gets away with too many things around here, taking shots, because trainers like Lonnie Arterburn, Bryan Webb,

Walter Greenman, and Terry Knight don't claim off of him. They've got this gentlemen's agreement between them and it's horrible. I love it when there's a lot of claiming. I think claiming is fascinating."

One of the persistent rumors around the backstretch at Golden Gate Fields is that trainers with small stables are afraid to claim horses off Hollendorfer because he'll bite back and take their good horses the next time they run. That's why they don't claim a horse like Lot's Curiosity from Hollendorfer when he runs him cheap. Umphrey didn't think the small trainers should be intimidated. "Good. Let Jerry play his game. They'll have money in the office. Hollendorfer has a lot more to lose than they do. I mean, why be scared of him. We know Lennie Shoemaker wasn't afraid. He took that horse Sumkindasign from him and moved him up. The 'Dorf' took that a lot better than I thought he would. I thought we'd have to have the suicide watch on him. He is rather temperamental, but you have to understand that about him."

Some jockeys complain that Hollendorfer is arrogant and abuses his power. Umphrey shrugged his shoulders and said, "Sure, he'll come out and holler at you for two minutes and then forget about it. But if you're riding for him in the next race, he'll be laughing. You just have to let him have his ego. You can't tell him to screw off, he's way too strong around here."

I asked Umphrey to talk about class comparisons between the different maiden classifications and the winner's races. How should a handicapper interpret the value of a maiden twelve-five win as opposed to a maiden allowance win, when the horse goes against winners the next time? "Well, when a horse breaks its maiden at twelve-five, it generally better get to the bottom of the claiming ladder real quick. Most of them will run back for $6,250. Yesterday is a classic example. This horse Serula broke his maiden impressively at twelve-five as a first-time starter and then got hammered against winners for eight. He didn't even hit the board. Clint Roberts got a little optimistic and claimed him out of that race. You can see the horse got bet heavily, even though there's not much pedigree. Freddie Marquez was probably happy to get rid of him. He's a pretty sharp trainer. In fact, there's some guys from Tijuana that are pretty slippery. Jose Silva does a good job with a horse, he's pretty slick."

Even though a maiden twelve-five winner will occasionally surprise everyone and climb up the ladder quickly, Umphrey emphasized that doesn't happen very often with older maidens. "But a three-year-old maiden winner can go anywhere. Like last week that little horse Comissio won for sixteen, and that's a character that has him, Abe LeMort, he's a slippery old dude. He runs him back a week later and gets beat a nose in a classified handicap by Ei's Hawkie. Now, off of a sixteen short, you'd think he was really getting his horse in trouble by going long against better. But, shoot, he ran good. With three-year-olds, I guess, you should watch where a trainer puts them. If a horse breaks its maiden impressively at twelve-five and a trainer runs it back for sixteen or twenty grand, that tells you they think the horse may have some ability and they want to find out. Sometimes a horse can break its maiden in a fast time but be crooked-legged. The trainer might run it back cheap because he thinks, 'Let someone else train this thing.' "

What about the top of the line, maiden allowance winners? Where would Umphrey run them back? "Well, if it was a four-year-old, I'd probably run him back at sixteen, because most of them are dogs. Although Lonnie Arterburn loves this horse, Hoofer. He told me to put the horse in the race because 'After Friday, he won't be a maiden any longer.' Hoofer might be a four-year-old that can win. Four-year-olds can be interesting. We had a four-year-old maiden race with six horses in it, and I got Laz Barrera on the phone at Santa Anita and said, 'Laz, you have this horse that isn't eligible down there. Run the horse up here. I've got a good spot for you. It's a small field, and your horse will be at least third and you can get everything going.' Then I find out that Jeff 'Scratchcard' Bonde has taken another horse out of a race. Thankfully, Laz sent his horse up. Well, the horse won. Laz couldn't believe it when I called him. He said, 'What, thee horse ween? He ween?' "

. . .

Before leaving the maiden ranks, Umphrey had an interesting observation about the bottom-level horses. "Where do all the maiden
twelve-five winners go? That is the mystery of the ages. Like yesterday I broke four maiden twelve-fives. It would be interesting
to know where they come back. Most of them won't run back here.
They must retire them and breed them somewhere, because they
sure disappear. They must get shipped to Portland Meadows or
into the abyss. We have better luck tracking the maiden twenty-
and-up horses because they're better horses and the purses are
good enough to keep them here."

Since Umphrey has worked as a Racing Secretary in both northern California and southern California, I was curious how he would
compare the two circuits. "We're like the Triple A and they're like
the Major Leagues. Most of our owners and trainers go down to
those two-year-old-in-training sales and buy horses for eight or ten
grand, while the heavy players think nothing of popping for eighty
or a hundred. It's just a different game. We have to create our own
good horses. That's why I run some short races. But I have to, to
keep us in existence. Or else it's going to be all like today's card,
with nothing but maiden twelve-fives and cheap sixty-two-fifties.
And that gets pretty ugly."

While the quality of horses is generally superior in southern
California, Umphrey has a lot of respect for trainers in the north.
"We have a good group of horsemen here. There's no doubt about
it. I'm sure that Hollendorfer, Webb, Gilchrist, Arterburn, Jenda,
and maybe a dozen others could win down south. They could win,
but it's tough down there. You've got a guy like Whittingham with
150 horses. When he loses a horse that's a Grade I stakes winner
he's got another at San Luis Rey getting ready to come in."

Umphrey's point was reinforced not only by Lloyd Mason but
also by Terry Knight's experience down south. "Obviously, I hate
to see our horses go down south. But the owners take a lot. Terry
Knight went down there, but L.A. proved too tough, even though
he won a nice stakes down there Wednesday with High Hatted.
Most of his horses are back up here now. Terry Knight's a good

trainer, but he got frustrated because he couldn't get anything in up here. Some of his races didn't fill at Bay Meadows. I try to run those races here, even if they have short fields. I write enough of them to where my comptroller starts reaching for her Valium, because some of these cards I'm writing are giving away $180,000 in purse money. I tell her, 'Hey, don't worry about it, it'll come around.' But I have to generate a lot of betting handle to keep my purse money up."

Umphrey believes that carding better races helps increase the betting handle. "We need to average $2.8 million a day to cover the purses. Even though I get flak for it, I feel I have to write some races for $60,000 purses to keep horses like Valley Land, Big Chill, and Second Legend here. If we have to cut back, I would prefer to cut purse money for all these cheap maiden twelve-fives. They don't help the program here that much. They win a purse and disappear. We have some inequities in the purse structure here. Horses at the bottom get too much compared to, say, a $25,000 claimer. The purse for a maiden $12,500 or $6,250 bottom claimer is sixty-two-fifty, whereas a $25,000 horse is running for only seventeen grand. I think the maiden $12,500 should be running for four grand and the $6,250 claimers for five, and the purses should be raised for the midrange horses where Bill Morey wants it put. I agree with him. Of course, I can't do it."

The reason Umphrey can't do it has to do with politics. "The HBPA would come totally unglued." He wiped some imaginary sweat from his forehead. "I'd be dead meat. All those little guys want their share. So what I've done, since I've been here, is raise the bottom-level races by about five hundred bucks, to keep everyone happy, and concentrate on raising the purse money for my allowance races and overnight handicaps up another six to eight grand. My allowance purses have jumped to as high as $27,000 for a non-winners-of-four going a distance, and the Overnights have a purse of twenty-eight grand. I'm trying to upgrade the program here and money talks. At GGF the purse money for claimers from $32,000 to $62,500 is roughly comparable to the purse money for the allowance races."

Even though horsemen are always complaining that there isn't enough purse money, Umphrey feels the program in northern California is a good one. "Right now, the purse money, if you compare it with most places, is awfully good. People here don't appreciate it as much as they should because of L.A.'s influence. This money would look good anywhere, but when you put it along-side Santa Anita, which has twice as much handle and purse money as we do, it doesn't look that good. But we do have some good horses here. Brown Bess, High Hatted, Owiseone, and even a horse like Casa Petrone went down there and won some nice money on both the dirt and the turf. So the better horses here are vastly underrated. A horse like Happy Idiot sprinted for $40,000 in eight and change. I mean, how good are those horses? If they ran down south for that figure they'd breeze. But then, of course, you lose them to the claiming box. So what good does that do?"

If Umphrey is right, why don't southern California trainers come up north and claim more horses? "Roger Stein does," Umphrey pointed out. "He comes up here, claims, and then runs them at the same level down south and makes money. He can do that because no one dominates the cheaper races down there. Up here the twelve-fives are like lifebloods, but down there the attitude toward them is, 'Phew, get this thing out of here.' They don't condition their cheap horses as well as we do ours up here. Even though we make fun of ourselves for some of our weekday cards, this is a vastly underrated circuit. The cards during the week are a little uglier because people have to pay their bills on these cheap horses and I have to let them run sometime. I don't want them to run on Sunday when I've got Fantastic Look, Knight in Savannah, and some really good maiden allowance races. I card fifty-seven races a week and probably three of them a day are maiden races."

Bill Morey had complained that, at $400,000, Umphrey was putting up too much purse money for a race like the Golden Gate Handicap. He would rather see the purse for that race reduced to $150,000 and the difference applied to supporting more races for midrange horses. Umphrey disagreed. "I like to see horses like the Great Communicator, Simply Majestic, and Frankly Perfect run in north-ern California. I get tired of watching these $50,000 stakes every week. I get tired of watching the same horses over and over. I put up $100,000 on Sunday and we're going to see Fantastic Look, Kelly, Variety Baby, Valid Vixen, and Luthiers Launch. I really like to see fillies of that caliber run, and I think a lot of people do. We need some variety up here, and we can build around our big events. California Derby day the purses will exceed $500,000 and we will probably handle $6 million. I have three other stakes going that day. Our hope is that one of these days we'll get lucky and have a California Derby winner that doesn't break down and is nominated, go to Kentucky and run good. Or maybe we'll get a late-developing horse up here for the California Derby and he'll go on to Kentucky."

Even though the California Derby is older than the Kentucky Derby and offers a $350,000 purse, in recent years it has not attracted the most sterling fields because of being sandwiched in between other major "preps" like the Santa Anita Derby, the Wood Memorial, and the Arkansas Derby. Umphrey agreed he was in a tough spot with the California Derby because of the competition and being so close to the Triple Crown races. "We've taken a new attitude toward the race," he explained. "We make an event of the thing. We want to be part of the three-year-old picture. That's why we simulcast races like the Florida Derby, the Jim Beam, the Santa Anita, and the Bluegrass. But the California Derby has had some great horses. Simply Majestic would have gone to Kentucky except for the fact he wasn't nominated. All Thee Power would have gone, but he broke down. Ruhlman was in that same Derby but unfortunately clipped heels in the stretch and hit the deck. But given our spot in the schedule, we are in a tight spot, and we need to get lucky to get a late-developing horse that needs the money and the conditioning to justify a trip to Kentucky."

Umphrey doesn't agree that the Cal Derby is too far away in distance and too close in time to the Kentucky Derby to attract a good field. "New York is no farther away from Kentucky than San Francisco is, and they have the Wood Memorial two weeks before the Kentucky Derby. The Arkansas Derby is also run then. So we must all be stupid to have a big race on that day."

Nevertheless, the Wood Memorial and Arkansas Derby seem

to attract horses from around the country, whereas the California Derby doesn't. Why is that? "That's because trainers outside of California know they're going to hook horses from L.A. That's a big factor in trying to draw horses to northern California. It costs money to ship horses, and trainers know they will have to compete with the likes of Sir Whittingham, Lukas, Drysdale, and Canani. You're shipping against the best horses in the world. So, what's so advantageous about shipping here? They might just as well ship to L.A. and compete in the Santa Anita Derby. But if we don't take a shot, we're never going to get lucky."

Umphrey believes that northern California's racing program is underestimated nationally. "The fact that we don't have a Grade I race irks me no end. Compared to some of the races I see run elsewhere that have that status, we certainly run races here that merit a Grade I rating. I mean the Golden Gate Handicap is a $400,000 race and has been won by horses like John Henry, Great Communicator, and Frankly Perfect in recent years. Horses don't get much better than that."

Just then the phone rang. It was D. Wayne Lukas returning Umphrey's earlier call about the Miss America Handicap. Lukas was confirming that Luthiers Launch would be running in the race. Umphrey leaned back in his chair and said, "All right, Wayne! That's with Ronnie Warren. Is she on Lasix? No Lasix, all right! Very good, sir. What? Warren. I gave you Ronnie Warren. We talked about that the other day. What? Oh, hell yes, for you, we'll do anything. Nice to hear from you. Now don't forget me."

Umphrey, in an expansive mood, told me he was pleased with the stakes program and mentioned that Brown Bess would be running in the forthcoming Yerba Buena Handicap and quite possibly the Golden Gate Handicap against the boys. I asked Umphrey, if he were in Suzanne Pashayan's shoes, how much longer would he run Brown Bess before turning her into a brood mare. Given her local following, I wasn't surprised by his answer. "I would never breed her," he exclaimed. "Not until she really tails off. Her pedigree is all right, but it's certainly not Raise a Native or Northern Dancer.

With a mare like that, as good as she's running, I wouldn't even think of retiring her. I mean it's not like Suzanne Pashayan has a lot of other horses running. That's her barn."

Since Chuck Jenda had screamed about the high weight Brown Bess had been assigned in the Bay Meadows Handicap before withdrawing her from the race, I asked Umphrey how he would resolve the weight question for the Yerba Buena and Golden Gate Handicaps. "Well, I got lucky because Tommy Robbins at Santa Anita already had to weight her at 123, and she got beat by Annoconnor. But Brown Bess needed that race and came back to nip Royal Touch in the Santa Ana. Neither of those two races was like the Yellow Ribbon. She was a steamroller that day. I mean I've never seen a horse win a Grade I stakes so easy and enjoy what she was doing. Her ears were just pricking, and all Kaenel had to do was just sit on her. Brown Bess would have beat the boys that day. There wasn't a horse breathing on the planet that day that could have beat her. I mean a mile and a quarter in 157.1 on the turf? C'mon, that's nuts! That and Wild Again's Breeders' Cup win are two of the greatest efforts I've ever seen."

Since Umphrey has to be a handicapper to do his job, I was curious how he does when he's away from his job and playing the horses. "I'm not very good at it," he laughed. "Certain races, I can kill. I don't bet when I'm here, but I'm one of these people who goes up to Tahoe and when I watch the races from Monmouth or Belmont, I get involved. I'm a very small player. I bet five-dollar exactas on races. I never bet at the track I'm working. That's just taboo. It's just not worth pursuing. But I can pick certain races just from being around racing so much. It's a tough game though, and I can appreciate what handicappers have to go through. It's not easy. My key factor in handicapping is who the horses ran with. If you've been running in class competition, that's a big key to me. I want to know what kinds of horses you have beaten or been beaten by. I'm a class handicapper."

Of course, I teased Umphrey, class would probably be a big bias for someone in his position. "Oh, absolutely," he agreed. "That's how you weight races. I have Lukas's horse, Luthiers

Launch, in at 117 because I saw she was running against Bayakoa at 113. Fortunately, Wayne is a guy who never complains about anything. I gave Luthiers Launch four more pounds, even though she did get dusted, because she finished second to Akinimod and Gorgeous. Some pretty classy fillies."

I could see the importance of class at the top of racing's pyramid, but what about in cheaper races? "Well, you have it even at $6,250. You'll see a horse who finished fifth in a good race, where all the horses subsequently prove they can run, come back in a weaker field and just crush them because he's just a better horse. It's tough to keep track of class at the cheaper level, though, unless you can find a key race."

Looking toward the future, Umphrey spoke about the direction racing should move. "If it were up to me I'd like to see double-wide turf courses like they have at Belmont Park. I think there's an increasing emphasis on grass racing because the horses last longer, fans bet more on them, and the aesthetics are great. I just think grass racing is far superior. Unfortunately, in California we're limited by the fact that the turf courses were built before the predominance of turf racing. All of them are inside of small tracks. And that's a problem because, when you put a turf course inside of a mile track, the turns are sharp and they can't be sweeping. In Hong Kong they actually have the turf course on the outside of the main track. There, if you proposed a race on the dirt on the inside for 1⅛ mile, they would think you were crazy."

Given the price of urban real estate, is it practical to build big turf tracks? "Well, no one is going to build a racetrack in prime urban land anymore. You have to do it in the outskirts where you can try some new concepts. Like in Minnesota at Canterbury Downs, they could have done whatever they wanted to."

The Ladbroke corporation, which runs the meet at Golden Gate Fields, may have some tough choices to make in the not-too-distant future about where to race. Golden Gate Fields sits on land owned by a development company that would like nothing more than to tear the track down and replace it with shopping malls and condominiums. With the lease due to expire in a few years, I asked Umphrey about management's position. "That's a good question, but I don't know that our lease with Santa Fe will expire. Berkeley and Albany accept Golden Gate Fields. Both cities do well off of their share of the track income. I'm sure they're going to fight any big development.

"If all else fails"—Umphrey smiled mischievously—"we might have to declare ourselves an endangered species. Our ponds out there in the centerfield have been declared a wildlife habitat for migratory ducks. We have some rare birds out there in those ponds, not to mention in the grandstand, that would put up quite a squawk if they tried to tear the track down."

11

WINNING PLAYERS
Playing the Odds

I ran into The Stone on a lazy Friday afternoon near the end of my tour of the backside. He was nursing a beer and trying to convince himself of the merits of two long shots in a cheap maiden race for three-year-old fillies. "Well, if it ain't the scribe," he teased. "Damn, I've been cold lately. I need to hit a big exacta to get even. Got any hot tips from the backside for this race?"

When I told him I didn't, he shrugged his shoulders and said. "Probably just as well. Most of those guys don't know anything anyway. If they did, they wouldn't be back there shoveling horse-shit. Still, there must be somebody here, besides Ladbroke and the state, that's making money at this game."

I was feeling a bit more chipper. I had come a race earlier and hit with a filly by the name of Donalda that had been on my horses-in-trouble sheet. She had aired at five to two, and I had had the rare good sense not to squander my winnings. In fact, the uncashed ticket was still in my wallet.

I wished The Stone better luck and headed toward Elrod Garcia, my favorite pari-mutuel clerk, to cash my ticket. When I got there he was holding down his usual workstation in the bowels of the grandstand. "I had the five horse in the third race, too," he beamed as he handed me fifty and change. "Saw the same thing you did on the reruns. But at the price, obviously a lot of other people did, too. Man, it's getting to be a tougher game all the time."

Elrod, who is an almost cherubic looking racetrack degenerate, has been playing the horses for twenty-five years. A retired telephone company employee, he fills in as a pari-mutuel clerk a couple days a week in order to get in free and keep closer tabs on the horses. While not quite an Andy Beyer clone in terms of his level of fanaticism, Elrod does keep charts, watches all the reruns, and compiles trainer statistics. "Hey," he cracks in sympathy with Beyer's monastic approach, "at my age hitting a fifteen-to-one shot is better than sex."

Elrod has the gift of gab and enjoys commenting on the foibles of the patrons at Golden Gate Fields. About his job he humorously insists that all the pari-mutuel clerks who have survived a meet should be awarded an honorary degree in linguistics. "Man, it's the tower of Babel around here. There's no such thing as Standard English. Everything's a mix of English with Tagalog, Cowboy, Black, Mexican, Indian, and Chinese. And you wouldn't believe the way some of these people bet. I just had a guy come up and say he wanted to play, 'Numbah wah-fie xacta bock for two dollah.' When I told him it wasn't an exacta race, he paused for a moment and then said, 'Hokay, gehme foe dollah winh on numbah seveh.' I mean, what kind of logic was going through his head? He wanted to box a one-five exacta, but then, when he couldn't do that, he throws the one and five out and goes to the seven horse for his win bet. Please. Explain that to me."

Ah, yes, one of the great mysteries of track life is how those numbers wind up on the tote board. People betting number systems, names of girlfriends, birthdays, and Lord knows what else. It all somehow gets mixed together and reflected in the final odds.

Given that level of competition, the game shouldn't be that hard to beat. Yet, for all but a few, it is. It was time, I figured, to go to the top of the mountain and talk to some handicappers who are good enough to support themselves.

One of the few horseplayers I know who regularly makes money at the track is wily Jack Matthewson, a nearly seventy-year-old renegade from New York. Jack grew up running bets for a local bookie and graduated to playing the New York–Florida circuit before moving to northern California some ten years ago. On dark days in the Bay Area, or merely to keep up with the New York and Florida tracks, he drives up to Reno and plays the racing book there.

Though he obviously loves the game, and is an everyday player, Jack is also one of the most patient gamblers I know. I asked Jack about that one afternoon. "Well, ya got to be patient in this game," he emphasized with his thick Bronx accent. "Otherwise, ya get your brains beat out. If you wait for the right spot, you can beat a race. But you can't come out ahead playing all the races. When I was young I was trained right. I was always sent out to put money on a specific horse in a specific race. When the horse won or came in the money, which was often, I brought the money back. So I learned early to be a spot player. I've never been tempted to play every race."

Besides being a spot player, Jack is also a high-rolling bridge jumper. His standard bet is between two and five hundred dollars to show, depending upon how much he likes a horse and what the probable payoff is. His minimum acceptable return is forty cents on the dollar. On an average week, he makes about ten bets and takes home around a grand. He typically waits for a sprint with a lone front-runner or one that sets up for a closer and then watches the show and place action on the board. "I prefer to play the speed because you don't have to worry about your horse getting in trouble," Jack will explain. "But a lot of times there's two or three speed horses that set it up for a closer to at least finish in the money. Since I'm normally betting show I don't have to win with a closer. He just has to be good enough to get up for third. What

I like to look for in a closer at Golden Gate is a horse with an outside post, because he won't lose any ground having to come off the rail or get blocked. Generally, he'll get a clean trip coming down the backstretch and get into position to cut in and make his move at the turn. My strength is in sprints. They're easier for me to figure the speed and pace on, though I know other people who do better with routes or the turf. It doesn't really matter what kind of race you play as long as you're good at it. If you're a smart player, you play to your strength. Why, for example, bet a turf race, if you're no good at it?"

Though Jack is primarily a show bettor, if a horse looks like a lock he'll sometimes bump his bet up to place to get his price. About his conservatism Jack says, "Hey, I've been playing the horses all my life, and believe me any horse can get beat. Even the way I play it, I only cash a ticket eighty percent of the time. That's why I have to get back at least $2.80 on a $2.00 show bet or I skip the race."

Jack isn't a guy who agonizes over the *Daily Racing Form*. Typically he scans it over coffee each morning and looks for his sprinter with the lone early speed. Failing that, he goes the other way and looks for a race with a lot of early speed that sets up for a free-running closer. His third choice is to play a route. "I'm not one of these guys who spends hours reading the *Form*. You don't have to do that when you play like I do. I can usually tell within fifteen minutes if there's any race worth playing on the card. When I find one, I study it maybe another ten minutes to make sure I haven't missed something important."

After picking a horse, Jack's real work begins. He watches the television monitor like a hawk for the probable show payoffs right up until the horses have entered the gate and are about to go off. On many occasions I've seen him get up to place a bet and then sit down when the show price has dropped below his minimum return on the board.

Jack figures the minimum probable show payoff for his horse by taking the total show pool less twenty percent for the vigorish. He then takes that figure and subtracts from it the total amount bet on the two heaviest action show horses plus his own. He divides what's left by three to get the minimum average return for each horse. The minimum payoff on his horse is then determined by dividing the actual show money bet on his horse into the average show return for the three horses. When two or more of the favorites finish out of the money, the show price of course becomes much greater because the average minimum return increases dramatically.

"You can get burned with some late action, if you bet too soon," Jack warns. "That's why I get in line and try to time my bets to the last few seconds." But Jack doesn't risk being shut out. He has a regular clerk he goes to who picks up his hand signals and punches out the tickets for him if need be. The clerk knows Jack is good for the bet and will tip him well for his efforts.

Jack says one of the reasons he's successful is that he doesn't have to pick winners. "I've known lots of people that are better at picking winners than I am. But almost all of them are losers because you can't beat the races that way. I go home with cash in my pocket. People like to put me down for being the kind of gambler I am and say it's stupid to bet the way I do. They don't think you can make any money. I always ask them, 'You wanna book my action?' I don't get any takers. Nobody wants to have to give me back $700 for $500 on the kind of show horses I bet. The average fan thinks that just because you bet a lot of money, it's a risky bet. That's why I got the edge."

Jockey agent Ray Harris is another person who found his edge after a number of dicey years in the grandstands at Suffolk Downs in the Boston area and then later at Golden Gate Fields and Bay Meadows. At forty-two, Harris is sitting in the catbird seat because he can apply the handicapping skills he's learned over the years and make money without ever having to place a bet. He does so by picking live mounts for two of northern California's top jockeys, Tom Chapman and Ron Warren, in exchange for twenty-five percent of their earnings. Unlike most jockey agents, Harris keeps detailed charts, trouble notes, speed figures, and track variants to aid him in his work on the backside. When Harris suggests to a trainer that one of his horses has a shot in a specific race in the

Condition Book, the trainer is apt to listen. Since fans are essentially trying to do what Harris has been doing successfully for a living since 1977, I thought it would be interesting to ask him about how he picks his horses.

We started off with the Condition Book. Is it really true, as Bill Barich humorously implied in his classic *Laughing in the Hills,* that a lot of trainers have trouble reading the arcane language in it? "No." Harris laughed. "They don't just toss their Condition Book into an empty feed tub. Once you get used to reading it, it's really pretty easy. What a lot of trainers do is point their horses for a specific race that is in the Condition Book. So it's an important part of what goes on. They'll see that in three weeks there's a mile race that fits their horse and begin to work it out or give it a prep."

Since one of the most difficult things for a handicapper to decide is whether a horse coming back from a rest can win off of workouts alone, I asked Harris what he looks for. If, for example, it's a mile race, would he want to see a good seven-furlong work as part of the training pattern? "Not necessarily," he replied. "Some trainers know how to get a horse ready, put some air into it, with long slow gallops. They might not work their horses to the clock for more than five or six furlongs. With the big horses, trainers will sometimes give them an easy race before a stakes event, so they don't get the weight put on them. I'm talking about a horse like a Sunday Silence or an Easy Goer that doesn't run very often compared to a claiming horse that might run twice a month. How often you work a horse depends upon the horse and what they're running for. Sometimes with a cheap horse they'll run him three times a month and you won't see too many works in between. With cheap horses it's hard to make money on them, so you run them more often and really don't care if you lose them."

Doesn't that kind of approach result in horses getting sore and maybe even breaking down? "Sure, that's there," Harris reflected. "It's just like people if they overexercise. It's the trainer's job to take good care of his horses and not let them cross that line. Most of the horses around here get good care, though. They get looked over every day. But that doesn't prevent some of them from getting sore or breaking down."

To do his job right, Harris has to think like a trainer. "If you want your jockey to get the mount on a stakes horse," he explained, "you have to anticipate from reading the Condition Book which race he's going to be entered in. Also, as an agent you don't want to promote riding too many cheap horses because your jockey just gets worn out riding them. If you're going to ride seven out of nine races, the two you don't want to ride are the cheaper ones, because it's harder to ride cheap horses and you don't make as much money."

Harris writes off horses as professional maidens after about ten tries, though sometimes he'll write them off earlier depending upon how much ability they have and who they've been running against. "If a horse keeps hanging against the bottom-level maidens, it may never win a race. I also listen to the jockey's opinion. When a jock gets on a horse in the morning they can pretty well tell how good a horse is by how he hits the ground and how he travels. They can tell if something is wrong. That's why you'll sometimes see me get them off a horse and go to another one. But we might also stay with a horse that seems a little off. Just because a horse has a little problem doesn't mean he won't run hard. In fact, sometimes the reason they're a little sore or stiff is because they try hard. So you don't necessarily want to get off those horses. They still win races. And another thing is that sometimes a trainer will work a horse in the morning without 'Bute' and he'll feel different and run different then than he will in the afternoon. So you can be fooled that way. It's something you learn through experience. Horses that don't run well in the morning will often warm up real good if they're on a little 'Bute' in the afternoon."

I noticed that Harris jots down adjusted speed figures on the bound copies of the charts he keeps and asked how important they are to his handicapping. "I think speed is very important, but pace always makes the race. If there's a lot of speed it sets up for somebody from behind. If there's less speed maybe a front-runner will steal it. So the old saying, 'Pace makes the race,' is very true."

What about studying the form cycle of a horse? "I guess that's important. But I think looking at the trainers that keep their horses in good shape is a better key. They're the best form to watch,

295

because if a horse is not doing well they're going to drop it down. If it's doing well they'll run it at a level where it's competitive. Trainers that aren't doing well tend to run their horses at a level where they're not competitive. So the best cycle to watch is which trainers, year after year, run their horses where they can win. Key races are also important. If you see a horse come out of a race in which several of the horses in that race have subsequently won, pay attention. Horses that come out of productive races, that's important information for a handicapper."

I asked Harris what the major difference was between himself as a gambler and fan in the grandstand and someone who now works on the backside. "Well, now I don't have to bet. So it's a lot less pressure. I try to pick my spots better. Rather than bet more races, I bet fewer races now. In terms of my handicapping, I think looking at the trainers is the number one thing. Some trainers consistently keep their horses at a higher level of fitness than the other trainers do. They also consistently put their horses where they belong. When they get sore or are going downhill they get rid of them, they run them cheap. When they get good they jump them up the ladder and maximize what they can get out of them. They know what they're doing. They can recognize when a horse is getting good and when it's getting sour. Once in a while they'll make a mistake, everybody does, but on the whole they know what they're doing."

What about trainers who claim a horse for $10,000, put it in jail for thirty days, and then drop it down to $8,000 and the horse wins? Harris feels that most often trainers who do that aren't just trying to cynically cash a big bet. "Despite the gambling aspect," he explained, "what they're trying to do from the financial aspect is minimize their losses. If they take a horse for $10,000 and it didn't win at that level on the day they claimed it, they might feel the horse isn't as good as they thought. So they drop it down a notch or two and hope to win the purse. So if they drop it to $6,250, it gets claimed, and they win the purse of say around $3,800, they'll be just about even."

While a horse's body language is important, looks can also be deceiving. "Some people are real good at reading body language in the paddock and post parade and as the horses warm up on the backside. But there can be some bad-looking individuals that run well and some good-looking ones that run bad. So there's no absolute rule. On the whole though, horses—like when they're in the paddock—will tell you some things. If they're nervous, washy, and lathered on a cool or normal day that's a bad sign nine times out of ten, because something is bothering them. They have other things on their mind than racing."

Does Harris use binoculars? "Absolutely. I have a very good pair and I watch how horses warm up. That's very important. I have friends who do their handicapping first and then see how the horse warms up. If it doesn't warm up well, they won't bet it. If it looks good, they load up."

Harris keeps his own speed figures and track variants because, like a lot of handicappers, he believes those listed in the *Racing Form* aren't very accurate. "It's true that the *Form*'s figures aren't that good. I keep numbers every day. I have my own track variant scale, and I'll say today was a plus 2 or a minus 2. But I still go back to the trainer as the most important key, because some trainers just consistently keep their horses at a higher level of fitness than other trainers do. Let me give you a good example of why Jerry Hollendorfer is such a successful trainer. Take this turf horse, Joys of Love, that he ran at a mile and three-eighths on October twenty-eighth. Before that race he gave the horse three good works that totaled twenty-one furlongs. He worked him a mile, another mile, and then five-eighths more. His plan was to get a lot of air in the horse and have him ready to win, and he did. Now let's turn it back to today's mile and an eighth race. It's been twenty-one days since he ran, and let's see what Hollendorfer has done to prepare Joys of Love for the mile and an eighth race today. Since it's a shorter race, Hollendorfer knew the horse would need a little more speed today. So if you look at the workout pattern you'll see that incorporated. Instead of working him a mile like he did before, what you see are three half-mile works. He knows the horse is fit and has just been trying to keep it sharp and increase its speed a little by working it four furlongs every seven days or so. In both races with this horse you can see the logic to what Hollendorfer is doing.

He's working the horse regularly, keeping it fit, and adjusting the distance of the workouts to the distance of the upcoming race.

"Now, let's take another horse, Glorious Amazon, that ran against Joys of Love in the same race twenty-one days ago and is running against him again today. What's been happening with him? He only worked twice in the same amount of time, which means he only worked nine furlongs while Joys of Love worked twelve furlongs. He also hasn't had a work in over a week, while Joys of Love worked four days ago. So the odds are that Joys of Love will be a fitter horse today. You can learn a lot about a trainer and a horse by looking at the workout patterns. When you see good recent works with a good trainer, it tells you the horse is fit and likely to run well."

Harris also has his notions about the relationship between foot size and a horse's ability to run in the mud or on the turf. "I like big feet on the turf and little feet in the mud. A lot of people think turf and mud are the same, but that's not true. Of course, the best indication in judging how well a horse is going to run on the turf or mud is if they've run well on it before. With horses that are starting for the first time, I look at the breeding to see if the sire was a horse that did well on the turf or mud."

What approach does Harris take to money management? "Well, I'm in a unique position now because I can do it more for fun. If you can keep your gambling down to that it's great. My advice to anybody, even if they only come once a week, is you shouldn't bet every race. Pick out three or four races that you're interested in. Maybe you want to bet a grass race, a sprint with older horses, and the feature race. Anyhow, pick out three or four and work really hard at them. Try and space them out so you have a couple of races in between and can take your time. Watch the track and see what's happening: is speed holding that day? But basically try and relax. Spend more time on fewer races and double or triple your bet on those instead of betting two dollars on every race. You should also make your biggest bet on the longest-priced horse that you like. That's how you get leverage and make money in this game.

"If you take this approach, you have a better chance of winning. First of all, you're spending more time on each race that you bet. Second of all, if you pick a winner, you really feel like you've accomplished something because you worked hard at it. Third, you get a better return because you're betting more than two dollars on the race. Approaching the game this way makes it more interesting and encourages you to dig deeper and work harder at it. There's a logic of the mind in the whole thing. Of course, there's some variables that you can't control. Jockeys make mistakes, the pace is too fast, the race is too slow. But it's really satisfying to figure out beforehand how a race sets up and then actually see it run that way. That's fun. The best way of figuring races will always be how much speed is in the race, are these horses going to push each other and push each other and set it up for the closers? Or are the horses on the lead going to have a relatively easy time of it and make it tough for the closers. Pace analysis will eternally be the best way to handicap. The only exception would be with a really good stakes horse, like a Sunday Silence or an Easy Goer, who can win with a slow or a fast pace. But those kinds of horses are few and far between. For everyday racing in a place like northern California you really have to pay attention to pace. Even King Glorious, as good as he was, got beat because there was another horse on the lead with him. Every other race he won on the front end with nobody that close to him. Now, don't get me wrong, I think King Glorious was a great horse, but I don't think he would have beat Sunday Silence or Easy Goer, because he wasn't bred to go the distances they were bred to go, at the pace that they could maintain."

While Harris is a believer in maintaining his own charts and adjusted speed figures, he thinks the recreational gambler can simplify things for himself in many cases. "Basically, you can go through a race, say a normal sprint, and ask, 'How many horses in this race can break :45.3 for the half-mile?' If there's only one horse that can do it, he's the probable winner. If there's four horses that can do it, then it could set up for someone to come from behind. Of course, you have to be looking for the horses that can finish on a fast pace. I generally prefer to bet races for older horses because they run more reliably. Three-year-olds are harder to handicap because they're still maturing. They can show sudden improvement or decline. The pace and final figures for four-year-olds and up are just a whole lot more consistent. It's just easier to predict how they're going to run."

While Ray Harris methodically works the trainer and pace angle to get his edge in the racing world, Ron Cox is perhaps the ultimate example of a total systems approach to the handicapping game. If they gave out PhDs to horseplayers, he would certainly have earned one. For the past eleven years Cox has put out *Northern California Track Record,* a weekly newsletter that looks comprehensively at the previous week's races, notes promising workouts, and compiles a horses-to-watch list. I first talked with Cox at the Pleasanton simulcast facility, some forty miles from Golden Gate Fields, where he regularly holds forth. He had just returned from a handicapping conference at the Mirage Hotel in Las Vegas, which was attended by over four hundred people, including such luminaries as Andy Beyer, James Quinn, Len Ragozin, and Steven Davidowitz. With the casual, almost jaded enthusiasm that only the cognoscenti can muster, Cox explained that he had been invited to lecture about different strategies for betting daily triples as well as to participate on two panels dealing with trainer patterns and exotic wagering.

Cox, who is a thoughtful man in his early fifties, told me he first became interested in the game while a student at the University of San Francisco. "Though I'm not a Catholic, it was some Irish Jesuits," he said with a laugh, "that got me into horse racing. They gave me a tip. The horse didn't win, but they told me to keep an eye on it and to bet it next time. It won coming back!"

Not surprisingly, Cox didn't immediately jump into full-time handicapping. Like almost every horseplayer, he had a few losing seasons to contend with. Throughout most of his twenties and thirties he subsidized his track education by first working in the restaurant business and then later teaching at Terra Linda High School. It wasn't until he was nearly forty that Cox decided he was good enough to take the plunge and become a full-time handicapper. A year later he was giving seminars and putting out the *Track Record* as an aid to local horseplayers.

While the weekend gambler may romanticize the life of a professional handicapper, living it is, of course, another thing. During the racing week, Cox is up by four each morning and handicaps for the next six hours. After that he heads over to the Pleasanton simulcast facility in time to see the head-on replays from the previous day's races as well as to settle in for the afternoon. By the time the last race is run Cox has typically put in a thirteen-hour day.

On Mondays and Tuesdays, when the track is normally dark, Cox devotes all his time to research and putting out the weekly edition of his *Track Record*. "On those days," he said in a detailed breakdown, "I review all the videotapes from Sam Spear's Golden Gate Fields and Bay Meadows Report, make horses-in-trouble and track-bias notes, and calculate track variants and fractional speed figures for each race that has been run during the previous week."

Cox next types up concise summaries for each race, which then become the *Track Record* for that week. The resulting product is mailed out every Tuesday evening, and subscribers normally receive it the following afternoon to add to their files. Over the course of a meet subscribers to the *Track Record,* which comes in a convenient punch binder format, wind up with a detailed analysis of every past race as well as relevant information about the workouts of first-time starters and horses coming back from layoffs.

One of the things you quickly appreciate about Cox, and the *Track Record,* is how eclectic he is when it comes to his information sources. Cox routinely draws from the work of a number of other handicappers and racing professionals. Generally, he trades his information for theirs. "Besides my own product," he explained, puffing on a Sherman, "I use the *Handicapper's Report* and the *Northwest Track Review,* which tell me respectively about shippers from southern California and Longacres. I look at the *Handicapper's Weekly,* which Tim Osterman puts out, for an update on the lastest training races and at Greg Lawlor's work on winning trainer-jockey combinations. I also tab the workouts from the

Racing Form and subscribe to the *Kentucky Bloodstock Report*, which is sent out on diskette and gives you such interesting data as the percentage of wins for first-time starters from each sire and dam, as well as how well they do on the turf and mud."

Even with all that information, Cox acknowledged, winning at the races is not an easy thing. "It took me many years to start making money at it. I think everybody, when they first start playing this game, spends all their time trying to pick winners. That's what the public generally does—bet who they think is going to win the race. They try and pick winners, and they wind up with two or three of the favorites every day, and someday they might even have all of them in a Pick Six and split the pool with a hundred other people. But when you consider the sixteen percent takeout of the win pool, in the long run you're going to lose taking that approach. It's only in the last several years that I really started making some money by working as hard on *how* to play the races as trying to pick winners. Picking winners isn't enough. You also have to figure out how to turn that skill into making money. Most handicappers you talk to say, 'My handicapping is super, but my money management is bad.' Well, that's because they're picking winners instead of figuring out how to make money at it."

Unclear about the distinction he was making, I asked Cox to elaborate. "Okay. I spent a lot of years playing Pick Sixes and thinking it was a horrible bet for the usual reason that you have to cover too many contenders. Well, when I finally started hitting— and in the last two years I've had the only ticket for $206,000, $85,000, and $137,000—the way I did it was by singling price horses. Like the general public, I used to be afraid to single a price horse. But I realized that if you single a long shot, now you can spread out in other races and play a reasonable Pick Six ticket. Even the professionals give the public bad advice on this. At the Mirage Conference a speaker talked about dutching two horses when you couldn't make up your mind. He said, 'If you have four-to-one and six-to-one you should bet them both, only with more on the four-to-one.' Well, I've learned that you should bet just the opposite. If you like them both the same, why would you bet more on the shorter-priced horse? If you're saying to yourself that you can't separate them, then you should bet more on the one that's paying the most."

Cox believes the same thing holds true for exactas when it comes to getting value for your bet. "You should never box three horses equally. Never. Because if you like all three horses equally, then you should be betting more on the combination that's paying the most. There's six possible combinations in a three-horse box, so you should be betting three times as much on the two that are paying the most, twice as much on the one in the middle and maybe one unit on the lowest payoff. Now, if you like one of the three horses the most, then that's a different story. You should bet him the most in relation to the highest payoffs. You should always be thinking about betting the most where the payoff is the most, because otherwise the takeout just eats you up. That's why you have real good handicappers that come out here every day, who pick more winners than I do but don't make near the money because they don't know how to play. And I did the same thing for fifteen years. I often came out here and picked four or five winners and went home with a hundred bucks in profit. Now I can pick one winner a day and I'll go home with a bigger profit."

I asked Cox if not picking winners means that he always avoids playing the favorite. "If you like the favorite in a race, you don't want to bet against him just to get odds," he cautioned. "What you should do is go for him in the exotics or don't play the race. When you look at each race, what you have to ask yourself is, 'How can I make money on this race? How can I play the horse and get my value in this race?' So if you like the favorite, don't bet the race, or find the horse that's going to run second to him in the exacta, or single him in the daily double, the Pick Six, or the triple. But don't bet the win money on him."

Given his comprehensive approach to handicapping, what is the first thing Cox looks for when analyzing a race? "The first thing that's important for me to do is calculate the pace in the race, and then I look for what the track bias is. Like today, when you came out, I told you the track is fair—your horse can be in front or a closer, be inside or outside. But when you know the rail is bad, now you're watching the race totally different. Because if you see a horse on the rail running *against* the bias and he's tiring and another horse closes *with* the bias on the outside, then you won't say, 'Ah man, that horse on the rail is a quitter, and the horse on the outside is a world-beater.' Well, in that situation I would be more impressed, for my next bet, with the horse that quit on the rail. My point is, you have to know what the bias is before you appreciate what's happening in the race.

"You also have to know what the numbers of the race were. For example, the other day, when Too Modest won, the guy in the *Racing Form* wrote an article about her saying what a great race she ran. But I guarantee you can bet against this horse next time around, because the pace numbers of the race were 92-96-100. You know those Quirin early speed points I showed you? Well, Too Modest had a seven and the rest had zero. So she was the only speed in the race. She walked out there. Nobody pushed her. So next time, before you get too impressed with her victory and time, see how fast the pace was in relationship to the final time. My point is that in evaluating any race you have to know whether the pace of the race was benefiting the front-runner or the closer.

"Last week, we had three days in a row where nobody could gain an inch in the stretch. Everyone was going wire to wire. So what you look for when you watch the reruns of those races is that one horse that made a little move against the bias and passed somebody. When you watch a race you have to know if the rail was dead and the outside fast, and whether it was a fast track or a closer's track when the pace was fast. In looking for that price horse in its next race you're looking for that front-runner who held on against the bias, or the closer that made a move against a front-runner's track."

That kind of attention to detail is fine for the professional, but what about the weekend fan who only has the *Racing Form* to look at? Is the *Racing Form* totally useless? "No. The problem with the *Form* is that everybody's looking at it. One of the lectures I give in my seminars asks the question, 'How do you know when you're getting value in a bet?' We know that if there were ten horses in a race, and there was no takeout, each horse would be nine to one if they were all bet equally. They would all pay $20, right? But instead, because of the takeout, they only pay $16.80. So if you bet $200 you're paying $32 for the right to bet that horse. So, you're losing by winning. The question every gambler has to ask is, 'How do you overcome the takeout?' You do it by betting horses who are not properly bet for their chances of winning. Now, they have to be badly underplayed just to make up for the sixteen percent takeout. So while the *Racing Form* is a necessity, everyone is looking at it. If you have a bunch of good handicappers all sitting in a room with no other information, they should all come up with the same horse and it would be tough to come up with a value bet. People who go to the track and only have the *Form* are going for the entertainment. They take fifty bucks to the track and bet two bucks a race and it's like they're going skiing or playing golf. So they don't mind losing. That's the cost of their fun."

But suppose Cox was limited to relying on the *Form* as his only source of information. What would he look for to get his edge? "Okay, that's fair. If that was the only thing I could use, then I would look for a horse that has early speed. Most California tracks favor early speed, and there's also less chance of a front-runner getting in trouble. As a matter of fact, I did well early in my career because I always did favor early speed. So if I was going just once a month I'd play the speed."

Another play that Cox advises for the recreational gambler whose only source of information is the *Racing Form* is "to look for a horse who has just run a competitive race and is taking a one-level drop. I call a competitive race being within two lengths at the stretch call or three lengths at the finish. If a horse has done that and is taking a one-level drop, he's very likely to run a decent race."

But isn't a horse coming out of a competitive race, I asked Cox, also likely to get bet? "Yeah, but not as much as a winner. He's definitely a better bet than a winner coming back at the same level, or a winner dropping. So the first thing that a real novice should look for when reading the *Form* is early speed and a horse taking a one-level drop out of a competitive race. Another thing that's really important for a beginner is to look at the money box that gives the lifetime record. He should look for a ratio that shows that a horse wins more than he comes in second or third. If you see a horse that has two wins and nine seconds, that horse is not a horse that likes to win. What you look for is a horse that wants to win races, that wins thirty percent of his races."

What about using the trainer- and jockey-win statistics that are usually listed in the racing program or in the *Racing Form*? "That's good. But the only trouble there is that the leading trainers don't usually give you the good-priced horses. If you bet the leading trainers you're going to wind up most of the time with the favorites, and you're going to lose money unless you crunch them in the exotics."

A third play that can give the recreational gambler a better chance of winning is to go for the third or fourth favorite in the race. "Statistically," Cox explained, "horses win in direct proportion to their odds. Since you know you're going to lose betting favorites, if you only go out to the track once a month or so, you're better off betting the second, third, and fourth favorites. Then if you win two races a day, you're probably going to break even. If you win three you'll come home ahead."

Cox also advises recreational gamblers to pay particular attention to track conditions in the first few races. "You shouldn't bet the first four races with your fifty bucks. Instead, watch to see if the front-runners or the closers win the first four races. If nothing but closers are winning, put ten or twenty on a closer in the fifth race. But you do have to be aware of class bias in doing that. What I mean is that good horses will overcome track biases and cheap ones won't. A cheap horse will quit on a dead rail every time."

Even though it's been a long time since Cox came to the track with only fifty bucks, I asked him to talk about money management from the perspective of a guy whose bankroll is that amount. "Okay, here's what I think he should do, whatever his basis of forming his opinion is. Let's say you have ten races. That means you could bet five dollars a race. Now, your chances of betting five dollars ten times and going home with any money are pretty nil. If you have to bet every race, split a two-dollar bet with a friend or whatever and then concentrate on two races and bet twenty on those two. If you do that, and win one of the two races, you're going to go home ahead for the day. You can even wait for the last race and bet all fifty dollars on it. That way you'll have something to look forward to. Sit there and watch the first nine races and then bet fifty on a ten-to-one shot and go home with five hundred or nothing. I'm not kidding. You'd be smarter to do that or even bet a fifty-dollar triple than bet five dollars on every race. Although, frankly, if I only had fifty bucks, I probably wouldn't play the exotics as my first choice because you don't have enough room. I think you should stay away from the exotics unless you can afford to play a lot, and you can afford to lose for a period of time, too."

Cox had an interesting perspective in terms of what kinds of races offer the best wagering opportunities. "Statistically, the cheapest races give the best return because the favorites are so much more undependable. So the cheaper the race, the more you want a long shot. You should look for playable long shots in cheap races and get closer to the favorites in your better races."

Going beyond the *Racing Form*, I asked Cox how important trip handicapping was to him. "It's huge," he emphasized, "because that's where you're going to get your price. You have a horse and he was on the rail against the bias the time before and it darkens his form and the public overlooks him the next time. That's your big edge. That's what you're always looking for. Earlier, I talked about how to get value and overcome the takeout. One way is to look at the *Form* and say, 'What does the public see when they look at this horse?' They're going to see certain things, and you're aware of what they see, right? So then you say to yourself, 'What do I know about this horse that the public doesn't?' You use all of your information sources. Okay, one of them might be trainer ability. Another might be the workout, how good was it for that day. If it's a trainer like Doug Utley or Greg Gilchrist or Bill Morey, somebody who always works their horses fast, then you're not impressed by a fast workout. As a matter of fact it's a negative, because the public thinks it's a good work and you know that those guys always work their horses fast, so it works in reverse. Like that horse Doc Murray today that was off for ninety days and had two bullet works and the public went for him at four to one. But I couldn't go for him at those odds because I know the trainer is zero for forty coming off ninety-day layoffs. That horse was a terrible underlay at that price. My point is, you have to look at workouts, trainer patterns, training races, shipper reports, anything to get an edge on what the public knows from just reading the *Form*."

Okay, suppose our recreational gambler decides to get a little more serious about his handicapping. What would Cox advise? "I'd watch the reruns of the races if a local station carried them. I'd find out about whatever seminars are going on. Why not go to a professional who's going to charge you ten or fifteen bucks and go to the track with some real information. Of course, the professional has to be worth it. I think you can tell how good he is by the kind of information he gives you. If you walk into the place and the guy tells you to bet the number three horse in the first race and the five in the second race, I'd leave. He probably isn't any better of a handicapper than you are. If, on the other hand, he explains the reasons why he likes those horses and it makes sense, then give him a shot. When I used to give seminars for the Golden Gate Fields meet, I always felt good after a seminar when people would come up and thank me *before* they ever went to the races and saw if the horses I recommended won. Because they knew I put a lot of work into it. Just like in today's third race with Doc Murray, I would have told them that in four years the trainer was zero for forty with a horse coming off of a ninety-day layoff. My point is that when you go to a seminar and hear something like that you know the guy has done his homework and you feel good about spending your ten or fifteen bucks."

I asked Cox if he had an opinion about the minimum amount of money people should bring to the track if they want to try to make a living from it. "That's a hard one to answer, but I would say whatever amount you're comfortable with. Whatever doesn't affect paying your rent. Once all your bills are paid and you have enough money to play, how much you bet depends upon the individual. I wouldn't want to have to win to pay my bills. When the bills are paid, then you know what your bankroll is. I mean if you can't stand losing, then you have to find some other game.

Because you can go weeks without winning and you're not going to win as often as you're going to lose."

Granted that the gambler's life is a precarious one, if Cox had $200 a day to play with, how would he allocate it? "It all depends upon what I like," he explained. "Some days I might only bet it to win on two horses. Another day I might think a horse is a cinch to be in the exacta and bet him top and bottom with four or five contenders, betting more on the top than on the bottom. Some days I might not bet at all. So it would totally depend upon the day, how I bet."

Weekend gamblers are notorious for their inability to stay out of races. Racetrack novelist William Murray has humorously referred to those who have the ability to sit out an entire card as having an iron ass. Are there days, I asked Cox, when he spends six hours handicapping, goes to the track and doesn't bet? "No," he laughed, "but there should be. There are days I've come out here not liking anything and gone home losing a thousand bucks and asked myself, 'How did I do that?' "

Since one of the things I learned from talking to backstretch people is the importance of patience, of waiting for the right time to bet, I mentioned that to Cox. "That's true," he agreed. "But you do know that the backstretch people are the worst handicappers at the track. They know their own horses, but they don't have time to do all this shit I do with all the other horses. There are a few good backstretch gamblers, but there are a lot more bad ones."

Red Lowery, like many horsemen on the backside, had told me that he would never bet a race unless he could physically see the horse. Since Ron bets almost exclusively at the simulcast facility in Pleasanton, I asked him how much he thought he lost by not being able to read the body language of a horse in the paddock or see how it warms up on the backstretch. His approach it seemed to me depends more on what a horse has historically done than what it might existentially feel like doing in today's race. "Well, if I wasn't successful doing it the way I am," Cox responded, "I'd probably go over and look at all the horses. Either that or I'd quit. But the tradeoff for me is the three hours a day commuting back and forth to the track. I'm not good in the paddock anyway. There are horses that wash out every goddamn time and still win. So if you keep records of that and can win, fine—if that's what you want to do. Every handicapper only has so much time to allocate to whatever he does. I showed you my schedule, and you can see there's not an extra three hours to spare, especially when I don't have the ability to read body language anyway."

Not that Cox hasn't tried. He once spent an entire meet in the paddock with a couple of guys who were supposed to be professionals at reading body language. "But they lost," he reflected, "because they weren't good at everything else. What they did was, they played horses that were physically at their best who were still not physically capable of winning. Some other horse that wasn't as good-looking to them was better. So these guys just weren't winners with their approach. It's very hard, for some reason, to put the combination of in-depth handicapping together with observation in the paddock. I have a friend that is very good in the paddock, but he insists on betting the horse that comes out looking the best, even if he's not the best. Now, if he would put the two together, if he would only wait until the horse that on handicapping factors was the best and looked the best, the guy would clean up. But he won't do that. And most of those paddock people won't do that.

"I know I'm losing something by not being at the track," Cox acknowledged, "because when I was able to watch the warmups it helped me. There's no doubt in my mind about that. I mean, a horse would come out onto the track and he's a closer, and he'd walk over to where the tractors are at the quarter pole and just stand there and not warm up. And I know from experience that closers don't run when they don't warm up. So I'm losing that information by not being at the track. But as far as I can tell, I'm better off having that extra three hours handicapping here, otherwise I'd be over there. I mean, even though I worked six hours this morning, I didn't have enough time to handicap all nine races correctly today."

A legitimate question that troubles a lot of racetrackers about professional handicappers is, Why are they willing to sell their information? As The Stone has often put it in his inimitable way,

"If these guys are so sharp, why don't they keep their insights to themselves and take advantage of the higher odds?"

Cox had a reasonable answer. "Well, I put out the *Track Record* because it gives me enough income so I don't have to worry about paying my bills, which makes me a better gambler. I can both be more patient and take more risks. But even more important, it gives me a reason to be disciplined as a recordkeeper. There are times when I get the flu, and have to get up at three in the morning and type this shit up, and I'm so sick I can't see straight. But if I ever got a week behind, I'd be dead. So by having subscribers to the *Track Record,* I have to do it. I'm obligated to them, and that gives me more discipline than I would probably otherwise have."

Cox acknowledged that when he first started out with the *Track Record,* it was for the income. "Now, I'm independent of that. I could raise my service to $2,000 a meet and have ten people who would gladly pay it. That would give me my $40,000 a year living expenses, right? But I do have some sense of loyalty to those people who have supported me since 1978, and most of my subscribers have been with me that long. I'm making less money now with sixty people, at $350 a meet, than I would with only ten guys at $2,000 a meet. Basically, I like the level it's at now and I'm not out looking for new subscribers. I have not advertised my product for four years. But the discipline thing and obligation to those people is really important because I have to sweat blood to get this sucker done. If I was only doing it for myself I'd probably take a break, and it would be damn hard to catch up. It takes me eight to ten hours a day to do this thing right—to watch the films, watch the bias, and get the variants and write up my notes. If I ever got two weeks behind, I'd never catch up and still be able to handicap every day."

Since maiden races make up such a large percentage of the card at most tracks, I asked Cox whether he agreed with the conventional wisdom, that they weren't worth betting. "I wrote a little editorial about them last week." His eyes lit up. "When I was at the Mirage Conference, I heard some guy who has a computer program say with total confidence, like this was the gospel, 'Oh, we never bet maiden claimers. They're too unpredictable.' Well, that's not a smart position to take when you're looking for value in a bet. You want to bet races that are *un*dependable because that means the favorites aren't dependable. Those are the races where you're going to get the long shot, because you have a bunch of slow and undependable horses. That's where you're going to get a nice value, if you have some reason to bet a horse."

With maiden claimers Cox looks for a pattern where a horse is improving at every call. He compiles pace numbers for every horse in every race and looks for a horse that does a little bit better at every call. "Talking numerically, a bottom-level maiden should go 92-90-88 at the three calls. When you have cheap horses they go slower later. When you get up to allowance horses, they go 95-98-101. Relatively, they go faster later, while the cheaper ones are slowing down. But let's say we have a horse that goes 85-87-89 the first time, then goes 87-88-89. Now he's still only getting a final 89, but he improved at every call, so he's getting better. That's a horse that might keep getting better and pay a big price, because very few people have both good pace numbers and final numbers. So if you get a horse that runs a better pace number at both calls, he's on the improve. And even though the final number is lower than another horse's, he might win because he's on the improve. So I don't mind playing cheap maiden claimers at all."

Another type of maiden that Cox likes to bet is a horse that has had two sprints, is bred to route, and is now stretching out. "Or a race where the trainer has much better stats with horses going a route, then sprinting. What you're looking for is some reason to play a long shot in this kind of race," Cox emphasized. "You aren't just playing him because he's a long shot."

Handicappers are always perplexed about what class to assign a horse that has just broken its maiden. How does Cox decide where it should be running next? "Very few maiden claiming winners will win back," Cox warned. "Usually, if they broke their maidens real impressively, they're pitched too high in their next race, where they have to beat proven winners. With straight maidens, who are running back in an allowance race, I like to bet them back if they're running against a bunch of horses who have already failed at that level. I mean, what is a good horse supposed to do?

A good horse is supposed to break its maiden and then go through his conditions. So if you get a straight maiden winner who wins impressively at a faster time than the average for that class, I love that kind of horse back in a non-winners-of-one allowance race. If he breaks his maiden in a slower than average time, that's another story. In northern California in the fall, we get a lot of horses that are proven failures in allowance races, and high claimers will often win these weak allowance races. So it's just a matter of what time of year and how impressively a straight maiden has won, whether they're a good bet back."

Interestingly, Cox thinks knowledge about pedigrees is a factor of growing importance for the serious handicapper. By way of example, he talked about an extremely sharp three-year-old, Knight in Savannah, that was the talk of the backstretch during the Golden Gate Fields meet. "Knight in Savannah is a good horse," he agreed. "He won his first two sprints in very good times. But he's not bred to stretch out. The average winning distance of horses from his sire, Knight's Choice, is 6.1 furlongs. I'm not as sharp yet in the pedigree area as I'd like to be. I've just got involved the last couple of years with the *Kentucky Bloodstock Report* to broaden my information base on breeding. Learning about pedigrees is getting more and more interesting to me as a handicapper because the information base available to the public is getting broader and broader. And knowledge about pedigrees can help you with evaluating first-time starters as well as horses running in the mud or on the turf. To stay ahead of the game, you have to keep getting a bigger information base. And one of the untouched frontiers for handicappers is in the breeding area. So if you get ahead in the breeding, you'll have a jump on most people, even most of the experts."

Cox elaborated about what kinds of information the *Kentucky Bloodstock Report* can provide a handicapper. "What they have is the average winning distances of a sire's progeny. So, like with Knight in Savannah, you could guess that he was bred to win early because of his sire's record. Knight's Choice progeny are bred to win early, sprinting. So Knight in Savannah winning first time out was no surprise. He's been running exceptionally, but he's not bred to route. So until he proves he can route, there's a question. In fact, I'll predict the first time he routes he will be totally over-played. [Cox was right. Knight in Savannah lost as the heavy favorite when he was routed.] So that's what the breeding stuff is good for. I use it to evaluate horses who are doing something they've never done before. Are they bred to do it? That's where you get the price, because people don't like to bet horses who have never done what they're being asked to do today. They look at their *Form* and see that a horse has never routed or been on the turf or mud before, and back off. They are not going to bet a lot of money because they just don't know. So that kind of horse won't be over-bet. If you know that a horse is bred to do what he's being asked to do today and the trainer is good, now you have a play, because the public doesn't know what you know."

Cox was cautious, however, about expecting too much from a pedigree independent of other factors. He echoed Jack Kaenel's advice about never asking a horse to do two new things at once. "The case where a horse is both routing and going on the turf for the first time, for example. Well, that might be a little too much to ask. But if they're only being asked to do one new thing and you know they're bred to do it, that gives you a big edge."

What about other professional handicappers? Who does Cox recommend people read to sharpen their handicapping skills? "Anything by Andy Beyer, Bill Quirin, or Jim Quinn. Also Steven Davidowitz, though he hasn't written anything for years. His work was early, before most people knew about biases and key race charts and that kind of stuff. I wish he would write again. His idea of a key race is still one of the most productive tools to use in handicapping. Sometimes you get a race that doesn't have good figures, and yet everybody that comes out of it runs well. The same thing with a race that looks real good, that isn't. You don't know what caused this race, if it was a timer malfunction or a fluke or what, but when the first two horses out of it come back and don't run their numbers, the next couple that come out of there you won't jump on while the public still will. The same thing with these races that look bad, but hey, horses coming out of them are winning. So you need to keep track of those races by going back to the charts and circling them in red when one of the horses in that race wins. If you see that three or four horses out of a race have come back to win—say the first-, second-, fourth- and fifth-place finishers—when the third-place finisher out of that key race runs back, you don't care what the numbers are. You just know it's a productive race and he's worth betting. In addition, you can see what numbers the other horses ran coming out of that key race when they came back to win and plug that in to compare with the other horses in the race. So keeping track of key races is important, and I do."

Ron and his wife, Cheryl, had an early dinner date and plans for the evening. I wrapped things up by asking him what the biggest change in his perception of the game has been as a result of the work he has done. "The biggest *surprise*," he replied, "is how little I knew about the game compared to what I thought I knew. When I started charging people for the *Track Record*, I thought I was pretty good. I didn't find out how little I knew until I really got into the work. When you start compiling all this trainer, breeding, bias stuff, you begin to realize how much it really takes to win. What I've learned is that you have to always keep working at it to find a new edge. The public keeps catching up. As a matter of fact, Andy Beyer at the Mirage Conference talked about how the edge is disappearing and how hard it is to stay ahead of the game. He was even talking about going to Australia, a new country, and do there what he's done here. Nobody was sure if he was serious, half serious or just bullshitting, but the public's information has caught up to the point where you have to keep working to stay ahead of the game."

INDEX

Hollendorfer, Jerry, 101, 107, 118, 139, 239, 269, 272, 278–79, 281, 297
Hollywood Gold Cup, 262, 263
Hollywood Park, 147, 262–63, 269
Horsemen's Benevolent and Protective Association (HBPA), 126, 127, 229, 235, 242–44
Hot walker, 39, 45
Houston, 276
Houston Post, 10
Hubbard, Nate, 125
Hummel, Chris, 121

Imaginary Lady, 117, 273
Inquiries, 210–11, 217
Interco, 240
Irish Look, 4
Irish Lord, 9
Isbell, Diane, 186–88, 191
Italian Derby, 253
It's a Boy, 10
It's Freezing, 131

Jamilla, 83
Jenda, Chuck, 14, 76, 86, 87, 93–129, 136–49, 202–3, 225, 249, 251, 254–55, 274, 278, 281, 286
Jim Beam, 284
Jockey agents, 39, 54–56, 293–98
Jockeys, 23, 48–92
  and courage of horses, 87–88, 145–46
  disqualifications and, 74–75
  equipment for, 61–62
  handicapping and, 306
  hand riding by, 81–84, 87
  income of, 29, 50–51, 56
  injuries to, 57, 69–73, 197
  inquiries prompted by, 210
  mental side of riding for, 66–68
  owners and, 258, 259
  substance abuse by, 125–26
  suspensions of, 75, 217–19, 221

track conditions and, 151, 154, 167, 169
  trainers and, 39, 41–42, 52, 55, 59, 66, 76, 107–8, 125, 133, 145
  veterinarians and, 192
  warnings to, 222
  weight of, 22, 57–60, 107–8
  whip use by, 84–85, 87, 219, 221
Jockeys' Guild, Inc., 50, 56, 57, 69
John Henry, 22, 120, 258, 285
Johnson, Ben, 205
Johnson, Tex, 26
Jones, Gary, 273
Joys of Love, 297–98
Judge Angelucci, 164
Judice, Joe, 222
Just Deeds, 8, 12–14

Kaenel, Dale, 50, 51, 91
Kaenel, Jack, 11, 48–92, 108, 109, 114, 125, 145, 157, 219, 221, 258, 286, 314
Kelley, T. W., 261
Kelly, 284
Kemp, Allen, 21–22
Kemp, Paula, 21
Kensington Handicap, 274
Kentucky Bloodstock Report, 302, 313
Kentucky Derby, 7, 20, 39, 43, 102, 146, 212, 284
King of the Bayou, 8, 9, 12–14
King Glorious, 299
King's Isle, 263
King Skipper, 7
Kleve, Larry, 226
Knight, Terry, 239, 269, 279, 281–82
Knight in Savannah, 283, 313–14
Knight's Choice, 313
Krone, Julie, 218

Ladbroke Corporation, 164, 261, 287, 289
Ladytron, 25